Uphill all the Way

Other Titles of Interest

The Long Way
Bernard Moitessier

This is Bernard Moitessier's incredible story of his participation in the first Golden Globe Race, a solo, non-stop circumnavigation rounding the three great Capes of Good Hope, Leeuwin, and the Horn. For seven months, the veteran seafarer battled storms, doldrums, gear failure, overwhelming fatigue and loneliness. Then, nearing the finish, Moitessier pulled out of the race and sailed on for another three months before ending his 37,455-mile journey in Tahiti. Not once had he touched land.

Handbook of Offshore Cruising
Jim Howard

"Accompanied by superb illustrations by Tadami Takahashi, the text of *Handbook of Offshore Cruising* touches on everything from boat design, construction and systems to voyaging safely, landfalls, health and communications...It is certainly one of the most thorough primers to come along in quite some time."
Cruising World

Sailing Alone Around the World
Capt. Joshua Slocum

Joshua Slocum's epic solo voyage around the world in 1895 in the 37 foot sloop *Spray* stands as one of the greatest sea adventures of all time. It remains one of the major feats of single-handed voyaging and has been the inspiration for many who have gone to sea in small boats.

Race Winning Strategies
Tom Linskey

The author explains yacht racing the way it really is–the situations, the tradeoffs, the decisions–and reveals why the same people win, race after race. Fifty up-to-date racing examples cover everything from teamwork, strategy, sails, starts, and rules, to the all-important psychological preparation that will help even the average sailor sail faster and win more races.

Uphill all the Way

A crew member's inside story
of the BT Global Challenge

Alan Sears

SHERIDAN HOUSE

This edition published 1998 by
Sheridan House Inc.
145 Palisade Street
Dobbs Ferry, NY 10522

Copyright © Alan Sears 1998

ISBN 1-57409-053-4

Printed in Great Britain

Library of Congress Cataloging-in-Publication Data

Sears. Alan. 1953-
  Uphill all the way : a crew member's inside story of the BT Global
Challenge / Alan Sears.
      p.   cm.
  ISBN 1-57409-053-4
  1. Sears. Alan, 1953-   2. BT Global Challenge (Race)
3. Toshiba Wave Warrior (Yacht)   I. Title.
GV832.S43   1998
797. 1'4'092--dc21
  [B]   97-48498
                                                  CIP

Dedication

For Pam
who was there when it started,
there when it finished,
and there in spirit during the best and the worst of it.

Contents

THE BT CHALLENGE –

ARCTIC
OCEAN

Southampton
July 1997

5300 miles
to Rio de
Janeiro

DOLDRUMS

INDIAN
OCEAN

7000 miles
to Boston

Cape Town
April 1997

6200 miles to
Cape Town

ROARING FORTIES

Kerguelen
Waypoint

Sydney
Feb 19

FURIOUS FIFTIES

winds

SEPTEMBER 1996 – JULY 1997

PACIFIC
OCEAN

3000 miles to
Southampton

Boston
June 1997

ATLANTIC
OCEAN

EQUATOR

Rio de Janeiro
Oct 1996

1200 miles
to Sydney

Wellington
Dec 1996

ROARING FORTIES

6600 miles to
Wellington

Waypoint

Cape Horn

STRONG WESTERLY GALES

Foreword by Sir Chay Blyth

There are few opportunties in life that test you to the full and which throw you in at the deep end right from the start. The World's Toughest Yacht Race is one of them. This is a Race which takes no prisoners and certainly no passengers.

I first met Alan at the Royal Ocean Racing Club in August of 1993 where I interviewed him for a place on the Race. He struck me then as someone who had set his heart on taking part and had all the determination and strength of character to see it through. I'm delighted to have had my initial instinct proven.

Following a training session, the skipper reported, 'He is very enthusiastic and gives 100 per cent all the time. He will be an asset on any boat and will be good for morale when everyone is down. Alan talks for England – as he says himself, he is the Honorary Secretary of the "Talk the hind legs off a donkey club!"'

As the Race progressed we witnessed that Alan's enthusiasm knew no bounds. He learnt quickly, giving his all to any task in hand, and his great sense of humour made him a well liked and popular member of the crew on board *Toshiba Wave Warrior*. He was also a great source of motivation to the other crew simply by his willingness to do things.

I am delighted to have been asked to write this Foreword and to be able to add my congratulations for Alan's fantastic achievement. It has been a pleasure to know him and I wish him every success in the future.

Foreword by Simon Walker

It was a great privilege and honour to lead such a terrific group of people on *Toshiba Wave Warrior* in the BT Global Challenge. To share the good times and bad in such a close-knit group under unusual circumstances was a real challenge; to achieve a good result was a tremendous reward for our hard work.

The conditions surrounding a race like this, in which amateur yachtsmen compete, give rise to personal stories of ambition, financial hardship, courage, fear, humour and introspection. On *Toshiba* I believe most of the stories have happy endings and our circumnavigation is something we will all look back on with satisfaction and a smile. Alan has turned it into a great story and I am delighted that he has achieved one of his ambitions of publishing a book so that he can tell it.

He strikes a balance between relaying his personal Odyssey and a factual account; and it makes an equally good read whether you're an experienced yachtsman or not. Its mix of humour and philosophical comment, sailing anecdote and personal thoughts made me reflect on my own impressions of the race. Some sections made me laugh out loud while others made me quietly consider the achievement of the crew and wonder how we got out of some of the more hair-raising situations.

Of course my memories overlay Alan's text to recreate my own private version of our race and I am grateful to him for providing the catalyst for this. Hopefully it will do the same for the rest of the *Toshiba* crew, and perhaps anyone else who has gone on a great journey of self-discovery of any kind.

Preface

'If you tell the truth, have one foot in the stirrup.'
Turkish proverb

I suppose it really started with Arthur Ransome, when the Walker children and the Blacketts went sailing down to Rio, led by Captain Flint and the old sea dog, Peter Duck; but the first time I really became aware of sailing was when Sir Francis Chichester completed his round the world trip. It was only then that I realised people really did such things, and somehow the idea stayed with me. Then I met Diccon and Jerry who owned a boat – and experienced for the first time the whistle of the wind, the tang of salt air, and the taste of breakfast making a second appearance. So we sailed in the Solent and I dreamed of ocean voyages, of crossing the Atlantic and sailing down to Rio. In between times I sailed in my armchair with Naomi James, Robin Knox-Johnston and Chay Blyth, watched Whitbread Round the World Races set off, and consoled myself that clearly one had to be born to it.

Pinned to the noticeboard above my desk is a rather dog-eared card. It is curling slightly at the edges, not surprisingly because it is already a good five years old. On it is written a list of ten highly improbable goals. Goal number two says simply 'Sail around the world'. This book is the story of how I came to do just that. It is a personal account of what it was like to sail on board *Toshiba Wave Warrior* in the 1996–97 BT Global Challenge. It is not necessary to know anything about sailing to enjoy this book, because the story of the race is, like all human endeavour, a story of the people who took part. On the other hand, to help the less nautical reader along I have attempted to explain something of what sailing a big yacht is all about, without cluttering the text with too much detail. I have probably failed on both counts.

I hope I have succeeded in conveying something, even if only a little, of what it was really like to be there, in the highs and the lows, in the storms and the calms. Of course the crews of the other 13 yachts against whom we raced will have different stories to tell. Indeed, my crew-mates on *Toshiba* will each have a different story to tell. I have tried very hard to be as accurate as possible, and if this account differs from others, or differs from the recollections of others, I can only offer that as evidence that the truth is never black and white, but always comes in shades of grey.

Acknowledgements

I have a confession to make: I frequently skip this section in other people's books. Nevertheless I have some very important things to say to certain people, which I could not really include in the main text, and I want to begin with a personal thank you to Sir Chay and Lady Felicity Blyth. To Chay because, without his vision and determination, there would have been no BT Global Challenge for me to take part in, and to Felicity for being such a constant source of good humour, inspiration and encouragement. Thanks, too, to Diccon and Jerry Scholefield for starting the whole thing off by taking me sailing in the first place, and to Martin Ley for helping me to keep on sailing.

Simon Walker was the best skipper anyone could have asked for; his dedication, perseverance and tolerance stand as an example to us all. Simon is not just a professional yachtsman, however, he is an adventurer, and during the voyage must have had cause to reflect upon the words of another noted sailor and adventurer, Bill Tilman, which he had inscribed in his volume of astronomical tables: 'Crew should be cheerful, equable, longsuffering, patient in adversity, tolerant of the whims and uncouth manners of others, neat and clean, adaptable, unselfish, loyal – in fact possessed of most of the qualities in which the majority of men are notably deficient.' To the crew of *Toshiba Wave Warrior*, who were all these things and more, I raise my glass in salute.

Yet where would the 'Wave Warriors' have been without Toshiba? A tremendous thank you, then, to all the staff of Toshiba Information Systems (UK) Ltd, led by the incomparable John Hill, and with special thanks to Toni, Sara and Gisele for all their extra hard work. There are many people without whom this trip would not have been possible, but particular mention must be made of Helen Wybrow, who stayed home to keep it all running, Andrew Roberts and Alistair Hackett, together with all the staff of the Challenge Business. Most notably the best maintenance team in the world – Chris, Garra, Peter Pearce, Peter Lucas, Fred and Martin – should note that tea (or beer) is always available at my home, or in any port in the world in which we find ourselves.

If it wasn't for your 'foulies' where would we be? So thank you to Nigel Musto for keeping us warm and dry, at least most of the time (!), and for a tremendous response when we did have a problem.

As we raced around the world we made friends wherever we went – too many supporters in every port, alas, to name everyone – but none are forgotten in our hearts, least of all the staff of the various Toshiba companies operating worldwide, who went out of their way to extend the most fantastic welcomes.

The BT Global Challenge was unquestionably a 'party' event, and much of the credit for that must go to BT's Director of Marketing, Richard Slogrove, who ensured that no event went unmarked and that the barrel was never drunk dry. Not to be outdone, we were superbly treated to a magnificent night out in every stopover by Business Club sponsor Duncan Spence. Duncan travelled the world to support the race and *Toshiba Wave Warrior*, and we all owe him a great vote of thanks and a good night out!

There are a number of very important people without whom you would not be reading this, and for the wonderful opportunity of writing this book I have to thank the 'Charley's Angels' of nautical publishing: my agent Gavia Wilkinson-Cox, Janet Murphy of publishers Adlard Coles Nautical, and editor Carole Edwards. Thanks are due also to Claire Gilbert and Joanne Adams for painstakingly typing up the transcriptions of my logs and journals, and to Ian Gilbert for doing the ironing.

Which leaves me with two further sets of 'thank yous'. To Maggie, my 'then girlfriend', still, and always, the greatest of friends, to Peta and to Chas, for taking care of Joe the dog at different times. To Pam, for absolutely everything, but most of all for 'being there', even when we could not be together, and for still being there when I got back. And lastly, but only because the Good Book tells us that the last shall be first, to my Mum. What can I say? It needs a book to itself. Thanks, Mum.

If this list seems rather tiresomely exhaustive I make no apology for that. If by some terrible mischance I have omitted anyone who should most deservingly be here, then I do most humbly apologise.

Prologue

'I have found that you do have only to take that one step toward the gods and they will then take ten steps toward you. That step, the heroic first step of the journey is out of, or over the edge of your boundaries, and it often must be taken before you know that you will be supported.'
Diane Osbon

It is January in the English Channel. A big powerful yacht is charging over the piled up waves. The waves are thirty to thirty-five feet high, breaking and foaming at the crests. Six people are in the open cockpit at the back of the boat as a particularly big wave sweeps up behind, picks up the back of the boat and starts to carry it forwards. Forty-four tons of steel are flicked upwards like a gigantic surf board in a mêlée of foam and spray. In the cockpit they are shouting in unison: 'Fourteen, fifteen, sixteen, sixteen point one, sixteen point two!' and a ragged cheer goes up as the white water foams under the hull and the wave charges on ahead.

'Is that a record?' shouts the man on the wheel. 'Must be,' the others tell him. And it is. It is the highest boat speed achieved in training for the BT Global Challenge with a crew volunteer at the wheel. A crew volunteer? Just that. The Challenge is a 'round the world' yacht race; round the world the hard way – the 'wrong way' against the prevailing winds and currents. The people sailing this yacht up the Channel in a force 9 are not professional sailors; they include a dentist, an accountant, an admin manager plus the butcher, the baker, and the candlestick maker! They have taken five days off work to share a place on a crowded yacht with thirteen other people. These 'volunteers' sleep in narrow bunks (when sleep is possible) to the accompaniment of the roaring wind and crashing sea only inches away, and battle against seasickness, cold and fatigue, while all the time they learn, learn, learn. Who does what? What goes where? What do all these different ropes do? What to do in an emergency? How to avoid the emergency before it happens. How to sail a full-blooded ocean racing yacht around the world in the shortest possible time. And all this in the certain knowledge that the Southern Ocean will be colder, the waves bigger and that the race will take them 2000 miles from the nearest land.

Two thousand miles! That focuses the attention when it comes to learning. If anything breaks, there will be no one else there to help fix it. It's a constant reminder, a constant theme: take care of your boat, take care of yourselves, take care of each other. So how do they come to be here on this bright cold winter day with the roar of the wind making conversation a hit and miss affair of a few shouted words at point blank range – anything else being simply inaudible – and these great rolling walls of water rising and falling all around? They have read about it, heard about it, seen something in the papers, picked up the phone and said: 'I want to sail round the world.'

That's all it took! A phone call – no who-you-know, no what-you-know, no previous experience required, just 'I want to do it.' Just one simple sentence down the phone line: 'Hello, yes, I want to sail round the world.'

1

No Experience Necessary

'The wonder is always new that any sane man could be a sailor.' Ralph Waldo Emerson

I made that telephone call from my girlfriend Pam's house. Having stayed for the weekend, I read her daily paper over breakfast. In amongst the sports pages was a short piece explaining that Chay Blyth proposed to hold a second round the world yacht race for amateur crews and was looking for volunteers. 'The question is,' the piece concluded, 'do you dare to pick up the phone and call this number...?' So I made the call.

'Oh, yes,' said a voice on the other end, rather matter-of-factly, 'if you send us a reservation fee of £100 we'll send you an application form. Seventy-five pounds of the £100 is returnable if you decide not to go ahead.'

For reasons that will become clear, £100 represented a considerable strain on my bank account so, without investigating too closely, I wrote a cheque and sent it off. Two days later, the application form arrived with an information pack about the race. 'I the undersigned make application for the reservation of a berth on Ocean Challenge 1996–1997 on the terms and conditions overleaf' it read, and as application forms go, it was a model of simplicity. I filled in my name and address, nationality and languages spoken, sailing experience, hobbies and interests, general health and education. So far so good. The stumbling block was the first stage payment. I knew that this adventure of a lifetime did not come free, but I expected to have some time in which to set about raising the money. A request for a first stage payment of £775 in order to get to an interview with Chay Blyth showed up a significant flaw in my plans: I had no money. I had no savings; I had no income and I had very little in the way of saleable possessions, but I did have a secret weapon. I had an overdraft! I telephoned my bank manager.

We exchanged pleasantries until inevitably he asked what he could do for me. 'I have a particular need for £800 this month,' I said. 'Of course we agreed that there would be no further withdrawals, but I am wondering whether I could take this from my number two account, which would in fact remain within its overdraft limit.' There was a pause. Any second now, I thought, he is going to ask me what I want the money for; I'll have to say: 'To put down as a deposit on a round the world yacht race,' and that will be the end of this conversation. 'Will you be making your usual repayment at the end of the month?' he asked at last. 'Oh, absolutely,' I replied with the air of confidence that is essential to these situations. 'Ah, well, that'll be fine then,' he told me. I intended to draw cash, drive straight to the Challenge Business and secure my place. 'First come, first served' they had warned, but some things are destined from the start. I wrote a cheque, and posted it first class.

St James's Place, London, 9 am on 24 August 1993: I walked through the appropriately portholed doors of the Royal Ocean Racing Club and found my way upstairs. Chay Blyth, hero of my bookshelves, a man who has rowed the Atlantic, was then the only person to have made a solo non-stop circumnavigation westabout and who had won line honours in the first ever round the world race with his crew of paratroopers, shook my hand, waved me to a chair and gave me a cup of coffee.

'So tell me about your sailing,' he began. I thought for a moment and then said: 'I was brought up having absolutely nothing to do with sailing or the sea, then I met two chaps who had been left an old boat by their father. Since then I've done some south coast cruising, a flotilla holiday in the Greek Islands and a week in the Med.' 'Perfectly qualified for round the world racing,' he remarked dryly.

One of the popular subjects of conversation on Challenge training sails was to become: 'How long did your interview last?' The longest anyone claimed was 15 minutes. Now that is not to suggest that Chay is either slipshod in his methods, or antisocial. He often invited people to share a meal with him and was always prepared to answer questions and to talk about the race in great detail. It is just that he did not need very long to make up his mind about people. He did, however, ask me one other question which caused me some amusement. Making no mention of my recently failed marketing business, I had stated my occupation as Music Teacher. Lacking any other form of income I had stepped back into my youth by taking on one or two guitar students, giving me a princely income of about £30 a week.

'So what about the money,' Chay asked, 'How does a music teacher afford £19 000 to sail round the world?' 'Ah,' I replied brightly, 'That won't be too difficult for me because I don't have a mortgage.' I did not tell him that the reason I didn't have a mortgage was because I had sold my house, moved in with my then girlfriend, put the money into the business, lost the business and the money, fallen out with the girlfriend and had no money, no income, no real means of support, visible or invisible and would have had nowhere to live had I not packed what little I had left into my car and gone home to mother!

The rest of the interview passed in brief discussion of the training programme and the comparative merits of the various stop-over ports, and there I was, navigating my way through the portholed doors again, unleashed on the world as a would-be circumnavigator. I do not know whether you have ever seen anyone in a business suit and tie skipping through St James's Park at 9.30 in the morning, but perhaps the commuters knew Chay was interviewing that day, because no one remarked upon it.

Back at home, things began in earnest. First question: how to raise £18 750 in stage payments whilst continuing to live and funding all the incidental expenses such as getting to Plymouth for training sails? I broke it down, calculating that what I actually needed to do was raise £20 a day. I brainstormed for money-raising ideas, wrote the best 20 on a piece of A4 paper and pinned it to my noticeboard, along with the schedule of payments. I wrote to everyone I knew, or whose address I had for whatever reason, explaining what I was doing and, highly fortuitously as it turned out, I started to send out a newsletter.

By the end of August I had received a letter from the Challenge Business introducing Helen Wybrow, Director of Planning for the business, Mandy Burnett, Helen's secretary and the major point of contact for crew volunteers, and Training Skipper Pete Goss. Now Pete has subsequently risen to international prominence following his rescue of Rafael Dinelli in the singlehanded Vendée Globe race, but his reputation travelled before him even then. An ex-marine, Pete had trained all the crews for the 1992–93 British Steel Challenge and then skippered *Hofbrau Lager* into third place on that race. By dint of reading everything I could get my hands on about the British Steel Challenge I also knew that Pete could climb up the backstay of a

Challenge yacht to the mast head 79 feet above the deck and then descend via the forestay; that he had raced *Cornish Meadow*, a 26 foot Firebird catamaran intended for day sailing 'round the cans', singlehanded across the Atlantic, and that he could cook a chocolate cake in a force 9 storm! Helen's letter also included the schedule of dates for training sails and, not wishing to seem slow in coming forward, I applied to be on the first.

A taste of the real thing

There once was a riding instructor of the old school who, so it is said, used to bribe a young lad to run along the outside of his riding school scraping a stick along the corrugated iron wall at least once during every lesson. As horses cavorted in all directions and riders were hurled from their saddles, he would survey the carnage grimly, crying: '*There's* a taste of the real thing for you.'

'You should join the yacht *Rhone Poulenc* at Queen Anne's Battery, Plymouth, between 6 and 10 pm on Friday 8 October. The yacht will be berthed on the red pontoon,' read the joining instructions. I particularly liked the bit about the red pontoon, it sounded vaguely reminiscent of that children's television programme where people used to go off through the round window or the square window. I think the programme was called *Playschool*, but somehow I didn't think we were going to be playing at this. The joining instructions included a suggested kit list containing such items as a warm woollen sweater and warm tracksuits or equivalents. Much thought went into the packing of my bag before I set out to drive down to Plymouth on the Friday afternoon and meet my brother Peter who lives nearby. Over the course of training for the Challenge I evolved a clothing system which worked fairly well, but which took up about four times as much space as the technical clothing we used for the race itself. My early efforts, however, consisted simply of as much warm clothing as I could possibly carry on to the yacht in one bag. Peter and I went for a drink and then set out to find the yacht. My first sight of a Challenge yacht came as we walked together along the marina wall, a concrete structure big enough to carry a road on top, and looked down on to *Rhone Poulenc* nestling quietly up against the pontoon some 20 feet below us.

'Good grief,' I remarked, 'Is that really big enough to sail round the world in?' Sixty-seven feet sounds big enough to join the navy with, over a couple of pints in a reassuringly land-locked pub, but now suddenly it did not seem so big after all. I carried my bag down on to the pontoon, said goodbye to Peter and swung myself up over the lifelines.

Even if, to my inexperienced eyes, a Challenge yacht did not seem that big when viewed from above, I knew that it was nearly twice the size of, say, *Lively Lady*, in which Sir Alec Rose had sailed round the world singlehanded; nevertheless the deck fittings are fairly imposing. The smallest winches on the boat, the mainsheet traveller winches, are about as large as you would expect to find as sheet winches on a 36-footer, while the spinnaker poles look as though they could just about be handled by a small platoon. In fact two of us manoeuvred them around the foredeck even in the hairiest conditions – any more people involved became a complication. Down below, two important principles were established immediately, the first of them being safety.

Lying on each crew member's allocated bunk was a combined lifejacket and safety harness; all recently serviced, all checked and numbered. Pete Goss casually picked mine off my bunk, slipped it over his shoulders and pointed out which toggle inflated it and which one turned the light on. I nodded sombrely, not because I was thinking about drowning but because I was suddenly feeling incredibly claustrophobic! We were standing in a three-man cabin, which is not very large even for two people, and I was eyeing the top bunk, my home for the next four nights. I have subsequently slept in smaller spaces on other boats but all I could think of at the time was: 'I'm not going to be able to do this!' Then it all seemed a bit silly. After all, the point of the thing was to have a big adventure, which is bound to mean facing up to some of your fears. But I just did not want to have to face up to this one. There was only one thing to do; grit my teeth, get through the training sail, and then quit.

The second abiding principle we learned that first night was that keeping a Challenge yacht sailing is a bit like painting the Forth Bridge; there is always something to do. I spent that Friday evening stitching loops into lengths of rope to make sail ties. This job had the great merit of at least being comprehensible. The crew member who heard Andy Hindley, then the Training Mate, subsequently Training Skipper and Skipper of *Save the Children* in the race, tell Pete that 'the port jockey pole dobber pin retainer needs fixing' merely remarked: 'Now I *know* you're making it up as you go along.'

Dawn on Saturday morning, and we were there to see it; training days started at 6 am. Later training sails began with a run and a swim but the early induction sails were designed to break people in gently. With no night sailing there was the opportunity for a drink in the bar after each day's training and a shower in the morning before going out. The men's showers were in two banks on adjacent walls of a communal changing area. The first few people in filled up one bank and naturally enough the next few people along used the second, wherein they endured a freezing cold shower for as long as they could stand it before emerging, trying not to look too fazed by the experience. Clearly they thought this was part of the toughening up process. Until Pete emerged, steaming hot and grinning from his shower cubicle to say: 'Oh, you don't want to use those, there's no hot water in there!'

We also learned the basics of hygiene and cleanliness at sea on these early training sails. Before we set out we were divided into two watches; one watch cleaned right through the boat down below, while the other washed the decks, a procedure which was repeated every day and carried over, in a modified form, into the race.

By nine o'clock we were heading for the high seas and it proved to be an interesting baptism. As we cleared Plymouth harbour break-water the wind was force 5 and picking up to 6. There had been three days of gales preceding us and there was a fair swell running in from the Atlantic. As the port watch struggled manfully to hoist the main-sail, *Rhone Poulenc* started to dip her nose into the waves and toss the spray back along the foredeck like a fresh racehorse resenting being held up. Hoisting the mainsail involved one hardy volunteer clinging to the mast about eight feet above deck level in order to attach the wire halyard to the top of the sail so that we could pull it up. Our volunteer committed a cardinal error: at a crucial point he hung on to the mast for dear life instead of hanging on to the halyard. This resulted in 85 feet of wire rope with a large U-shaped shackle on the end whipping round our heads with enough force, it seemed, to start removing them from our shoulders. Eventually one of us grabbed the wire as it slashed overhead and was rewarded with a cheery word of thanks from Andy.

As soon as the sails were set, we had to change them all around again, just for practice, but then that's really the point of a training sail, isn't it? By now we had 28 knots of wind across the deck. If you are not a sailor you might find it easier to relate to inland con-ditions in a force 7 wind (classified as between 27 and 33 knots) which is described as 'near gale, whole trees in motion, difficult to walk into wind'.

On board the crew had divided into three groups. One third were hanging over the side indulging in what a nautical friend of mine

8

calls 'avast heaving' or 'bringing up alongside'; another third were feeling distinctly queasy and incredibly thankful not to be hanging on the rail, and the rest were completely untouched. This last contingent comprised Pete, Andy and the only two members of the crew with considerable ocean sailing experience! The next four days combined exhilaration and exhaustion in roughly equal amounts and left most of us with our enthusiasm for sailing at an all time high in spite of the fact that, as we stood on the foredeck sweating, breathless and panting after a particularly vigorous sail change, some of us concluded that if the sea did not leave you feeling sick the exercise certainly would. This only served to make Pete Goss's parting words even more appropriate. 'The real training starts next time,' he said with a grin, 'You'll need to be fit, so start running and join a gym.'

One other thing happened on this first training sail which was to have a profound effect on me. During our final debrief in the saloon the subject of THE MONEY came up. Did anyone have it? Was it just a question, for some people, of writing a cheque? If not, and *not* was the common answer, how was each of us going to set about paying off nearly £19 000 over the next three years? I raised the subject of sponsorship but found myself in a minority of one when I said that I thought personal sponsorship for a project such as the Challenge was at least as valid, and possibly more so, than giving to charity. Now lest anyone should misunderstand, I am a great believer in giving to charities and try to practise what I preach, but the effects of something like the Challenge are potentially life-altering, and one person on a mission can often do more than all the organised charities in the world put together. Think of Martin Luther King, or Gandhi or, nearer home, Bob Geldof. So if you personally sponsor someone whose life is touched in such a way that they go out and do something to change the world ... I could see from the faces in front of me that I was not winning, and then I glanced over at Pete. He was standing very quietly with a smile on his face and his right hand held in front of his chest showing 'thumbs up'. I determined to get myself sponsored and started with a method Pete had used to raise money for *Hofbrau Lager*'s crew fund: selling postcards to be posted back from the points of call.

It was always part and parcel of the Challenge that we would all train together before being selected into crews and matched up with our race skippers and yacht sponsors. In the early stages the race had no title sponsor, and although several of the yacht sponsors from the first British Steel Challenge had signed on again, that all seemed rather distant. With the start still three years away, what we had was each other.

Not everyone on that first training sail made it to the start of the race, let alone the finish, but of those who did I can say that all are friends and some have become very dear friends to me, most notably Mark Earle. Mark runs a tree nursery near Lymm in Cheshire, has a passion for racing motorcycles, great taste in music and an appetite for simply being at sea which never deserted him. That, together with his unquenchable cheerfulness and his previous experience crewing on yacht deliveries, made him a natural choice as a watch leader when we were united on *Toshiba*.

To foster this spirit of being one big happy family, the Challenge Business organised a number of crew outings, the first of which was a day, courtesy of Nuclear Electric, at their Oldbury Power Station. This proved to be hugely entertaining, both in terms of the official content of the day, and because it provided a meeting ground for us all to get together and see who else was involved in this crazy scheme. It was also the first exposure for most of us to 'The Life and Times of Chay Blyth'. Chay gave a hilarious talk which seemed to be illustrated largely with slides of enormous seas or boats floating the wrong way up, during all of which he remarked once every three or four sentences: 'Well, you've got to have a sense of humour!'

What we did have to sustain us and nurture our initial enthusiasm was plenty of news. The Challenge Business moved its headquarters to their present location at Liskeard in Cornwall; Mike Golding announced that he was going to attack Chay's record for the non-stop singlehanded westabout circumnavigation in *Group 4*; and Time & Tide signed up as yacht sponsors. These last two events had interesting repercussions. *Time & Tide*'s fantastic bid to complete the race with a crew all suffering from some form of disability became the focus of a huge amount of media coverage and their fantastic achievement stands as a tremendous example to all those facing any kind of handicap or prejudice. In the meantime, Mike's phenomenal solo effort secured him a permanent place in the history books but raised the interesting point that Group 4 Securitas, having bought the *Group 4* yacht, were sponsoring their skipper to sail the race course, albeit on his own, thereby providing an opportunity not available to others to study weather and currents and plan race tactics well in advance.

In March 1994 BT announced that they had taken up the Titleholder position for the race, the training yacht was re-named *BT Global Challenge,* and in May Andy Hindley succeeded his former skipper on *Hofbrau Lager* as the new Training Skipper. Having handed over the reins to Andy, Pete soon moved on to plan and begin raising sponsorship for his entry in the Vendée Globe race. For all that, he remained very much in touch with what we were all doing and, for those of us who trained with Pete in the early days of the BT Global Challenge, there is no-one who so exemplified the spirit of what this endeavour was all about. For even during training, for some of us, there were dark moments of self-doubt and despair.

The Challenge training programme was divided into four parts: induction, continuation, assessment and placement. Induction training consisted of day sailing from Plymouth. Every day began with a complete stem to stern, whether cleaning the yacht or naming all the parts of it. Time at sea was spent changing sails, learning good safe techniques for winching and handling equipment and learning safety procedures. There is a standard man overboard routine on all Challenge yachts and we were drilled in it until we could do it automatically and talk it through both individually and as a group. 'What is the first rule of man overboard?' would come the inevitable question. 'Don't fall overboard!' we would yell back.

One of the interesting things about a man overboard routine as a piece of teamwork is that everybody has to know, and be able to do, every one of the jobs involved; you simply do the one you are nearest to. So we would fly into action, pointing to our 'casualty' in the water, starting the engine, bringing down the sails, in a tremendous flurry of activity, which would always conclude with us 'ferry-gliding' down, oh so gently, towards our target, boat hook over the side, and another rescue would be complete as we hauled our fender safely back on board. This left us to the sombre reflection that this was only a fender after all, not a crew member wearing thermals, mid-layer, foul weather gear and a lifejacket; that we had a few pounds to lift out of a slightly choppy sea, and not sixteen stone to haul up out of a heaving ocean. But for now our fender was safely back on board and we could put everything away again – until the next time.

A taste of the real thing? Well, continuation training involved putting out to sea and staying out for at least 48 hours; assessment meant starting each day with a piece of hallowed Challenge tradition, a four mile run and a swim in the sea. One of these was particularly memorable. We were anchored up in Cawsand Bay and at 6 am we pumped up a 14-man inflatable dinghy and set out, Hawaii Five-O fashion, for the shore. This definitely smacked of Marine training; we were half expecting orders to take out the entire village in one lightning strike, but all that happened was that we got soaking wet. We pulled the inflatable up on to the beach and jogged through the sleeping village. A quick round of warm-up exercises and we were off, running side by side in pairs. What we did not know was that our route would take us from the lowest point, the beach, to the highest, which happened to be the church, and back. There was some speculation as to whether the church was for saying our prayers or for burying those who expired on the way up, but in the end we all made it back to the beach.

'Right,' said Andy, stripping down to the bare essentials and heading for the sea. 'You are joking, aren't you?' cried one hopeful. 'You're not getting back on my boat without a wash,' replied Andy, plunging in. It was only September, after all. Training went on all year round and, yes, we went in in October, November, December, January, February and March as well. We towelled down on the concrete ramp leading up from the beach to the road. Imagine if you will, the face of the chap who came by walking his dog, especially since we were a mixed crew! I cheered myself up for ages thinking about him. I kept expecting him to turn up on *Strange but True?* reporting a ghostly, if not ghastly, apparition on Cawsand beach.

The temple dogs

Outside Eastern temples, guarding the entrance, are often to be found a pair of fearsome figures. Commonly, although not always, these are in the form of huge and ferocious-looking dogs. Early Western travellers assumed that these figures were intended to frighten off infidels such as themselves and leave the temple within undesecrated, but they missed the point. The point is that inside the temple lies the way of enlightenment, the way to find one's true self and the spiritual reality that lies there. The guardian figures represent the fearsome difficulties you will have to overcome if you are to reap the rewards.

It was on a training sail that my particular 'difficulties' manifested themselves – in fact, all my worst nightmares came true at once. Black night, big seas, 45 knots of wind and the boat beating to windward behaving like a rocking horse from hell. I certainly picked the wrong training trip to try omitting the seasickness pills. To say I was ill is like saying Bill Gates has done quite well out of computers. I spent most of one night grimly hugging the staysail winch on the low side, leaning out every half an hour or so to retch horribly and puke another few spoonfuls of green bile out over the toe rail. I winched with all the strength and power of a three-year-old when we tacked, I lurched and vomited my way to the foredeck when asked to check on something, but mostly I hung on the staysail winch and consoled myself that the chap in front of me and the chap behind were doing just as badly. But really there was no consolation. These were the western approaches to the English Channel, not the Southern Ocean. This was one night, not one night out of 40. This was a wet, windy, watery Hell on Earth. There was, I could see, no way of continuing. If an air-sea rescue helicopter had flown over they could have had everything I possessed, or ever would possess, if they had simply taken me out of it all then and there. Yet at the back of all this lurked a bigger dread. I had heard of people being sick for weeks on end at sea. It was unbearable even to think about, but how could I possibly write to everyone who had bought a postcard from me and say I was backing out?

Sir Francis Chichester is to blame, and he did not even want to be sponsored. When Sir Francis made his solo voyage around the world he was sponsored, with much publicity, by Whitbread, the brewers, and by the Woolmark. In his book *Gypsy Moth Circles the World* he explained that the night before setting out he felt extremely appre-hensive. So apprehensive that all his seaman's instincts told him not to go. But what of the sponsors? In the end he felt he could not let them down, so he went and he found his true greatness. I knew, even before Pete Goss had mentioned postcards, that I needed to be sponsored. I knew I would need some leverage to help me through the testing times. Sponsorship became the sword in my sheath when it came to walking past the temple dogs.

In the middle of the blackest part of this dark night of the soul for me, we needed to make a sail change. Ill as I was, I had to play a part and was assigned to a role in the cockpit, but the foredeck team got into trouble. As the wind and the tension increased I was sent forward to find out what the trouble was and report. I made the journey along the side deck four times before communication was established and things were sorted out. Someone said to me when it was all over: 'You looked like the ghost of the Ancient Mariner coming down there, I really thought you shouldn't be here'. At the time I could not have agreed more wholeheartedly.

At the end of this sail I stepped off the boat with a heavy heart. Martin Ley, newly appointed Training Mate, stood in front of me.

'All right, Al?' he asked.

'Not exactly,' I replied.

'Reckon it might not be for you then?' he suggested after a pause.

'Something like that,' I said disconsolately. He looked me up and down.

'Reckon you'll be all right,' he told me. I looked up, slightly surprised.

'You think so?' I asked and he nodded as we shook hands.

Some time later I discovered that Eleanor Roosevelt had summed it up rather pithily. 'You must do the thing you think you cannot do,' she had said.

2

It's Only Wind and Water

*'A man who be not afraid of the sea will soon be
drowned for he will be going out on a day he should
not. But we do be afraid of the sea and will only be
drowned now and again.'* Displayed on a plaque at
the NSRI station in Cape Town

Sailing a big boat is all about teamwork, but it is an interesting
form of teamwork. Most of the operations we had to carry out
were really sequences of events, so the art lay not in actually doing
things together a lot of the time, but in doing them quickly and efficiently in the right order. Take tacking for example. A yacht cannot
sail directly into the wind, but a well-designed one can sail at an
angle of about 30 to 35 degrees to the wind direction. So if you want
to sail to where the wind is coming from and the best you can do is
to sail 30 degrees, say, to the left of that line, after a while you need
to stop doing that and 'tack', ie sail 30 degrees to the right of the
line, zigzagging to where you want to go. It's called 'tacking'.

Teamwork on the tack

The main point, especially if you are racing, is that the bow of the
boat swings right through the wind, and when the boat is actually
head to wind the sails do not drive. Only momentum will carry the
boat past this critical point. Since there is a point where there is no
forward drive at all, boats lose speed when tacking. The object is to
lose as little speed as possible and get up to speed as quickly as
possible on the new tack. How do you do it?

We are creaming along close-hauled, sailing as near to the wind as we can, on starboard tack. The helmsman is concentrating on his course, the skipper is standing by his right shoulder watching ahead to pick his moment. The crew are seated along the windward rail; every bit of weight on the high side will tend to keep the boat more upright and sailing faster.

'Ready about!' The skipper calls for action; the crew peel away from the windward rail and head to their designated positions in the cockpit. With six crew on watch we are one to a winch and the crucial one at this point is the leeward runner. From either side of the boat at the back a wire runs to a point part way up the mast. The one on the windward side has to be winched up tight to counteract the pull of the staysail in front of the mast. Since the boat is about to change its angle relative to the wind, the runner, which is currently slack, has to be made ready to take the strain. The one currently in use will be released as we go through the tack.

In the back corner of the cockpit the line holding the slack runner is released from its cleat and the runner is pulled tight to its winch. When the winch handle is in and ready to wind, the man on the runner calls: 'Ready!' Ahead of him the crew on the staysail and primary winches stand ready to cast off the ropes currently taking all the strain of the sails; on the other side of the cockpit the winch crews have already taken three turns of rope around the winch barrels ready to haul in. Behind them the starboard runner crew is ready to let his line fly. When the skipper has 'Ready' from everyone, he signals the helmsman who starts to turn the wheel. There is a trick in this: if he spins the wheel right over, the rudder will act as a big brake and slow the boat down, if he does not go into the tack fast enough we will lose the momentum to carry us through.

'Helm's a-lee!' calls the helmsman.

'Seven point eight,' the skipper reads the speed from the instruments and glances ahead, eyeing the oncoming waves.

For a calm, quiet moment, *BT Global Challenge* carries her way forward, sails full, crew poised. Then the whoosh of the sea streaming past lessens, she straightens up slightly and begins momentarily to slow. 'Seven point six.' The yankee curls out of shape. Deprived of the airflow from the sail in front, the staysail slackens. The wind noise lessens, the crew wait. Finally the yankee folds in towards the centre of the boat, the deck rolls suddenly flat. 'Lee-oh!' from the back of the cockpit. The yankee and staysail sheets are whipped out of the self-tailers on top of the winches which hold them locked, and four turns of rope around the barrel are spun away. With the rope gone, the person on the port primary winch steps smartly across the forward part of the cockpit to the winch opposite; now there are two people hauling in armfuls of rope, one behind the other. It is a race to get all the slack in and the rope secured on the winch before the sail re-fills on the other side of the boat and pulling it in by hand becomes impossible. Further aft, the staysail sheet is being hauled into the cockpit as if life depended upon it. The old windward runner, strain released when the wind went from the staysail, has been cast off its winch and on the opposite side the new runner is being aggressively wound up to its mark. 'Runner on!' between panted breaths gets a quiet: 'Well done,' in return, as the winch handle is slid back into its pocket.

From calm to madness. As the sheets stream out, the sails crack in the wind, the ropes fly across the foredeck snapping and jerking, the winches clack and clatter. 'Seven point nought!' 'Winch!' yells the front man on the big primary as he passes the fourth turn around the drum and brings the line around once more, locking it into the teeth of the self-tailer. The winch handle clicks into the top of the winch; two people: four hands, bodies swinging together, drive it round in high gear. 'Six point eight.' 'Other way.' The winch grinders reverse direction, winding faster again now in lower gear to bring in the last few feet. The forward facing grinder has his eyes up watching the slowly circling forefinger of the sail trimmer who in turn stares up at the changing shape of the sail as the sheet gradually winds in.

BT Global Challenge shoulders her way on to the new tack, heeling over again now as the wind presses the re-set sails, and the noise picks up. The wave whoosh is back. The sail trimmer holds his fist clenched. The winch grinders pant with relief. 'Good on the yankee. In on the staysail.' The lone winch clatters on. 'Staysail's good. Seven point two. Seven point four.' We are accelerating back up to boat-speed, still trimming the headsails, adjusting the set of the main, on course on the new tack. It has taken about a minute – and any moment now we will be doing it all again.

Cooking up a storm

They told us placement training would be tough and it was. Intensive day sailing, starting with a run and a dip in the sea at 6 am. We learned to hoist, peel and gybe our spinnakers or 'kites', the large (often brightly coloured) sails flown when sailing downwind. They operate on a different principle to the headsails and involve the use of a pole to hold one corner of the sail out. They generate phenomenal loads: the strongest ropes on a Challenge yacht are the spinnaker guys and halyards which have a breaking strain of 13 tons, and handling them required us to become adept at ever more complex sequences of events, each person playing one small part in the grand scheme of the operation.

Sometimes these training sails took us out into winds gusting up to 60 knots and more. The description from the Beaufort scale for this sort of weather reads: 'Force 10, 48–55 knots. Storm. Very high waves with long overhanging crests and dense streaks of foam making the sea white; heavy tumbling sea; visibility affected. Probable wave height 30 ft. Probable maximum wave height 41 ft.' The description of conditions on land is: 'Seldom experienced inland; trees uprooted, structural damage occurs.'

On one occasion we had anchored in the River Fal after a trip around the Bishop Rock lighthouse in very heavy weather, when two Customs officers came on board. 'Where have you come from?' they asked Andy. 'Plymouth,' he replied, 'We're training for the BT Global Challenge.' 'You were off the Lizard earlier on, weren't you?' said the Customs man suspiciously. 'Yes,' said Andy, 'We've been round the Bishop Rock and back.' The Customs man eyed him up and down, then cast an eye round the deck at the rest of us. 'How was it out there?' he asked. 'It was all right by me,' Andy told him, 'but this lot found it a bit rough!' The Customs officers shook their heads quietly, climbed back into their launch and left.

On another occasion we were called to pay attention and told: 'These are just the kind of conditions in which it is possible to be knocked flat. If we are knocked right over, hang on, and when we come back up again listen for instructions!' That caused a moment's quiet reflection among the crew. On the lighter side as we coasted back one night in light airs and pitch darkness someone remarked to Mark Lodge, later the skipper of *Motorola* for the race, 'I thought you said there was no night sailing on Assessment.' 'This isn't night,' replied Mark, peering into the blackness, 'It's just dusk!'

Some of these moments were shared with people who were later to become great rivals on the race, others with crewmates of the future. I shared a trip round the rock with Geoff Ward who was, amongst other things, our 'Chief Engineer' on *Toshiba*. Geoff has been described as a professional Yorkshireman (though not by me!). He has an encyclopaedic knowledge of cricket, a bedside manner that would do credit to a sergeant major and a liking for ready-rubbed rough-cut old shag that followed him round the world. At 55 he was our oldest crew member. Fit as a fiddle, Geoff could mend anything on board in any weather and did everything he was ever asked to without complaint, except eat curry! Jo Dawson was another who rode out some wild weather with me on early training sails. A corporate bank manager, and much travelled back-packer with a taste for adventure, Jo became *Toshiba*'s controller of the crew fund, tireless leader of the sail repair team and founder member of the 'Tosh Blondes'.

The other major part of this final training sail in the sequence was to complete our knowledge of the boat's systems. There is, after all, no-one else to help once you are well and truly out there. You need to know how to fix the water maker, how to operate the GPS navigation system and the radar, you need to be able to strip a winch down and re-assemble it, and you need to know how to clear a blocked toilet, as well as know where all the different bilge pumps are located. Under the floorboards are four freshwater tanks, five diesel tanks and a 'slurry' or waste tank. They are surrounded by a maze of piping and stop cocks. You need to know where all the hull fittings are; the places where pipes go out to or come in from the sea; drawing in sea water for the water maker, for cooling the main engine and the generator, and for use in the galley to conserve fresh water. We need navigators, tacticians, radio operators, weather experts, sail makers, and riggers, and there ain't nobody here but us chickens!

So on Assessment Training, at the end of each day's sailing, we went through the boat's systems. Those we had already learned about – the safety equipment, the main engine, the plumbing – we had to regurgitate in the form of training lectures to each other. The remaining ones we learned and did our best to memorise.

We also studied routeing charts, which show the statistical like-lihood of winds blowing at various directions at various speeds; and a glance at the Southern Ocean showed us why they call this route 'the wrong way round'. Above all we learned a sense of adventure. Even our 'bedtime story' about Rich Wilson and Steve Pettengill being capsized by a giant wave off Cape Horn in their trimaran *Great American* became an inspiration. They were subsequently turned back the right way by another enormous wave, and eventually rescued by the container ship *New Zealand Pacific*.

Through all this period of training and learning, other people's lives went on exactly as before. I suppose that when someone you know says they are going to sail around the world, starting in three years' time, you wait to see whether they are really going to do it before you worry about it or even think about it too much. So for

Pam and for my mother not a lot changed, except that I would be away for a few days every couple of months or so.

Pam has two startlingly attractive daughters (it is easy to see where they get it from) and was busy in a post-bringing-up-the-children managerial career. That of course meant that her week revolved around work, as mine did around teaching guitar, and weekends we spent together, usually at her house. Life would look very different once I was away.

Involvement in the Challenge brought me the opportunity to sail on other boats from time to time, most notably with Paul Waxman, a long-time member and officer of the Royal Ocean Racing Club. Paul very kindly included me in his crew for a number of offshore races, including the 1995 Fastnet Race. He had borrowed a bigger boat than his own for the race and it needed quite a lot of work doing on it, so the whole thing took on the air of a proper campaign with all the preparation that entails. Although the boat was rather slow, we had a fantastic time and I had the thrill of being at the helm as we rounded the Fastnet Rock. Paul remarked, 'Quite emotional, isn't it, coming round here? Think what it will be like when you round Cape Horn.' The idea was certainly hard to grasp.

What was easy to grasp was the need to keep sending cheques to the Challenge Business to keep one's hopes and aspirations alive. In the end I had a full time guitar teaching practice with every day full from mid-afternoon to late evening, Saturday solidly booked and a fair few students coming along for lessons in the mornings. It was an extraordinary example of focus. I simply held my faith that I would meet every payment as it fell due. The result, predictably, was to put pressure on my social life. Teaching every evening and spending a lot of weekends away sailing is not conducive to domestic harmony and looking back on it I am surprised that Pam bore it with the fortitude she did. On the other hand, we are both great believers in 'going for it', and the bigger the challenge that someone takes up the more important it is that you get out of their way and get round behind them where you can help and support.

Cell mates

A year has always sounded like a long time to me. The seasons roll by: autumn leaves, Christmas coming, New Year, spring and summer. A lot can happen in that sort of time scale. And then someone says: 'Only a year to go, then' and it sounds like nothing. Hang on a minute, I've got things I need to organise. Who is going to deal with everything at home while I'm away for a year? What do I need to know? What do I need to take? Are you sure about this? A year doesn't seem very long to sort all this out. And inevitably, inexorably, the London Boat Show was drawing nearer.

Suppose you were asked to spend nine months in a 67 foot by 17 foot tin shed, boiling hot in hot weather, freezing cold the other half of the time. You will do hard physical work with a high risk of injury, eat dehydrated food, be woken up to work every four to six hours and frequently have to spend long periods out of doors in the worst weather imaginable. On top of all this, you have to share this space with 13 other people. Would you not be interested to know who those other people were and what they were like? Dr Johnson said that a ship is a prison with a risk of drowning. On the Challenge, the London Boat Show was where you found out who your cell mates were.

The room was large, big enough to hold a fair size dance. Mandy Burnett greeted us as we crowded in through the doorway. At the far end a microphone and a screen for an overhead projector signified the business afoot. STRICTLY CREW ONLY read the signs. There was wine on hand and an expectant edge to the hubbub of conversation. Several boats were still without sponsors so this was going to be a real lucky dip. People formed up into ragged groups, laughing and joking, and there was high excitement in the air. Eventually Chay called the room to some sort of order and made a few preliminary remarks, the main thrust of which was that 'You can't have Utopia,' by which he meant you will not necessarily be with everyone you wanted to be with, and you will not necessarily get along with everyone on your boat.

Then the fun began. The first boat came up on the screen, a sponsor's name, skipper underneath that and then 11 members of the core crew. The two remaining places on each yacht would be taken up by crew sailing one leg of the race only. The hardest thing in all this was watching the names of old friends go by and seeing those people start to move out towards the edges of the room to meet their skipper and crew mates for the trip. *Toshiba* came up quite late in the proceedings, late enough to make me suffer childhood pangs of 'I'm being left out!' and then suddenly there it was: *Toshiba Wave Warrior*, skipper Simon Walker and a list of crew.

I knew next to nothing about Simon. Two people who had sailed with him had told me he was fantastic, but they were both young and pretty, and neither of them was male. What did that tell me? I also knew that he had been the Mate on *Rhone Poulenc* in the British

21

Steel Challenge and rumour had it that he had been the mainstay of that crew during some difficult times. The crew list showed up Mark Earle, Geoff Ward and Jo Dawson, three familiar faces from training at least. Mark, I knew, was a keen sailor, with several transatlantic delivery sails behind him, although the majority of his sailing had been with his partner Claire. Geoff, by contrast, had never set foot on a yacht before training for the Challenge. Along with his sea-legs he brought his own mixture of paternalism and abrasiveness, and whilst sometimes outspoken was never disliked. Jo, bright, blonde and bubbly, had the strongest competitive streak of any of us, and that sometimes showed a darker side when things were not going well. Prepared from the start to give up virtually everything for the race and to work heart and soul for the boat, she sometimes became upset when she thought her efforts were not appreciated or that others were not so selfless.

We were not a complete crew, but we had a sponsor and we had a very happy-looking skipper who immediately made a good impression on me, dressed as he was in blazer and tie over his chinos and polished shoes. Ciara Scott I had met whilst crewing on a couple of corporate hospitality days in Southampton. At 22, Ciara was the third youngest person on the race and the second youngest girl. Still in her last year as a dental student, she had her finals to contend with before getting to grips with racing round the world, and had the interesting distinction of sharing the race experience with her father John, who sailed aboard *Global Teamwork*. Although she said later that she had found it difficult to settle in at first, being the youngest person on board, it did not show, and she always pulled her weight, literally as well as metaphorically. Possessed of a strong sense of humour she was not slow to say what she thought if anyone upset her.

I scrutinised the new faces present. Spike is only ever called Stewart Briggs in official crew listings and by certain members of his family! Formerly an engineer on North Sea oil rigs, he had given that up to retrain as a doctor and was working in the intensive care unit of Southampton Hospital. Someone who needs little sleep, is fascinated by winds and weather systems, and has rock climbing, wind surfing and driving much too fast among his hobbies is likely to be an asset aboard a racing yacht. When that person is also ultra-fit and comes on board as the boat medic, the gods are smiling on you.

Ben Pearson, who became our Mate, and Mark's opposite number leading the starboard watch, came, fittingly, fresh from the navy. As a navy and marine dentist, Ben was fit, ready for anything and able to see the funny side of absolutely anything. His tremendous enthusiasm and zany sense of humour only ever deserted him when presented with a steaming dish full of McDougall's minced mutton just after being woken up. One of the strangest things about life in a watch system is that you keep eating breakfast. That is to say that at all different times of day you are shaken awake, crawl into some kit and stagger to the galley to be confronted with a meal. This meal may actually be breakfast, lunch or dinner, although if you have never been on an ocean racer for any length of time you would probably not recognise any of them as such, but nevertheless it is served to you immediately upon rising. Some of us simply ate whatever was offered, whenever it was offered, and came back for more, others found the 'wake up, eat up' routine more difficult.

Of our two non-British crew, Kobus was still in South Africa tending to his chicken farm, but Drew had flown in from his home in Newport, Rhode Island, home also of American yachting, bringing his camera. Drew is a photographer who wanted to combine his chance to race around the world with an unrivalled opportunity to get some great pictures on the way. Coming from Newport it was understandable that Drew loved being around boats and had long cherished an ambition to race around the world. Like Kobus, Drew had a certain culture gap to cross in getting to grips with our sense of humour. Kobus is an Afrikaner to whom English is a second language, and his more philosophical statements sometimes acquired an interesting opacity. Having crewed previously on a long ocean passage, he had some experience and a taste for the sea.

Fittingly for the first time any of us had united under the Toshiba banner, we were promptly each given a red jacket to wear and whisked off for a team (or part-team to be accurate) photograph. From there we went on to another hallowed 'Team Toshiba' tradition – the good night out. We caroused the evening away in a nearby restaurant, during which Simon took the opportunity to try to find out who we all were and how we might best fit together.

The following morning he telephoned me to say, among other things, 'I know you said last night that you were really interested in the food on board, so I'd like you to start to think about our food programme.' I did not like to tell him at that point that it must have been somebody else who had been so keen, since I had always said it was the one job on board a boat I did not want! It goes without saying that I had a great time doing it once I had got stuck in, although I very rapidly became second lieutenant to the incomparable Joe 'Woolly' Watson once she joined the team and took charge. Joe was an eternal bright spark. Her helming efforts in the Southern

Ocean earned her the soubriquet of 'The Mighty Atom' – she is only just tall enough to peer over the wheel, but helmed brilliantly. A 'foody' undeterred by the rigours of being at sea, she was the world's greatest in the galley. She denies that she is permanently cheerful, but by most people's standards she is. She also won the 'Best Body in a Bikini' competition in a very closely fought competition.

Interestingly, I had another experience similar to this later on, when Simon asked me to take care of all the paperwork that is involved in entering and leaving each port, and fulfilling the requirements of the various customs and immigration authorities. In 'real life' I absolutely abhor this kind of thing and can't stand filling in forms or dealing with any kind of bureaucracy, but in the cause of getting us round the world as smoothly as possible, I found it quite an entertaining task.

Of the three crew who could not join us that night, Guy Bell had originally been assigned to another boat, but had a slight difficulty with the sponsor. It is always a little awkward when your company is suing your boat sponsor, even if the cause of the problem is nothing to do with the race, and so Guy, an ex-Sandhurst City man with a wickedly sardonic sense of humour, joined the Wave Warriors, as did Woolly. When Joe joined us we had the problem of two people with the same name, given of course that the 'e' in Joe is silent. Communication on board a big yacht is of paramount importance, and it is also often very difficult. We struggled through our early sails on board *Toshiba* with Simon calling 'Jo D' or 'Joe W' and we tried various nicknames, but these never work of course. Good nicknames arise naturally and so when Joe let slip that one of her family had been nicknamed Woolly we fell upon it with glee. It has nothing, by the way, to do with the practice of tying spinnakers up with wool to prevent them opening whilst being hoisted, and everything to do with ... but that would not be fair! Guy was an experienced sailor and a good helm. Intellectual, although he claimed that the copy of Marcus Aurelius' *Meditations* he had on board had been given to him, and deeply cynical, he was, nevertheless, the only one of us to stick up pictures of his family by his bunk! Guy was often very funny, a master of English understatement and, along with Ben, one of our two great patriots on board. So that was our 'core crew'.

It was always part of the Challenge plan that two crew members on each yacht would be rotated for each leg and the original idea was that one of these 'legger' places would be filled by someone from the company or organisation sponsoring the yacht. Because Toshiba UK run a very tight ship in terms of staff numbers, they opted to give their places to the RNLI, who in turn offered them to active lifeboat crews from around the UK. Part of the selection procedure for the RNLI leg berths was a commitment from each volunteer to raise £5000 towards the cost of a new lifeboat and Chris Gaskin, a 25-year-old science teacher from the Wirral, had by doing that won his place on the first leg of the race. Ebullient and quick-witted, a skier and windsurfer, Chris was fit, strong, and raring to go. A tendency to distract himself from the job in hand in order to deal in the much more important task of trading insults must, we concluded, have been the product of that near-Liverpool upbringing.

What then of the opposition? Five sponsors from the previous race had elected to go again: *Group 4*, *Commercial Union*, *Heath Insured*, *Nuclear Electric*, and *Courtaulds*, racing under their own name this time rather than the *Interspray* banner. *Motorola*, Rover, sailing as *Ocean Rover*, and late arrivals *3-Com* took up the Challenge, along with three yachts bearing the names of charitable foundations: *Save the Children*, *Pause to Remember*, supporting the Royal British Legion, and of course the indomitable disabled crew of *Time & Tide*. *Concert* was named for the joint venture between BT and its US counterpart, MCI, and *Global Teamwork* for a consortium of information technology companies who not only all supplied BT, but who had joined forces previously to go yacht racing. Fourteen identical yachts, fourteen crews selected to be as evenly matched as possible. Who would fare best?

We had a crew, and unlike many we had a sponsor and were profoundly grateful for it; what we did not have at this point was the boat. Along with all the other yachts, *Toshiba Wave Warrior* was still undergoing her final fitting out at the DML yard in Plymouth so, perhaps taking a cue from Chay's Whitbread campaign of many years before, Simon arranged for our first team training session to take place in a house in North Wales. The house was situated conveniently close to the Welsh Outdoor Activities Centre, Plas Menai, where, it turned out, we would go dinghy sailing. The Menai Straits in a force 6 in January is not a bad place to begin a bit of Southern Ocean training. The waves are not quite so big, of course, but the temperature is about right. It was freezing! But it was great fun. Spike expertly rigged his dinghy very quickly and set out across the straits with Jo, travelling fast until they wiped out in a big capsize. As the rescue boat came over, Spike learned that there are three bungs you need to secure in a Wayfarer dinghy, not two, if you want to stop it sinking! It was some time before he was allowed to forget that.

For two days we raced against each other and were put through our paces on the water, and in the evenings we talked through every aspect of the race; prepared and delivered short talks on all sorts of different topics: food, weather, watch systems, sail trimming and so on; and listened avidly to Simon's plans. In fact Simon had been planning this campaign virtually since he had stepped off *Rhone Poulenc* at the end of the British Steel Challenge, and it showed. His overall grasp of the project, coupled with his impeccable attention to detail, went a long way to meld us into a fighting unit with some chance of winning even at this early stage.

The pages of history are a record of great meetings: Livingstone and Stanley, for example, or Antony and Cleopatra, and in Wales we met John Hill. John was then General Manager, Corporate Marketing for Toshiba in the UK, and as such the mastermind of the sponsorship programme. He travelled up to meet us with his wife Sue and got the full blast of the 'Wave Warriors' letting their hair down over dinner after the day's exertions. Completely unfazed, he pitched straight in with the spirit of the thing and immediately sealed a fantastic relationship. Throughout the entire race, Toshiba were a wonderful sponsor and John was our number one supporter, our chief ally, and a tower of strength behind the scenes.

We also spent a weekend training in the Solent on board *Maiden*, the boat used by Tracy Edwards and her all-women crew in the 1989–90 Whitbread Race. There is often a little bit of magic which attaches itself to boats with a history, and *Maiden* is no exception. I had sailed on her once before at Pete Goss's invitation and was delighted to be back on board. This was our first weekend sailing together as a crew on a big boat and, unlike a Challenge yacht, *Maiden* has hydraulics, 'coffee grinders' for powering up the winches, and genuine running backstays – that is to say, no fixed backstay. In layman's language that means she has lots of toys to play with but if you get it wrong you start breaking things in a big way! But we functioned well together, learned a lot and kept everything in one piece. It was a very promising start.

Avoiding breakages is of major importance. It is fairly obvious that to stand a chance of winning a long ocean race you have to conserve the gear on board. On the other hand, in a one-design race where all the boats are identical, unless you drive the boat as fast as possible, you will be beaten by someone else doing just that; and of course driving the boat to its limit means that you are much more likely to suffer damage. It is an interesting game and one which was to cause conflicts and controversies later on.

In May 1996 the entire Challenge fleet was assembled for the first time in Queen Anne's Battery Marina; 14 bare boats moored up together alongside the pontoons. The week that followed was like every yachtsman's dream of Christmas. Everything you needed started to arrive by the van and lorry load, all of it brand spanking new, and in identical sets of 14. Word would ripple through the fleet: 'Our spinnaker poles are here,' or 'You can collect your storm stay-sail from the end of the pontoon' and off we would go to pick up another sail or collect some other part of our inventory. Best of all though, without a shadow of a doubt, was taking our big red boat out sailing at the end of the week. For the first time, although we still did not have everyone aboard, the 'Wave Warriors' took to the high seas on *Toshiba*.

High seas is a bit of an exaggeration, actually. Like any prudent mariner we conducted our first sail trials inside the Plymouth Harbour breakwater and then made our first passage, in company with the rest of the fleet, along the south coast to rendezvous at the Needles for a helicopter photoshoot and then proceed to Southampton, our home port for the next few months.

For the next four months, under Simon's ever patient tutelage we learned to race the big red machine. We learned the skills of helming upwind and down, improved our tacking and our sail changing, spent many hours calibrating our optimum boat speeds under various different conditions and, above all, we learned, in a phrase Chay was to make so famous that Challenge crew would yell it at briefings before he could say it to us, to *trim, trim, trim*. Sail trim is almost the be-all and end-all of racing yachts. Good or bad helming makes all the difference in the world, but after that your boat speed depends on how you set your sails.

Of course the Solent is a sheltered stretch of water, and even the English Channel is usually pretty flat in summer. All those heavy weather training sails seemed a long time ago, and in many ways the Southern Ocean seemed a long way ahead, but it haunted me. I would wake in the middle of the night and be unable to get back to sleep imagining the roar of the wind and the slam of the waves crashing against the hull. How would I stand up to continual exposure to that kind of weather? The fear of being disabled by seasickness, of being unable to function properly as part of the crew, lurked in the back of my mind. I had always said that the only thing I really feared, apart from continual seasickness, was serious physical injury; a broken leg or something of that order. As the race drew nearer I was not so sure – perhaps I was most afraid of letting down those around me. Or perhaps it was just a case of nothing to fear except fear itself. In Herman Wouk's novel *Don't Stop the Carnival* someone asks a navy frogman what the motivation of his men is. 'Poverty and fright,' he replies, 'It's double hazardous duty pay, you see ... and I guess most of us are cowards who have to keep proving to ourselves how brave we are.' I thought about my motivation.

Call to arms

'It's not a race, it's a training sail,' Chay kept telling us at the briefing, but of course no-one believed him. A thousand miles from the start line off Cowes, to a waypoint off Ushant on the north-west corner of France, up to another waypoint in the Irish Sea, round the Fastnet Rock and home again. Full race crews, full race rules, just one funny quirk. Each yacht was to carry a number of packets containing sealed instructions. If so instructed by Race Headquarters (universally known just as RHQ), any given yacht was to open the appropriate package and carry out whatever exercise was detailed therein. Ostensibly this was to enable the race organisation to test various communications and emergency procedures, but we had our doubts. This was our first and only chance to race against each other before the real thing, and we meant business – or did we?

'We don't really want to win it,' Simon informed us with a grin. 'We want to have a good run round, have fun, not break anything – that's very important – and come in somewhere around fourth or fifth. That means we'll look quite good but we won't have shown our hand too early.'

In the event we had a tough beat out to the first two waypoints in about a force 6 with the typical short lumpy seas you would expect in this part of the world, but the atmosphere on board was tremendous. Everyone seemed to slip into the watch system very comfortably and, in my case at least, the seasickness pills were working to the extent that I could keep on working. Coming back from the Rock, however, we had just about the best sail any of us was to have on *Toshiba*. In winds of 30 to 35 knots we kept the flanker, our heaviest spinnaker, up all the way. We had a top boat speed of over 19 knots and, more importantly, scored a 24 hour run of 269 miles – within 3 miles of the all-time record for a Challenge yacht. This was my first experience of helming a spinnaker downwind in anything like these conditions and it was fantastic fun. Our plan for a conservative finish went by the board, however. 'What happened to fourth or fifth?' John Hill asked with a big grin. 'The problem was,' Simon explained, 'that we had got up to second, and there were about another five boats not so very far behind. So if we had slowed down we might easily have come in around seventh, which was *not* the plan.'

Nuclear Electric took the honours and *Toshiba* followed not long after in second place, to a tremendous champagne welcome organised entirely by Lou Foord, Simon's partner and mother of their young son, Jack. We felt that we had done very well. After all, our sealed instructions had required us to take the mainsail down and sail at reduced speed under trysail for four hours, but we kept quiet about that!

August and September went by in a welter of anticipation and a flurry of activity. There was simply so much to do: vaccinations and visas, bank accounts to sort out, a power of attorney so that someone can act for you, a car to take off the road and lay up, pupils, friends and loved ones to say goodbye to ('This is it, I'm really going') and a great many heart-to-hearts with Pam. Pam and I had known each other about two years when the race came up. She is a sharp, intelligent, sparky woman and I loved her great sense of fun from the moment I met her. It was probably helped by the fact that she was wearing a purple evening dress slit so high that you began to wonder what else she was wearing. We were not starry-eyed youngsters in love with love itself, and we had had our ups and downs, but we had formed a pretty solid partnership, whilst telling each other it was probably not for ever. How do you deal with relationships under these circumstances? If you are solidly married, perhaps with children, and your decision made about who you want to spend your life with, then a year away is perhaps not such a big test. If you think the experience might alter your life irrevocably, and that is a very real possibility, then what do you say? 'I love you, I'll be faithful, it'll be just the same when I get back'? That is not being very honest. And what of the person left behind, the person with the really tough job? After all, we were all off to see the world on a big adventure, whereas partners left behind had by and large the same life as before but with one of its mainstays removed. We talked and talked, largely without resolution.

Other relationship issues were brewing as the countdown to the start accelerated. Spike, Ben and Guy all achieved the astonishing feat, for three single and eligible men about to go off around the world, of starting new relationships, while Simon went through all the joy, and stress, of becoming a father for the second time when Jack's sister Charlie was born in August.

September saw the 'Bye Bye Ball' go by. The Challenge Business organised a superb evening at the Grosvenor House Hotel with the joint aims of allowing us all to have one jolly good last fling together before setting off, and of raising money for Save the Children. Save the Children was the nominated charity of the BT Global Challenge, the Princess Royal being the patron of both, and the interplay between the two was hugely successful. The Challenge Business, via such enterprises as the ball, and the crew volunteers using an incredible variety of fund raising activities, raised in excess of £1 000 000 for the charity, and of course Andy Hindley and his crew carried the name around the world on their yacht *Save the Children*.

Our last minute preparations included an excellent day's sailing with Peter Vroon of Hood's, the sailmakers for the race. Peter naturally divided his time equally amongst the boats in the fleet and was always careful to be completely impartial with his advice. Nonetheless, it was perhaps helpful to us that Simon and Peter were great friends and Peter obviously enjoyed the fact that we paid very close attention to what he said. Sail trimming, especially trimming the main, which had become one of my specialised tasks, can be something of a black art. The problem is that it is partly a left brain activity and partly a right brain one. You need to be clear and logical in making the basic adjustments, and you need a good analytical understanding of how each of the various controls affects the shape, but the final tweaking is all feel and art, not exact measurement; right brain, not left. We had a good day on the water – sunshine always helps – and with just over two weeks to go to the start we were looking fairly good and feeling reasonably confident.

There is something very exciting about preparing a boat for a long passage. The tiniest job inspires the thought, 'Is this good enough?' or 'Will this survive the Southern Ocean?', in short: 'Have I done it well enough?' It is an attitude manufacturing companies would kill for, but then again, this was *our* yacht, our home, our cocoon of survival for the next ten months.

Whilst buying something in the chandlery I was seduced by the sight of Umberto Eco's then new novel *The Island of the Day Before*. I lusted for it, but realised that a thick, heavy hard backed book has no place on an ocean racer and reluctantly I left it on the shelf. These little moments, these epiphanies, continued to crowd in upon me; the tiniest things took on a great significance and there was the continuing feeling of 'this will be the last time I do *this* particular thing before we go'. Then I realised that in not much over a month we would be looking at a street plan of Rio.

One week before the start most of us moved on to the boat. The hardest part of that was saying goodbye to Joe, my dog. He is a beautiful Border Collie bred on a farm in the middle of Bodmin Moor. I bought him when he was eight weeks old; he was nine when the race began and in all that time I had not spent more than two weeks away from him, so saying goodbye was a wrench. Pam drove me down and helped put my kit on board, then we went off for a cup of coffee. Everything was fine until just before she left to drive back to her house, when she became a little tearful.

'It's *next* weekend we're going,' I pointed out.

'I know,' she said, 'I'll be all right. It's silly, really.' She then promptly drove the wrong way out of the car park and had to U-turn and come back. She passed me with a wave and turned right instead of left at the car park exit into a dead end, so we had to have a reunion while I explained to her how to get out of Ocean Village!

This last week was a time when specialisms came to the fore. The Challenge Business had arranged earlier in the year for each supplier of equipment to the boats to run a training course and so while some went off to learn about the rigging and spars, others spent time in the sail lofts or learning about the engine or the heaters. Thus Spike, who had done the rigging course, spent most of his time dangling from a halyard up the mast along with Kobus who, being small, light and agile, was a natural choice for bowman. Drew became an expert in the care of our Harken winches, Guy checked and re-checked the charts and the navigation marks for the start, and everybody carried, fetched, cleaned and stowed. One difficulty with this is that 14 crew, plus various helpers including some of our 'leggers', soon make even a 67 foot yacht a very crowded place to be. We had our first taste of the frustrations of working at such close quarters and the difficulty of trying to get things done when you constantly have to make way for other people so that they can get their work done. It was a considerable relief to me to be detailed to pack the food for the first leg, since this operation was taking place at Spike's flat in nearby Romsey.

It was one of Simon's prime considerations that we should eat well on board and the food programme had been the subject of a great deal of research and effort. Simon had arranged a tailor-made course for Woolly and myself at Brooklands Technical College where, for several months, we spent every Monday morning in the company of department head Marco Zachariah rehydrating dried food and experimenting with stocks, sauces, spices and herbs. All the foods were designed to be light and easy to carry, to provide interest and variety, whilst providing the necessary energy and nutrition. We had researched quite heavily into previous races of similar duration and developed an eight-day menu which we thought fulfilled all the requirements. The whole programme was ingeniously set up on one of our Toshiba lap top computers by Woolly and Simon, the idea being that if you put in a number of days at sea as a starting point, the computer would produce the total quantities of each foodstuff required in the form of a shopping list, whilst also keeping a running tally of the calorific value and the cost of each meal. That just left the small matter of going shopping and packing it all up.

The shopping was good fun. We formed a SWAT team (special weapons and tactics, if you do not know your US Army jargon) and descended like locusts upon Makro and Tesco. Packing it up was quite good fun too. Eight days' food for 14 people at sea fits into four plastic boxes, each about 24 in x 18 in x 12 in, but in order to make the system work we had to do a great deal of splitting down from bulk packs into the amounts required for just one meal. Ease of preparation was a prime requirement on board, so there was a great deal of weighing and measuring to be done. As the race went on, we were able to simplify this part of the process considerably, compensating for it with increased galley skills among the crew!

One of the real difficulties with many of these jobs is actually finishing them off. There always seem to be odds and ends left to do. Perhaps that's just life, but this was life with a deadline! Without in any way wishing to insult anyone who has only a short time to live, I often referred to this period as like having a terminal illness. All known life ended on Sunday 29 September, and a new world would begin.

Pam came down for the weekend of the start, and on the Friday evening Toshiba held a dinner for the crew, but 27 September is Pam's birthday and we wanted to be alone so, excusing ourselves, we found a very nice restaurant where I arranged to have some fresh flowers on the table and champagne on ice when we arrived. We then ate a very good meal accompanied by an excellent claret, at the end of which my ability to add up was slightly impaired. Never one to stint on these things I added what seemed like a goodish tip to the bill and paid with a credit card. While we were waiting for a taxi to take us back to our hotel the restaurant owner sidled up to me in an almost conspiratorial fashion and murmured: 'Thank you so much for coming, Sir. If you should come again do just ask for table twelve.' She pointed to a table nestled snugly into an elegant bay window. 'I'll try to make sure it's kept for you.' In the taxi on the way back I managed to work out that I had in fact massively over-tipped, and had obviously been taken for some sort of high roller, rather than an impoverished yachtsman! As Bob Dylan once said: 'Money doesn't talk, it swears,' but what is money to a heart full of adventure?

3

Our Kind of Weather

'The real voyage of discovery consists not in seeking new landscapes, but in having new eyes.' Proust

Was it an omen? We woke up on the morning of the start of the Challenge to the sound of rain spattering against the hotel windows and a moaning, blustering wind that would have sent my heart down to my boots had we been going out on a training sail. Yet this time even windy, wet Southampton failed to dampen my spirits. This was it, the culmination of three years' training; we were setting out to race around the world. Pam and I took a last walk together around Ocean Village, hugged, kissed and managed to smile at each other.

There was keenness mingled with anticipation on board. We grinned, asked each other whether we were 'all right' a lot, and grinned back as confirmation that we were. Just before the first of the fleet untied, a small rubber dinghy came skimming across the marina. It headed straight up to the end of our pontoon and out stepped the smiling, if rather wet, figure of John Burnie. John without doubt qualified as one of my two greatest sponsors and supporters, having produced for me, at his own expense, a beautiful four colour brochure designed to help me raise funds. He shook hands, wished us all luck and promptly said: 'I want a set of postcards from you, Alan: send me one from each port.' And with that he thrust five ten pound notes into my hand!

Minutes later we slipped our moorings, each yacht in turn enjoying a cacophonous send-off of cheers, yells, shouts and horn-blowing that left me feeling very proud. It was rather as if we carried with us the hopes and aspirations of all those we were leaving behind, almost as if we were doing something for them as much as for ourselves.

Then the last mooring rope slid off the pontoon cleat; the few feet of water between hull and the pontoon widened as we slipped backwards, and I realised that the next land I would step on would be in Rio de Janeiro! A very odd sensation. We took in the fenders and coiled the mooring warps; the ordinary, everyday things we did every time we took the yacht out, were now seemingly packed with meaning. 'Won't need these for the next 5000 miles then,' said Ben cheerfully as we stowed them below.

Motoring up Southampton Water, with the wind smashing the white tops from the waves and the rain washing the salt from our faces, we had another visitor. A small yacht came bashing up towards us, motorsailing through the chop, and as it neared, a voice yelled: 'Ahoy, *Toshiba*, is Alan Sears on board?' I stepped from the mast to the rail and saw Chris Adigun, a classmate from my yachtmaster exam course, waving furiously. It was no surprise he hadn't recognised me in full foul weather gear with hood up and face guard pulled across; the only way we could tell each other apart on deck was by the names stencilled on to the backs of our hoods!

The Solent was in fury, with the ebb tide beginning to set against the full force of a south-westerly gale, as we motored to the start line, oriented ourselves with what we could see through the gloom, and checked the direction of the wind and the set of the tide. Our plan for the start was first and foremost to stay out of trouble, and Simon gave us a comprehensive and cheerful briefing to explain how we were going to achieve that. His wry closing remark: 'That's if we can see anything when it comes to it,' proved to be prophetic. During this whole pre-start period I was amazed at my self-possession. I had expected to feel nervous, sick and distracted. Instead I found myself cheerful, very determined and rather cool. I could almost say I felt rugged! I certainly did not give a damn for the weather. This was supposed to be the world's toughest yacht race after all, and even if we were starting into the teeth of a full gale, we were well equipped to face it.

With two reefs dramatically reducing the area of our mainsail, a small No 2 yankee and the staysail set, we jockeyed for position at the start. Challenge yachts, being principally designed for sailing upwind, carry three different yankees, headsails with a high cut 'foot' so that the waves do not catch the bottom of the sail, and one large No 1 genoa for use in light airs. The No 2 was an almost universal choice, but many of the yachts flew it in conjunction with their bright-orange storm staysails, and some opted for only one reef. Our plan for the start was to gain clean air and clear water, that is to say we were more concerned to avoid a collision and have space to sail in, where the wind was not being interfered with by the other yachts' sails, than anything else. That did not mean that we meant to start almost at the back of the fleet! It was a nightmare. In spite of the weather, there were spectator boats everywhere; it was impossible to see anything and, worst of all, the noise of wind, motorboats and helicopters made it impossible for us to hear each other on deck. Add to that, sailing at very close quarters in a lumpy sea and you begin to get the idea.

We set about making amends for our start when disaster struck. We tacked, and as the staysail flew across, the knot holding the sheet on to the sail came adrift. We had to tack back, re-tie the sheet and tack again. Now that sounds simple when you read it because you cannot hear the gunshot cracks of the loose sail flogging, you are not in danger of having an arm taken off by a flailing rope, nor are you heaving and wrenching at a winch with all your might while the boat lurches this way and that beneath your feet. The stark reality of it all, the wrenching wind, the slap of the rain and spray against your face, the sheer volume of noise – like a rock band at full power – the pent-up, wound-up nervous tension of it all is impossible to convey.

In the midst of all this I glanced back at Simon from my position in the cockpit trimming the mainsail, to see a look of horror frozen on his face. As the foredeck crew struggled with the sail and the sheet, *Toshiba,* having lost way dramatically as we went straight from the new tack back on to the old one, was being swept by the furious Solent tide down on to a channel marker buoy. We slithered past with only feet to spare as the huge iron mass rolled and twisted ominously on the waves. It was nearly a disaster, but we rescued the situation and set about sailing up to our best. Our route down the Solent was exemplary. In a tremendous display of skill and determination, Simon called the tacks from the wheel, looking all the time for every slight advantage we could draw from the tides. Our teamwork was quick and slick after our initial clanger, and by the time we had reached the Needles we had worked our way through the fleet and were anticipating getting on level terms with *Group 4* and *Save the Children* who led the charge.

We sailed fully-crewed, with everyone active, for the start of each leg, but as night came on we swung into the watch system. The starboard watch, led by Ben, consisted of Guy, Drew, Kobus, Joe and Chris Gaskin, our RNLI 'legger'. Mark led the port watch with Jo, Geoff, Spike, Ciara, myself and Mike Hutt, our non-RNLI legger. Almost a Southampton local, Mike took time out from running his business to sail on leg one. In love with the whole idea of the

Challenge, and by nature a mild man, it took a lot to rouse Mike, but other people's attitudes managed it occasionally. A wonderful chap to share a cabin with, I enjoyed Mike's company immensely.

The first night demonstrated the value of our preparations. There is a great rule of yacht racing, known either as the 5-P rule or the 6-P rule depending on whether you opt for the clean version or not. The 5-P rule states that: 'Perfect preparation prevents poor performance'. Part of our preparation was that we had a crew agreement to take our seasickness pills, and that included most of the people who had never been sick. As a result we had a full working crew through the night, with only one or two people feeling queasy. Seasickness saps not only the strength but the resolve. It is a pernicious thing in an environment where you need to be physically and mentally strong. Some yachts reported having up to 10 out of 14 crew sick on this first night, and clearly, their ability to race would have been dramatically affected. We were not without drama, however. Geoff was hurled across the cockpit when a huge wave struck, and bruised himself badly and extensively on the ribs and thigh, smashing into two different winches. He was considerably hurt and, on reflection, was lucky not to break any bones.

Ocean races are won and lost at night. Bashing across the Channel into force 10 winds we worked and worked, tacked as and when we had to – and not just when we had to but every time it was beneficial to do so. At one point we made three sail changes in half an hour, and it all paid off. We were second to *Group 4* by daybreak and in the lead by mid-morning. It rained most of the day and was still pouring down by mid-afternoon, but being in the lead felt fantastic.

By the evening of our second day at sea, the wind had freed us; we had a spinnaker up and were heading down towards Ushant in rather more pleasant conditions. It had been a hard start, but I had been sustained throughout by the thought that, contrary to some reports, we had seen much worse in training, and consoled by the fact that on this leg at least we were heading towards the sun.

The Isle of Ushant lies just off the north-west corner of France and is what sailors call a 'tidal gate'. If the tide is favourable you can negotiate the narrow, rocky channel that separates Ushant from the mainland; if not, you have to take the long route round the outside. We took the inside course, sliding dramatically down the right side of the channel with the rocks lying just off our beam and the red and white lights marking them gleaming across the water. It was a tense and tricky piece of navigation and we did not quite make it. With the situation becoming critical (sometimes where you can steer is ruled by which sails you have up), Simon called for us to drop the kite. We swung into action, hoisting the No 1 yankee as the first part of the manoeuvre, and then hauling the race spinnaker in under the boom.

These spinnakers are *huge*. There is something like 6000 square feet of nylon in each one and the method of taking one down is this: the bowman climbs up to the end of the spinnaker pole, which is, typically, out over one side of the boat and about 15 feet above the waves. Two or three crew position themselves on the roof of the dog-house where they take hold of a rope attached to the back corner of the kite. The bowman releases the shackle holding the spinnaker to the pole and the gatherers gather the sail in with all their might. When they have both the bottom corners of the sail on board another crew member lowers the halyard so that the whole sail can be hauled in under the main boom. Simultaneously, someone in the cockpit feeds the vast mass of material down the companionway hatch so that it all goes below and does not billow about the decks causing mayhem. There are other ways of doing it but we stuck almost universally to this method.

Unfortunately, on this occasion the spinnaker caught on something and we tore it. This was aggravating as we had gone to a great deal of trouble to try to eliminate 'sharps' that might snag our sails, and make sure that all were taped up or protected in some way. Jo and Ciara spent the rest of the watch and the next one stitching and patching it. Chris and Ben stayed up to let the girls get some sleep and then we sorted ourselves back into our proper watches.

As promised, Simon became nocturnal, which was just as well because we had some hard nights: pitch-black and cold. Things became complicated tactically heading down towards Cape Finisterre off north-west Spain. Coming up on deck at 2 am for a night watch, we were greeted with the news that *Concert* were ahead of us by six miles and that we had made a mistake: the waypoint of Cape Finisterre had been entered wrongly into the GPS and we had been heading too far west.

Now, the development of a GPS (Global Positioning System), which typically can track any vessel to within 100 yards or so, has changed the navigator's job irrevocably. No longer is it a case of: 'Where on earth are we?' It is a case of: 'We know where we are, but where should we be?' The function of the equipment which enables us to key in the latitude and longitude of any chosen point and then relate our position to that, not only simplifies navigation, but leads on to the be-all and end-all of modern ocean racing: the waypoint closing velocity, or WCV. Put simply, the WCV is a measure of how fast you are going towards where you want to be. It tells you whether you are on the right tack or not, or if travelling downwind which gybe is favoured. It will tell you whether or not it is better to sacrifice wind angle for boat speed, and it can even reveal which of two different sail plans is actually more effective, but you *do* have to put the information in correctly in the first place!

Simon was quick to point out that we could turn the situation to our advantage. Heading back towards the east would actually put the wind sufficiently on our beam that we could fly the flanker and gain from increased boat speed. We set to the task with a will, but as soon as we had the flanker ready to hoist, the wind gusted up beyond a safe limit for the sail. We changed everything around again and set up to hoist the No 1 yankee. Then the wind died again. We went for the flanker a second time and back came the wind more strongly. We then made a positive decision, hoisted the No 1 and within minutes down went the wind and up went the flanker! This sounds amusing after the event, but the sheer physical effort involved in moving these sails around and hoisting and lowering them is tremendous, and everyone working on the foredeck came back very wet and very tired after a long stint.

Where are you? How are you?

When the first round the world yacht race set off in 1973, the crews agreed to keep a daily radio schedule with each other, reporting their positions and any other news. In those days that would have been about the extent of any communications once the yachts had set sail. Blessed as we were with a 'satmail' system giving us instant access to RHQ and to anyone else with a fax machine, we nevertheless maintained the tradition of the twice-daily 'chat-show'. There was a noticeable difference between the yachts, *Group 4*, *Concert*, and *Toshiba* in particular, who simply reported a position and 'All well', and some of the others who liked the opportunity to swap jokes, insult the rest of the fleet, or complain about the weather. Not that we were being aloof, we just did not like to give too much away! Apart from radio contact, each yacht sent a daily report to RHQ, and we communicated with Toshiba in Weybridge, where John, Toni and Sara took time out from busy schedules to send us a stream of funny stories, encouraging messages and jokes of varying quality!

Towards the end of our first week we had our first real spinnaker disaster. I had just woken the new watch at 2.30 am and was going round to check they were stirring when a cry of 'all hands on deck' went up. I dashed up to see the head of our race spinnaker flying from the halyard and below it a huge space. On the lee rail the on-deck crew were hauling yards of red nylon from the sea. The sail had ripped right up one side (where the fabric is stitched into a 'luff tape' to form the edge of the sail) across the top and all the way down the other side. We had been well within the wind range for the sail and the likely cause seemed to be, once again, an 'untaped sharp' on the rig. We had the flanker up quicker than any training routine and lost only 0.7 of a mile on *Concert*, to whom we were third by 2 miles, *Group 4* being a further 2 miles ahead. Just a little while earlier I had been on the foredeck, *Tosh* had been creaming along and I'd been thinking how wonderful it all was. Now it was 4 am we were an hour into our off watch, due back on watch at 6 am, tired, upset and facing a massive spinnaker repair.

Shortly afterwards, as if that was not enough, we suffered the biggest spinnaker wrap in history. A 'wrap' is when the spinnaker winds itself around any, or all, of the fixed wires running from the deck to the mast, or indeed anything else it can find, and, horror of horrors, because of the damage to the race spinnaker, we were flying the promotional kite, with an eight hour penalty on its head. One of the objects of the Challenge is to promote good seamanship, including good husbandry of sails. For this reason there were penalties for sails damaged beyond repair, and the promotional spinnaker, with the sponsor's logo on it, carried the highest penalty of all. We wrapped the promo. We wrapped it around the forestay, the inner forestay, the shrouds – you name it – we wrapped it. It looked like Christo's wrapping of the Reichstag in polythene sheets, except that he claimed his effort as a work of art and we knew ours was a disaster! Unbelievably, after a huge effort and inspired helming from Simon, we got it down in one piece. In a one-design race you cannot afford to give away eight hours to your rivals on a penalty. From one slight lapse in concentration we had come within a hair's breadth of throwing away the first leg, and a sense of relief that we had rescued the situation was tempered by the realisation of how close it had been.

We had saved it, but what an effort. With the sewing circle still in session in the galley working on the race spinnaker, and the need to check the promo for damage, we carried on under flanker – slower because it is a smaller sail, but safer because it is stronger. We also had time to reflect on whether we had been unlucky or whether it was bad sailing. Either way, it was very annoying.

In spite of this, with the south-westerly gale of the start behind us, and sailing downwind in bright sunshine over blue seas, we started to settle in as a team. Not that life was without its little moments. Geoff was very irate when Ben's watch forgot to make breakfast one day, and again when he washed up more mugs than we had people on-board – clearly a cardinal sin. I was on the wheel another day when Spike came up with a message from Jo D saying that half the supper washing up was done, and could I complete it when we changed helms? I said, 'Of course,' pointing out though that we had plenty of people sitting on the rail if it needed doing now, but Spike remarked ruefully, 'No, I think it was a personal message.' Now I am not the greatest galley hand on a boat so I do try to make sure that I do a reasonable share and, having washed up lunch, reckoned it was someone else's turn.

One or two of us tended to become exercised around fair shares of different types of work, and indeed about some working harder than others. I had remarked to Pam just before we left that, in my opinion, the only thing to do is to try to be one of the people who work hard and say nothing about it, but that is not always easy. I think that one of the wonderful qualities most of us could learn from Simon is the ability not to make judgements about people, or if you do, not to mention it or act upon it. Interestingly, those who seemed to be most judgemental (and it really is a disguised form of criticism) were also most prone to eruptions of temper; those who seemed genuinely happiest made no comment whatsoever about their fellow crew. My pet hate was the other watch being late on deck, and some of them kept doing it. In an odd contrast to all this Mark read us two poems written by his daughters to send him on his way. They were quite lovely, and Mike remarked: 'If only all kids were like that we'd all be okay.' Of course the answer to that, alas, is that not all dads are like Mark.

Reaching the first official waypoint of the course we gybed round Berlenga Island off southern Portugal and set course for Madeira. Now these are romantic words, and for me much of the romance of what we were doing lay in this first leg of our journey. The Southern Ocean was always the big dare, but I did not view it so romantically. Passing so close to Lisbon put us in conversation about Henry the Navigator and the early mariners who plied the trade routes, navigating with the backstaff. Then we got on to John Harrison and his invention of the chronometer. History seemed to be all around us. Just before we gybed, the moon rose: a glimmering half-circle sitting just above the horizon. It was a clear night with a brilliant display of stars. There is simply nothing like being at sea for giving one a sense of the planet as part of a system with its sun and its moon. To be perfectly alone on the ocean with a circular red sun setting in the sky and, diametrically opposite, at exactly the same altitude, a perfectly round moon rising is like being at the centre of a mediaeval painting. What seems really odd is how small a space one appears to be in. In all the vastness of the oceans, you can only see as far as your own horizons, and they seem very close. It is the smallness of that circle that strikes me almost more than the inconceivable distances beyond it.

As we slipped away from the coast, the shore lights twinkled merrily at us and it hit me that this is where the adventure began. Until now we had crossed the Channel and sailed down the coast past Spain and Portugal. Having done that, I had a much better idea of how mariners of old did it, even with simple instruments, but now we were about to cross an ocean. Here be dragons, possibly; here be adventure, certainly.

My romantic feelings took a rude blow the following day when I hurt myself trying to put an extra turn of rope around the winch holding the spinnaker guy. The boat rolled, I lost the tension, the top turn of rope jumped off the winch and the guy, under terrific load, streamed out. Luckily I had sailing gloves on so I grabbed it, held it, went to get a turn back on the winch, and was promptly pulled off my feet and slammed into the forward corner of the cockpit, by the companionway steps. The rope streamed out again, I grabbed it again and on about the third attempt secured it around the winch. The price was a 'dead-leg' which lasted, stiff and sore, for several days and two large blisters across the ends of my fingers, unprotected by the gloves. (Sailing gloves usually have the ends of the fingers cut off, partly so that you can use your fingertips, and partly to avoid the ends of the gloves becoming trapped in ropes and winches, pulling your fingers in.) An hour and a half soaking in cold water finally took the sting out of the blisters. The bruises on my leg, lurid, bluey-purple masses, were with me for a lot longer and I started inwardly to think of the most dire consequences: of infection setting into my fingers, or the recurrence of an old bone injury in my leg. I observed that even in a tiny bit of adversity I tend to go for negative thought patterns and the sympathy vote.

Rolling down the trade winds

The trade winds are every sailor's dream. Day after day, night after night, you come on deck to find the same steady constant breeze bowling you along. We had some tremendous downwind sailing, averaging about 12 knots, with long surfs on the tops of the waves and white foam hissing alongside. It was a joy to be on the wheel. We gybed down towards Madeira, losing a little ground to *Group 4*, but making distance on everyone else.

Our crisis management came to the fore again when a spinnaker sheet let go one night. We got the flanker down with some difficulty, and a very quick and sweaty re-pack followed down below. Flushed with success, and too much clothing, we heaved it on deck, rigged it and re-hoisted it. The halyard was fouled at the top of the mast. Down it all came again, with difficulty, for a second re-pack and a second hoist, this time successful. In between the two hoists we had gybed, but now decided the first gybe had been better and so had to gybe back! Mark was clipped round the head by one of the heavy metal clew rings to which the sheets are attached, but Spike's diagnosis was: 'No stitches required,' so we had only blood on the flanker and Mark's sore head to show for it. I worked out that in a four-hour watch I had helmed for one hour, sat by the mast holding the kicker (which controls the height of the boom) for an hour, cleaned the heads, wiped down the companionway walls, pumped out the slurry tank and the bilges, been on the foredeck for a spinnaker gybe, made tea and helped stitch up our damaged spinnaker – never a dull moment.

The job of holding the kicker rope is an interesting one. Running downwind it is possible for the boat to set up a side to side roll, a 'death roll' as it is known. If the whole thing gets out of control the spinnaker takes charge of the boat, swinging up into the wind until the boat 'broaches' sideways on, and is knocked flat by the wind. One of the things which tends to trigger this off is the end of the boom dipping into the water as the boat rolls, so that the boat starts to pivot around it. The person at the mast, by releasing the kicker if the boom is about to dip, can avert this. It is known as the 'chapel watch', but whether that is because one sits in silent meditation as the boat roars along, or because you should be praying that the helmsman doesn't broach the boat and turn it over flat on its side, it is hard to say!

With position reports forwarded by RHQ every six hours, there was never any respite from the need to keep trimming and changing sails to best advantage. But those people who can make a meal or wash up, or change a jubilee clip on a water pipe under difficult conditions, become as valuable as those who can steer a good course or trim a sail. Right from the beginning, we tried to make *Toshiba* an 'equal opportunities' environment, where the chores were shared equally and everyone could have a go at everything. Naturally, there are times when you need to put your fastest people on the wheel, but our boat protocol was to share the skills and try to raise everyone's capabilities. It transpired that not everyone in the crew felt this was working.

'Assumptions about capabilities' was the phrase used, and the complaint was about roles and divisions of labour. I was surprised. Surprised because here we had people who could talk eloquently about teamwork and yet miss one of the most basic rules: never nurse a grievance. I felt it was not so much assumptions that were at fault, so much as the failure of the 'assumed against' to say clearly, and without rancour, what it was they wanted. The other bone of contention was 'shoulds'. 'He should do this, the other watch should do that,' and so on. Of course we operated the watch system on an agreed set of 'shoulds', but there was aggravation when some people thought that they had been let down by the other watch, missed out on a round of drinks, or been kept waiting past their time. This is all on the easy leg, I remember thinking: what will it be like in the Southern Ocean?

As we raced towards Madeira, *Group 4* chose a course to the west, clearly setting to leave Madeira to port. *Concert* were away to the east, perhaps looking for a different wind near the shore and around the Canaries. Our theory was that the eastern Madeira convergent winds should produce high pressure, lots of wind, and fast sailing. To the west, divergent winds traditionally produce lower winds. In a nutshell, winds change direction as they change in speed when going from land to sea or vice versa. Sometimes this effect yields two wind masses which converge, producing higher wind speeds; sometimes they diverge, producing lower speeds. We discussed at length Mike Golding's tactics in going west. After all, he had sailed the route twice before, so should we take note? The straight line to the next Great Circle waypoint went slap through the middle of the island so we had to make a choice. Our weather information from before the start suggested leaving Madeira to starboard – that is the generally accepted thing to do – and in the end we followed the advice we had been given.

The BT Global Challenge specifically prohibits 'weather routeing' – the practice of having on-shore meteorological experts not only transmitting weather information to yachts, but also suggesting strategies and tactics to take best advantage of the conditions. BT yachts were, however, allowed to consult anyone available up to the start of each leg. We had opted to use some of the money we had raised for our crew fund to purchase weather information from the world renowned guru Bob Rice, while *Group 4* threw their lot in with winning Whitbread weatherman Vincent Geake.

The subject of what is, and is not, allowed affected us greatly. Weight distribution is incredibly important in a racing yacht and because of this, a lot of equipment has to be carried in specified places under the rules. The origins of this are interesting. Many years ago people ballasted racing boats with sand bags and employed teams of people simply to shift the bags about. To prevent this practice, the rules were changed to outlaw moveable ballast. Some modern yachts use water ballast which can be pumped from one side to another, but only when this is specifically allowed under the class rules. One of the few things that we were allowed to move was ourselves, so we slept on the high side or the low side, amidships or aft as the conditions dictated. We became nomads, and I am not talking about wandering the seven seas, I am talking about 'hot bunking'. Have sleeping bag, will travel.

'Physician heal thyself,' says the Good Book, but as Spike found out, that is not always so easy. Having been spending a great deal of his time swinging from a climbing harness, either as bowman at the end of the spinnaker pole or up the mast trying to track down our sharps, Spike developed an abscess at the base of his little finger. Self treatment with antibiotics having yielded no result, he had to have it lanced by Ben, proving as he did so the old adage that doctors make bad patients. He probably was not helped by a large and delighted audience, all taking photographs. Mark dutifully took over the bowman's role and had to go to the end of the pole for a spinnaker peel during the night. Spike helped him sort out the harness with all its various lines and strops and when he was finally ready to go Mark burst out laughing, saying: 'I've got so much safety equipment here that if I try to move I'm likely to trip over it all and break my leg!'

We re-established our lead for a short while, but our jubilation was short lived. We fell into a hole in the wind and found ourselves back behind *Group 4* again. The fleet began to bunch up, with *Save the Children* storming through to be third, about 14 miles behind us. Finally, after five days, our repaired race spinnaker went up again amidst much joy that we had managed to repair it, together with a certain amount of apprehension from Jo, Geoff, Ciara and Kobus, who had borne the brunt of the stitching, about whether it would take the strain. The basic method of repair was to stick the pieces back together with double sided sticky tape, stitch it all back together and then iron on self adhesive patches of Dacron sailcloth. The kettle made a fine iron. We later discovered that *Concert* had managed to obtain a stapler and a supply of suitable stainless steel staples to obviate the need for thousands of hand stitches. Even though we subsequently did the same, we found that our efforts with this system were not as effective and we went back to sewing.

By now, the end of week one, the fleet had split and the boats taking to the African coast started to do well. We dropped to fourth place on the leader board, the lowest we had been, and that immediately sparked off a lot of doom and gloom, and 'we're doing badly', without a complete analysis of the positions. We were still making good progress in relatively light winds: rolling along at 8 knots, running down towards the Cape Verde Islands. At this point we intended to leave the islands at least 60 miles to the east and did not expect to see any more of them than we had of Madeira or the Canaries. How things change!

We crossed into the Tropic of Cancer on Wednesday 9 October, day 11. We had also covered our second 1000 miles, and celebrated with cocktails in the cockpit. Since I was in charge of this I tied my Toshiba headband into a white bow tie, wrote 'smooth talking bar steward' in marker pen on strips of duct tape, stuck them to my shirt and served daiquiris made of Bacardi, Limoncello (a lemon liqueur from Italy I found in Tesco) and Rose's lime juice, which were very well received. These occasional 'happy hours' were just about the only times that the whole crew was together, which usually meant that we had a jolly good laugh about something. Working a two-watch system as we did (some boats opted for three) means that you only really see the other watch as you change over, and people are not always at their best immediately upon being woken, so these occasional celebrations were always held in something of a party atmosphere. With impeccable timing our first flying fish landed on deck later that evening, and Simon remarked on how its wings made a perfect fully-battened sail. The analogy is absolutely extraordinary, man having produced by design, study and development exactly what nature has produced by evolution.

We began to consider a change of plan. Making 9–10 miles every hour, but with the easterly boats still gaining, we began to consider going between the Cape Verde Islands rather than to the west of them. The wind was basically coming from the north-west which meant that the eastern boats near the African coast would have to run dead downwind to leave the Cape Verdes as close as they dared to starboard. We had less distance to go and would be able to sail faster, but were losing a mile or two to *Group 4*, still to the west of us, every six hours. The science behind the plan to go through the middle was that of convergent and divergent winds again. It was the most direct route; going round them meant more distance, and there

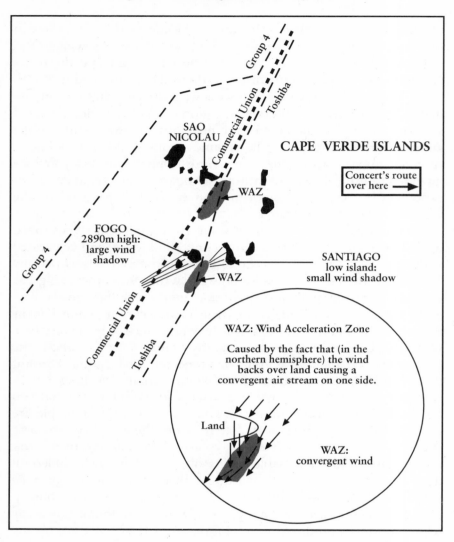

FOGO
2890m high:
large wind
shadow

SAO
NICOLAU

WAZ

CAPE VERDE ISLANDS

Concert's route
over here ➡

SANTIAGO
low island:
small wind shadow

WAZ

Group 4

Commercial Union

Toshiba

WAZ: Wind Acceleration Zone

Caused by the fact that (in the
northern hemisphere) the wind
backs over land causing a
convergent air stream on one side.

Land

WAZ:
convergent wind

was good reason to believe we could pick up breeze by going
through the gap in the middle. Tactical decisions aside, life went on
as normal. With the race spinnaker holding up, the repairs to the
promo, necessitated by 'the great wrap', were going on apace. We
were on our second kite, and already we felt like expert repairers.
Expert or not, we certainly had a claim to professionalism: although
no-one was actually paying us it was certainly a full time occupation.

Our full time preoccupation was the heat and the problems that
come with it. By now the sun on deck was very hot, even though the
breeze, a steady 20 knots of true wind, was pleasant. Below it was

sweltering. With the air temperature at 28 degrees we were bathed in sweat. Active work below decks, packing spinnakers or cooking, was just like being in a sauna, but we were denied the luxury of the plunge pool, tempting though the cool water looked from time to time. This brought issues of personal hygiene to the fore. For my part, I was completely amazed at how much of their 5 kg personal weight allowance some people had used up in cosmetics; the heads looked like a small branch of Boots the Chemists. On the other hand there were dark mutterings from some quarters about insisting that people take showers – and I thought it was meant to be a ruffty-tuffty yacht race! In fact, given that it was possible to shower in the heads, and to wash clothing in the hand basins, things remained very civilised, if rather amusing, with strings of underwear hanging out to dry across the stern rail.

Spinnaker repairs took place in the main saloon (there was nowhere else suitable) so all the time this was going on, the saloon table was buried under seemingly endless yards of red nylon and meals were taken wherever we could stand, wedge or squeeze into a corner to eat them. Things like this made life difficult and some of the frictions were still showing. It is interesting, although perhaps obvious, that you cannot build a team until people drop their personal issues, and the strength of the team is directly proportional to the extent to which you do that. Very often, I suspect, successful expeditions or adventures are made up of like-minded people or people with similar back-grounds – English public school to take one familiar example. The Services build teams by instilling an attitude of duty before self, which is an effort to submerge individual issues without dealing with them – not unreasonably perhaps: the military life is not designed to be a substitute for psychotherapy.

With less than 3000 miles to go to Rio we were back in third place, had taken some miles out of *Group 4*, and were back on the roll again when we received a message from RHQ telling us we were almost exactly where the fleet had been on the same day in the 1992–93 British Steel Challenge, the difference being that we started three days later than them. Andrew Roberts, project director for the Challenge Business, apparently felt that crews might have been driving the boats too hard. At the time, we were running straight down the rhumb line, well within the wind limits of the race spinnaker and our full main. 'So what are we supposed to do,' asked Chris, 'Chuck a bucket over the back to slow us down?'

We bit the bullet and headed through the Cape Verde Islands. We gybed in, left Sao Nicolau to starboard, and gybed back on to port to leave Fogo to starboard as well. Sure enough we picked up a convergent wind to the east of Sao Nicolau and hoped for the same from Fogo. With over 10 knots of boat speed we felt very optimistic, waiting to see how it all panned out when the leaders had all passed the islands. *Group 4* went round to the west, but *Concert* led, having gone down the African coast to come round under the Cape Verdes. We were in the middle, hoping posterity would record 'a brilliant tactical move by Walker'!

Our careful planning took a slight knock when we almost lost the wind completely coming round Fogo. We had an intense period of very tricky sailing, during which things were very hot and sticky and all rather tiring. In the end, though, we seemed to have sailed quite well and, once we were clear of the islands, we were second again to *Group 4*. The results vindicated the decision brilliantly, and we were in a very self congratulatory mood when Spike pointed out that, on closer inspection, the tide tables we had used, as provided by the Challenge Business, were actually for 1997, not 1996!

More discontent began to foment about who should do what, but the real issue seemed to be about people wanting to have their abilities respected and not ignored. This was one of the great issues of the Challenge. Everyone had paid for their place, and no-one had paid to be a galley hand for the entire race. On the other hand, we were involved in a fiercely competitive struggle for the lead. What should a watch leader do? Stick to the people he thinks are best at each job, or allocate fair shares for all and risk the boat's performance declining? The problem was taking more resolving than I had expected.

Other problems of a more expected nature manifested themselves, tiredness being one for me. We decided to start with a watch system operating three hours on and three off through the night and four on, four off during the day. Now psychologically this suits me very well; I like short bursts of effort with frequent breaks, but spinnaker work is hard work and it was beginning to tell, especially when driving the boat at night. This is the sailing equivalent of driving down a motorway, and the tiredness problems are exactly the same. The instruments swim in front of your eyes, the boat seems to keep turning even though you know it's going straight, the instruments tell you you are on course or off course, but your instincts disagree and you become confused. And all this time there are the twin requirements to sail as fast as possible, and not make a mistake that will damage the spinnaker. All you can do to relieve the pressure is to rotate helms, that is change drivers. There are no service stations or lay-bys on the ocean.

A lot of people were, by now, complaining that it was too hot to sleep below. Waking the new watch to come on deck became a matter of searching the forepeak for figures recumbent on top of the sails, checking the seats in the saloon under the open cockpit hatches for slumbering crew, and avoiding treading on sleeping bodies on cabin floors. I slept in my bunk (or one appropriate to good weight distribution) right through virtually every off watch for days on end and still felt tired quite often. In fact my chief dissatisfaction at this stage was that I was spending all my off watch time sleeping so that I could keep working on watch, and had no time for anything else. I was feeling the lack of intellectual stimulation. The silver lining to this cloud was that to get ready for lots of hard work in the doldrums, we decided to drop two crew out of each watch for each of three nights to help people catch up on a little rest.

The common perception of the doldrums, or the Inter Tropical Convergence Zone (ITCZ) as it is correctly known, as a place with no wind is not entirely accurate. Whilst it is true that yachts frequently are becalmed there, the real nature of the doldrums is the dramatic changes that take place as squall clouds and thunderstorms bring gale force gusts of wind with little warning. The trick is to sail with the clouds, where the wind is, and try to avoid the dead spots. For years, racing through the doldrums has been considered something of a lottery, and it is. But there is no doubt that skilled reading of the conditions and a willingness to work very hard in terms of changing sails, getting the weight, that is the crew, in the right place all the time, and paying attention to the other thousand details that make yachts go more quickly, will always pay off. Simon briefed us thoroughly to this effect.

We were aiming for a very narrow section of the ITCZ, hoping to get to at least 7 degrees north before we ran out of wind, and to pick up a tropical wave front (the wave in question being a feature of the weather, not of the sea) so that we might not run out of wind at all.

The worst job in these very hot conditions was cooking. I spent what seemed like a whole afternoon in the galley on one occasion and by the time I was through I was incredibly hot, absolutely shattered, and my morale had reached an all-time low. I felt very emotional and upset. Mike Hutt, with whom I was sharing a cabin, spotted it, bless his cotton socks, and produced, from a secret supply someone had given him just before departure, a very large whisky. What a hero! I felt better at once, but then the restorative powers of alcohol have never ceased to amaze me.

When our first doldrums cloudburst did strike, the romantics all grabbed their soap and shampoo and rushed on deck to wash.

Now I do count myself a romantic, but this did seem to me like wanting to live out the ritual, since the boat was equipped with a water maker and two showers anyway! Nonetheless it cooled everybody down and cheered us up, so that was all to the good. There was a very strange contrast here between the rain which, if not cold as it flooded down over us out of a black night sky, was at least cool, and the sea water coming over the foredeck, which was so warm it felt as if someone were throwing buckets of water drawn from a hot tap over us.

We slipped through the ITCZ with hardly a murmur. We saw some characteristic squalls and a lot of hugely spectacular lightning, but managed to keep moving virtually throughout until we slipped quietly out of the bottom and into the south-east trade winds. With that, although it was still hot, we were at least out of the blast furnace for a while.

On these predominantly warm legs, even though the work can still be hard, there is some time for reflection and I concluded that we had two underlying causes of friction. One was that a little learning is a dangerous thing: some knew more about sailing than others when we started, some remembered different things from training to others, some were more adaptive learners; but we were all still on a steep learning curve about how to keep the boat going fast and about our protocols, the way we did things. The upshot of all of this would be disagreements and, like a lot of disagreements, these frequently put egos against one another. Underlying one debate about the correct number of stops to put on a spinnaker leg was a fierce, 'I'm right, you're wrong'. The answer in this case really was, it depends. It depends on what the weather conditions will be when you hoist it, which will to some extent be dictated by which spinnaker it is, but you can't be exact. It also depends on whether you will be hoisting it in place of a headsail, or peeling to it from another spinnaker, which can't always be predicted.

There was, however, a second, more interesting cause of friction. We were all working for the common cause, to win the race, but we were working for the cause as individuals, which is not quite the same as teamwork. Some people would remember a particular point from training, and mention this detail every time it came up, and be congratulated for it. But often it would not be long before 'why am I the only person who remembers to do this?' would be heard in one form or another. In all this we played 'Simon says,' backing up our arguments with outside authority. This is merely another disguised form of the 'I'm right, you're wrong' gambit.

I had a taste of my own problems during a nightmare watch where nothing I did was right. To make things worse, it was a lovely morning with great sailing, but I didn't feel very awake. I was trimming the mainsail and everything I did was wrong, including when I did nothing. I began to find this quite painful. Although Simon made no admonishments and whilst his focus was on boat speed, he nevertheless continued to explain his reasoning on the trim to me. My problem was that I had thought I was beginning to get the hang of this job and now it appeared that I wasn't. Eventually I said something about my poor performance, causing Ciara to comment, with a grin, 'I have to say I think Simon's probably right, Alan.' I said, 'Well I'm perfectly happy to give this to someone else, given how badly I'm doing.' Geoff promptly sang out, 'Don't be a quitter, Alan,' which was exactly the right thing to say. It reminded me to just sit in the pain of having the problem and hope the learning would come along. Not only the learning of how to trim a main sheet on a close reach, but of how not to dissolve into jelly internally, with its associated feelings of wanting to give up, go somewhere else and do something else when I feel I am failing horribly at something I want to be good at. It is hard, sometimes, to take any form of correction or even well-meant advice without a feeling of being hurt. When the hurt turns into anger things get even worse, so I sat in my problems and sat in my hurt, did not get angry, and things got better.

During all this, Simon taught us the art of cloud spotting. Cumulus clouds fall into two categories: rain bearing and non-rain bearing. The rain bearing ones have a gust front associated with their leading edge, which can mean more wind, an area of very light wind behind, and a flat calm directly underneath. For those reasons you have to be very careful which side of them you go, and the occasional judicious course amendment or tack saved us considerable anguish.

The days and nights rolled by, sliding into one another as watch on followed watch off and it was beginning to seem to me that this was a great long way and a great long time when we reached a very significant point, and everything changed very rapidly.

Neptune rising

On Thursday 17 October at 0814 GMT we crossed the equator. Most of the crew were poised to photograph the GPS, which most disobligingly flicked from 0° 00'.2 N to 0° 00'.2 S, and never actually showed a line of zeros! While this was going on Ben was jumping up and down with excitement saying, 'We've got to do it, we've got to do it!' The next minute he was deep in consultation with Woolly and Ciara about the on-board video camera. Then all three of them started laughing fit to burst. Finally Ben said, 'Oh, all right, then, I'll ask him,' and went off with a manic gleam in his eye. The next thing we knew Ben was on deck, delivering a geography lecture in a commendably accurate 'piece to camera', demonstrating the equator, the continental land masses, and our course from Southampton to Rio by drawing in felt tip pen on a shiny brown globe. At the end of the 'lesson' Geoff's smiling face slowly rose into shot to reveal Ben's globe as his bald pate, now covered in blue and red marker pen!

The tradition that newcomers to King Neptune's kingdom shall be put on trial is so hallowed on board sailing ships, that even racing yachts make time for it. The customary order of events is:

1 The case for the prosecution
2 The verdict
3 Sentencing and punishment
4 Pleas in defence and mitigation
5 Tea and light refreshments

Since Neptune was clearly going to be very busy with 14 yachts to attend to, he delegated his role to Simon, who duly appeared swathed in the red ensign, with the boathook converted into a trident and wearing a crown made from an old Weetabix packet. Since Kobus had actually crossed the line under sail before, he was given the task of being clerk to the court and as such he read out the crimes. These included crimes under the gratuitous sewing and malicious damage act – failing to read the small print and instructions on spinnakers resulting in tearing not one but two; and privatisation of the water supply – instigating a drought whilst using the shareholders' money to purchase expensive sports cars. That one was a dig at Mark who drives a TVR and was the person most in touch with which water tanks we were trying to fill and which we were trying to leave empty.

We had charges of attempting to convert the crew to foreign religions and recruit virgins for his harem, directed at Guy, who had been wearing a Lawrence of Arabia-like burnous to protect himself against the sun whilst steering. Spike was accused of refusing to treat himself for sleeping in public places, and of desertion: trying to leave his own watch by always being on deck with the other watch. Drew was declared to be in contravention of the IYRU rules for sneaking his own personal 20 horsepower snoring engine on board and was also found guilty of exposing excessively large lenses in public. I was announced, rather oddly, as a man of few silent words but well chosen ones (irony or what?) and accused of contravening the privacy act by always taking notes. I was further arraigned for filling people up with endless garbage in such a way that they believed me, and charged under the indecency act for walking about with puffed eyes and hideous-looking underwear before coming on watch. Geoff was accused of waking people up sergeant major style then placating them by making tea and telling them it was all right. Mike was charged with failing to share his personal fan, and of excessive use of sun cream. Ciara was found guilty under the indecency act of exposing bits of flesh while sleeping, thus arousing the puzzled mind of a cabin-sharing crew member, and of forever being on the lookout for food or goodies even when in a state of nocturnal shutdown. Jo D was found guilty of using the chart table for purposes other than navigation, while Joe Watson was tried under the commodity control regulations part 4 sub-section 2, jams & preserves, for hoarding a jam mountain in an attempt to control world markets; and under the prohibited communications control act for consorting with the enemy (her boyfriend, Mark Baptiste, was sailing on *Motorola*). Joe was also found guilty of the particularly heinous crime of putting couscous on the menu.

Now, the punishment in King Neptune's court is universally the same; it is to have an appalling conglomeration of slops from the galley copiously ladled over one's head. Porridge, chocolate sauce and rice pudding work particularly well, but it must be said that for this purpose couscous comes into its own! The court sat, the punishments were administered, and the cleaning up took some time.

The clerk of the court didn't in fact escape scot free; he joined the nick-name club. When we discovered in conversation with Kobus that South Africa is home to several species of Dassie, 'small, stoutly built, tail-less animals with short legs and small, rounded ears,' according to my *Field Guide to the Mammals of Southern Africa*, there was no stopping us. Ben chortled for days, but retribution was swift. All Naval dentists carry the rank of Lieutenant-Commander ... Elsie it was, much to Ben's chagrin.

The south-east trades reminded me of just how wonderful sailing for the sake of sailing can be. We were constantly pushed along, blessed by the wind, cradled by the waves, drawn on towards the new horizon. And the nights! The Bible-black nights of the first two weeks were swallowed up astern. Overhead, the sparkling jewel box of the equatorial sky was thrown open for us every night. Orion, the great hunter, climbed up on our left, arching across to dominate the whole of the night sky with his shield and his upraised club. All around us the constellations glittered. Venus and Jupiter shone bright, as we sat on the rail following Simon's outstretched arm as he pointed out the stars: 'There's Betelgeuse, Bellatrix, Rigel and Salph; off from Orion we go to find Procyon, Alpheratz, Castor and Pollux. Here are the Pleiades, there is Scorpio, and soon we will be looking at Crux, the Southern Cross.'

The further south we went, the more the tension built. *Group 4* were still out to the west inexorably making ground, a mile here, a mile there while *Concert* led the raiding party from the east. We were very conscious of the fact that *Concert*'s skipper, Chris Tibbs, had competed in both the 1985 and 1989 Whitbread races; was his experience about to pay off? *Toshiba* had become the meat in the sandwich, but we were sliding from front to back causing a contingent of the crew to slide further into doom and gloom with each six-hourly position report. I wrote: 'Attitudes are more important than facts' on the notice board in the starboard head. Well, at least one person added a message of agreement. On deck things became tense and gritty; controversies flared. Some felt we were not trimming determinedly enough; others thought that we were interfering too much with the set of the sails. Arguments surfaced: opinions differed as to how well or how badly we were doing. I suppose it was a measure of what we expected of ourselves that all this grief was not because we were tenth, or even, say, fourth, but just because we were not winning. It took Simon to say: 'Cheer up, we are still second – and it is only a yacht race!'

In our efforts to keep the pace piled on, we blew the flanker. It went with the classic tear across the head and down each side. It blew out just after midday on day 21 and we dropped the remains of it down on to the foredeck, hoisted the No 1 and the staysail, and then set about the repair. The head was sticky-taped together on the 'coffee table' – the liferaft container in the centre of the cockpit. Next we unpicked the luff tapes and took it all down below. We worked until about 2330, by which time I was fit to drop. Simon had told us to stop at midnight, but I left Jo and Geoff still sewing. I was so shattered that, when I lay down, I nearly cried out as my body relaxed. We split into teams, two people from each watch sailing the boat through the night, leaving the others free to sew. I came on watch again at 2.40 am when my on-deck team were woken. The flanker was finished at lunch time on the following day, which was an amazing feat of sail repair. We had a team round the galley table patching and sewing the head, while the rest of the sail went up the steps out of the saloon, past the 'foulie' locker, on past the chart table, down the steps into the companionway, where Chris and Kobus sat opposite each other, one in each toilet compartment, stitching the luff tapes.

Chris remarked: 'What a wonderful thing it is when something goes wrong on board. All the bickering promptly evaporates and everyone just gets on with the job in hand.' Unfortunately it was not long before the slide started again, notably with poor old Drew who said he wouldn't sew. He had been having a very bad trip and I suspect didn't feel well enough to work down below, but his refusal did not go down well with everyone. I felt rather sorry for Drew. He had been dogged by slight sickness for a lot of the leg. He absolutely hated the food, hated the heat and found the privations of being at sea for weeks on end difficult to bear. In the face of all that, unsurprisingly, his usual good humour deserted him and with it, alas, went a lot of the sympathy he would probably otherwise have had.

Rolling down to Rio

To lighten things up a little, a message came through on day 24 saying that a French rocket had come down in the sea off French Guyana, and could the BT Global Challenge fleet keep a look out for wreckage? It was, needless to say, a wind-up, but it seemed to have some of the fleet fooled for a while!

We had more doom and gloom in the saloon as the positions indicated that once again we had lost a little to *Group 4* and been caught a little by *Concert*. It was annoying and frustrating to see our best efforts going unrewarded and rather dampening to our spirits. As always we split into optimists and pessimists, this time by gender: the guys were okay about it and the girls were down in the mouth.

Finally it all cracked wide open. We took a big chunk of mileage out of *Concert* and, up ahead, *Group 4* sailed into a hole in the wind. Under brilliant blue skies we were treated to a wildlife display; there were dolphins everywhere, and they were spectacular, so fast and so quick to manoeuvre. They do not just swim alongside and then flip out of the water every few minutes. They charge under the bow, turn and dash away, circle round and flick in and out in a series of never-ending acrobatics. On a good day, dozens of them appear and they can keep the display up for hours. Then we saw something truly spectacular.

On the morning of Wednesday 23 October we gybed on to starboard for the first time in 2274 miles and saw a fantastic sight. Two humpbacked whales – not only spouting, but driving up out of the water vertically towards the sky – their undersides gleaming in the morning sun. Like all these moments, it was too fleeting. We saw more fins and one lovely fluke rising from the water and splashing down again just like all the photographs, but the first leap was like a moment of ecstasy, wonderful but gone in an instant. These snapshots of nature do make you realise just how much we are in their domain, not ours. The skuas winging their way lazily round the mast; the gannets folding their wings and diving at up to 60 mph into the sea on target for a meal of fish; the dolphins feeding, and these huge, glorious whales, perfectly adapted, made us, in our boat of steel and aluminium with our Dacron and nylon sails, seem like aliens from another planet. We certainly came from another world. It is, after all, only our technology that enabled us to be out on the oceans.

There was now a much improved atmosphere in the cockpit perhaps because Simon had stepped up his previously not inconsiderable activity level. The difference, I think, was that Simon's presence removed our doubts and differences of opinion about trim so that our efforts were more coherent. Perhaps that's what leaders do, they get teams to cohere.

Then we had our first sight of Brazil. Tubarão appeared as a grey lump, about one thumbnail wide at arm's length, and half a thumbnail high. We were tearing down towards Rio at 10 to 12 knots in 22 knots of breeze, with the race spinnaker flying. This is just about the upper limit, if not slightly beyond it, for this sail, so the occasional gust of 30 knots required steady nerves on the helm! Then suddenly, of all the cheek, we were beating – forced to tack into a wind blowing straight up the narrow corridor between the coast and the Pampo oil field, which was a no-go zone for us. The wind had gone round from practically a dead run into a dead beat, so here we were finishing a glorious downwind bash with a beat to windward, at least as far as Cabo Frio, the last corner before Rio.

But all at once, everything stopped. At Cabo Frio the wind died. We spent a whole watch staring at the rocky coastline with its passively intermittent lighthouse winking a leisurely eye at us as we sat motionless, a few miles offshore. Gradually, painstakingly, we crept along, and along, but it was no good. We were slowly, but inexorably, heading inshore. 'Three quarters of a mile!' came the shout from the chart table. 'Half a mile.' 'Point four.' We tacked, *Toshiba* quietly swinging her bow through the almost non-existent breeze. We crept, cat-like, across the deck to take up station on the other side. Cabo Frio sat impassively before us. The lighthouse cast an impartial glance our way and swung its beam serenely on.

Every yacht in the fleet suffered this same torment, but we had always seen Cabo Frio and the run in to Rio as a potentially decisive part of the course. Consequently we had attempted to research it thoroughly before the start, with the help of weather expert Roger Badham. Our 'secret formula', consisting of differences in air and sea temperatures, the amount of cloud cover, and whether it was day or night, was supposed to yield an answer in terms of whether we should be inshore or offshore to pick up the new breeze. We fed in the numbers, did our sums, and went offshore.

Eventually there was a flicker of breeze. We crept a little further offshore. Now there was almost enough breeze to fill our sails. Gradually, almost as if pulled on invisible lines, *Toshiba* started to slip across the surface of the flat sea. The wind held, then we were moving, sailing respectably, and in the right direction. We added our sighs of relief to the warm night air caressing our faces. Rio beckoned and Rio tantalised.

The next position report showed clearly how the gods had smiled upon us. Virtually the whole fleet was stopped. From *Group 4* in front of us to the last of the 12 boats stretching out to something like 500 miles behind us, hardly anyone was moving. Yet *Toshiba* flew on, all the way to Copacabana beach and the Rio fairway buoy. The breeze, described by one writer subsequently as 'Walker's private wind', held all the way to Rio, but went lighter and lighter as finally, in daylight, we approached the Rio fairway buoy.

All the way through this last part, the sky was very overcast. We could not see the famous statue of Christ on Corcovardo until we were quite close, when it suddenly appeared through a brief gap in the cloud and mist that shrouded the peaks surrounding the city. The cloud thinned, and dissipated momentarily, Jesus blessed us with out-stretched arms, and was swallowed up again in wreaths of grey. It struck me with an awful irony that here was a city entirely dominated by the image of a man who said 'suffer the little children to come unto me', and where policemen are accused of culling homeless children on the streets; simply shooting them to reduce their numbers.

We floated down towards the fairway buoy under our lightweight spinnaker but could not make it without having to gybe. It was slow, it was messy and we should have bitten the bullet earlier and made a series of gybes to the buoy. A strange accent came over the radio: '*Toshiba, Toshiba*, you are going the wrong way!' At the chart table Guy started patiently explaining the principles of yachting over the radio. 'Tell him to Foxtrot Oscar,' yelled Simon from the cockpit, wanting to be rid of the distraction, but the voice persisted.

Finally we closed the buoy, dropped the spinnaker, hoisted the headsails and slid past, turning left to run alongside the golden sands of Copacabana beach. Chay came out to meet us in a motor launch, zooming towards us, yelling encouragement as we inched along the beach looking for the yellow buoy and the flagpole that marked the finish. It seemed to take for ever, but finally we crept past the buoy, doing about one knot in about one and a half knots of wind. A huge cheer erupted from the launch and they swung in towards us aiming a volley of bottles of champagne and cans of beer. We were bombarded but still managed to catch nearly everything that was thrown at us. We shook each other by the hand, hugged, drank and grinned wildly at each other. Done it, done it, done it! Crossed an ocean and second into Rio!

'Thank God we made it when we did,' I said to Simon. The wind had died to nothing, not a breath. 'Thank God we did,' he replied. We were two hours and four minutes behind *Group 4*. The wind, agonisingly for the other crews, had gone for the next three days, but Guanabara Bay was before us and Rio, 'The Marvellous City', beckoned us with open arms.

Amazingly, Katsuhiko Iwasaka, the Diretor Presidente of Toshiba's operations in Brazil, had arranged a champagne reception for us. We moored up alongside on the fuelling pontoon and were served champagne, in flutes this time rather than from the bottle, and canapés – which were slightly surreal, given the huge pasta meals we'd been used to on the way across. We were met by the crew of *Group 4* who had finished after a much more frustrating time in light winds than we had experienced, watching us whittle away their lead. After much champagne and a lot of chat, we finally motored off, picked up a mooring buoy and were ferried, with our kit, to the shore and into another world.

4

Speak English?

*'Brazil is not a serious country and should not be taken
seriously.'* Charles de Gaulle

*'Romantics lose their hearts in Rio. Social scientists lose
their minds.'* Edwin Taylor

The yacht club of Rio stands, in contrast to the poverty of much
of the city, in its own compound, with its swimming pool beside
the restaurant and its tables and chairs looking out over the bay. But
the most wonderful luxury there, for me at least, was, oddly, to be
served a beautiful meal without having to order it. Since there is no
choice at mealtimes on the boat, this struck me as rather a strange
luxury. The meal however, arranged for us by Katsuhiko, was perfectly
chosen. A fresh salad, which included asparagus and artichoke hearts,
followed by fillet steaks with a side dish of potatoes, onions and
bacon in gravy – a feast! We followed that with a suggestion from
Fernando Fay of Semp-Toshiba that we try papaya and vanilla ice
cream and, having started with beer and moved on to red wine, we
finished with caipirinhas – cane sugar rum served with lots of ice,
chunks of lime and sugar to taste. Oddly, not everyone seemed to like
these; people kept surreptitiously passing me full glasses. Since
Katsuhiko was kind enough to order several rounds, I did rather well.

There was much elation and excitement round the table. If we had
differences they were put away for a while. It was part of our crew
ethic that we intended to be a happy crew and enjoy the race, and in
our first end-of-leg celebration we lived up to our ideal.

Since we had finished in the middle of the afternoon, even a
lingering dinner did not take us late into the night, but it felt like it

after a long day, and there was a reasonable willingness to pile into a pair of minibuses and be driven to the Rio Copa Hotel. This short drive was interesting, chiefly because it passed through a long tunnel under one of the huge plugs of volcanic rock that make up the region. The coastline approaching Rio could almost be a lunar landscape, with massive mounds of rock surging up hundreds of feet and sinking away just as rapidly, giving a lumpy, switchback look to the country. Rio is built on this landscape, scrabbling up from the bay along the marginally shallower slopes and surging out around rock faces which are too steep to build upon, like a larval flow of concrete and bricks, capped, in the case of the more traditional buildings, with fluted orange roof tiles. Twentieth-century technology brought the means to pass through the rocks and so Rio is a city of tunnels.

There was a move to walk to the Scotch Bar, infamous by reputation from previous yacht races, but we were too early for it to be lively, and some of us were too tired to wait until the place got going. Those who turned in slept. Those who did not were full of tales of dancing girls the next morning, or too hungover to talk at all! The walk to the bar and back was like walking down London's Oxford Street – full of noise and traffic, the pavements full of people wandering, standing, gesticulating on street corners or waiting for buses, with a constant roar of diesel engines and rush of taxis passing by. The hotel, by comparison, was an oasis of calm and sanity. Coming back to it was like going below decks when there is a gale blowing up above – it may not be exactly where you want to be, but it does seem like an improvement at the time.

Rio by day was a considerable improvement for me. Opening the curtains on the morning light revealed another of the 'Marvellous City's' contrasts. Nestling into the hillside behind our hotel was a beautiful old villa, built on two levels, with railed balconies and blue shutters standing out from its peeling white painted walls. Alas, now it looked out over a splash of tiled roofs dotted with TV aerials and satellite dishes, and on to the concrete slabs and air conditioning units of the hotels which line the Avenida Atlantica. I went for a walk.

Coconut coolers and smoking brakes

Across the Avenue lay Copacabana Beach. It is quite strange that a broad strip of sand washed by Atlantic rollers should have become quite so famous – as beaches go it is very nice, but it is still only a beach. Between the beach and the dual carriageway drag strip of

Avenida Atlantica, the drinks vendors flourish. A kiosk, a plastic table with four plastic chairs, and a fridge full of canned drinks are the essentials. The main attraction, however, is the huge bunches of green coconuts with which each kiosk is festooned. Your coconut is selected by some judicious squeezing, it is twisted off its stalk, and, once free, carried back inside the kiosk. Here the performance calls for nerves of steel, from the onlookers at least. The coconut is held in one hand; in the other hand is a meat cleaver. The cleaver swipes down into the top of the nut once, twice, three times and a neat triangle of coconut husk is flicked aside. In go two straws and your coconut vendor, still unbelievably the possessor of eight fingers and two thumbs, hands you your drink. It is clear, thicker and sweeter than water, and miraculously cool. On a desert island this would make you believe in manna from heaven. Even among the noise and diesel fumes of the Avenida Atlantica it is not half bad.

Periodically, the police wander by in small groups. The military police not only carry guns but, rather intimidatingly, spare ammunition in belts at their waists. The other police carry long batons and, additionally, very much longer batons; half way at least to a quarter stave and something like two and a half inches in diameter. I usually find the presence of policemen reassuring, and in their shorts and T-shirts the non-military police looked, for the most part, very young and rather amiable. But there was something about all this firepower that was unsettling. As Mark Twain aptly observed: 'When you have a hammer in your hand an awful lot of things look like nails!'

Walking back to the hotel someone called out to me: 'Hey, do you speak English?' Not a Brazilian I thought, an American perhaps? He came up to me wearing shorts, sandals and a short-sleeved shirt. 'Listen, I'm really sorry to bother you,' he began, 'but the kids got me, some of the kids on the street, and they took everything I had. Could you lend me five bucks so I can get a taxi back to my hotel? I've been walking for miles.' Did I believe him? Would you? How far would you like to walk on a hot day if everything you had on you had been taken at knife point? The Koran says: 'If asked for alms, give.' I am not a Muslim; I gave him ten *reals*.

Chay had always said that this race was about people, and in Rio it started to come true with a vengeance. Guy was flying home to see Gisele, Simon was, understandably, flying home to see Lou, Jack and Charlie and now, suddenly, Mark was flying home to see Claire and their children. For me being away from home was part of the adventure, but Marshall McLuhan was right, we live in a global village, and even round the world sailors can phone home and fly home every six weeks if they wish. Spike drove the crew volunteer Land Rover, very kindly loaned by a local Rover Dealer, and I went along for the ride while we took Simon, Mark and Guy as well as Richard Tudor, Derek Day and Paul Egan from *Nuclear Electric* to the airport. Richard was making a quick trip home, but Paul had finished his sailing. Having been around the world from Rio in the British Steel Challenge he had signed on for the first leg of our race to complete his circumnavigation. Derek, sadly, was giving up. This was a subject people did not talk about lightly, but there was a faint whisper around *Toshiba*'s crew. Some felt that not all our core crew would make it all the way around. As usual, I was so far off the grapevine they could have been making wine and I wouldn't have known, so I contented myself with being quietly curious.

Other than continual seasickness, reasons for giving up tended to be complex. A mixture perhaps of being physically uncomfortable, not enjoying the sailing, missing people and things from home life, and sometimes just not fitting in on the boat, had, for some, formed a brew of discontent which then simmered slowly in the heat. One 'returner' I spoke to had been unable to come up with the balance of the berth fee for the rest of the trip but said he was looking forward to getting back to the UK and being busy sailing there again.

The journey was a revelation in a number of ways, mostly because of the extreme difficulty we had in getting to the airport even when in the close vicinity. Every sign saying 'Aeroporto' seemed to face the other way down a strip of six-lane highway. Having obviously overshot our destination we roared up a slip road marked 'Ritorno – Rio de Janeiro' but instead of finding ourselves going back down the other side of the same road, we were routed along a potholed one-way street, our Land Rover receiving odd looks from the few cabs and many buses, which finally coagulated into a grinding traffic jam, as opposing election buses blared samba music and high volume rhetoric at each other and their respective entourages. When we did finally arrive I said to Richard, who had been at some pains to check with me earlier in the day: 'I told you our driver was all right, but I forgot to mention the navigator. Good speed. We just had a bit of trouble with the airport closing velocity!' The drive back was uneventful, until, just cruising under the outstretched arms of Christo Redentor on his hunch-backed mountain, we stopped, nose to tail, and there we stayed.

Traffic jams are a way of life in Rio, and Spike is a perfect Rio driver. Red lights are optional, so are lanes; left or right turnings can be approached along the adjacent kerb or from the farthest lane away. The horn is used continuously – it means 'I am coming'; from behind, from in front, from inside, from somewhere, anywhere, it doesn't matter; and nobody wants to stop for anything. Jams around town are the occasion for more demonstrations of horn technique, shouting, gesticulating and shoulder shrugging, but when you can see a mile of stationary tail lights in front even the Cariocas give up, get out and light a cigarette. Spike and I don't smoke, so we discussed philosophy. There are about one and a quarter million vehicles in Rio in a space which, at a push, might handle about one third of their number. It is a good job that when Rio was developed in the 1920s they built the main Avenidas with four or five or even six lanes on either side because at least two lanes of most of them are permanently double parked. The third parking row is often the pavement, although apparently every so often there is an official blitz on this. What the motorists do then is anyone's guess! City of tunnels, city of cars, and city of taxis. Yellow taxis with a blue stripe along each side, and everywhere they circle, they hover, they buzz back and forth like a swarm of metal insects flying about the city at street level.

Eventually the tail lights up ahead began to move, but the driver of the car in front was nowhere to be seen. Spike tried to pull into the next lane; a volley of horns sounded inches away and we could not escape. Spike selected reverse, sounded 'I am coming' and backed up a foot. More horns sounded behind, accompanied by furious yelling. Spike hit the brakes, the driver behind tried to pull out around us, when suddenly the driver of the car ahead made a 'Le Mans Start' running to his car, diving in through the half opened door and roaring off. Spike floored the throttle and we surged forwards triumphantly, honours even in the great game.

The rules of the game are: lane markings are an insult to the motorist's creative driving style, taxi drivers have stronger nerves than you do, carving up the driver in the next lane is de rigueur and the buses run on Caribbean rules. Caribbean rules were once explained to me by an old yachtsman as 'De biggest boat has de right of way' and so it is with Rio's buses. They are the biggest thing on the streets so the divine right is theirs.

There's Glory for you

On our first weekend in Rio we were invited to join the fun at the yacht club, after a local regatta. Cutty Sark were the sponsors, and their wonderful whisky, 'The wine of the country' as my old friend

Harry Callaghan used to say, flowed all night long! The food was served on a buffet system which meant that the Brits formed an unbelievably long queue and the Brazilian naval cadets adopted a more forward thinking strategy of asking to be served. After a very long time being British I found myself being apologised to, on behalf of the cadets, by a striking lady standing behind me. I assured her that no apology was needed – it was clearly just a cultural difference – and asked did she live in Rio? Yes, she did. Then could she tell me what I should go to see in Rio? Yes, she could. Would she accompany me? She might. Her name? Glory McKnight.

On our first day free from working on *Toshiba* we took the Land Rover and, with Spike at the wheel, Jo, Joe, Ciara, Ben, Geoff, Drew and I set off for the summit of Corcovado via the Tijuca National Park. This is an area of some 3200 hectares of sub tropical rain forest cut through by about 60 miles of road, with spectacular viewing points; but the view from the top of Corcovado, at the foot of the statue of Christ, surpasses them all. Here is Rio laid before you, just like looking at a map. There, away to your left is the airport and the marching concrete spans of the Rio-Niteroi Bridge stepping across the bay; here is the great circle of the 180 000 seater Maracana Football Stadium; then downtown Rio, Flamenco and Botafogo beaches. Dead ahead is the Sugar Loaf, with the entrance to the bay beyond, then Copacabana, Ipanema and Leblon. With the enormous placid surface of the lagoon just behind, from the beaches to the mountains it is all quite extraordinary and quite fabulous. Indeed it is the very stuff of fable. Little wonder that sailing down to Rio passed into mariners' folklore centuries ago, and for some of us has remained, as a passport to adventure.

Jo, Joe, Ciara and Ben headed off to the coast resort of Buzios for a few days. Chris returned to the UK, his part of the adventure over for now; he planned to head off to France for the ski season with his girlfriend. Geoff and Spike went to the boat and I spent a glorious few hours, completely absorbed, sorting out my kit for the next leg. In this *gestalt*, this being 'in the moment', being here, now, not off somewhere in the imagination, in this, I thought, surely lies the key to the next leg.

As we drank a farewell beer in Chris's room people were already talking about the leg to come; comparing clothing and kit, pulling on ski masks and balaclavas, combinations of wool and rubber gloves, technical waterproof socks and boot liners; and there was much discussion of the relative merits of our two-piece foul weather suits and the one-piece survival suits with which most boats had equipped themselves. So much for the externals. I was more concerned with the mental preparations: the attitudes, the affirmations and the mental anchors that would see us through. Then we received a shock.

Sitting in the press office one afternoon with Drew, who was sending a story back to a US magazine, we heard that Peter Vroon of Hood Sails was seriously ill in hospital. He had felt unwell the previous day, had gone down to reception at his hotel at about 3 am to ask for a doctor, and had collapsed. At about 5.30 pm Drew and I found Spike and told him, and when he went to see Peter at the hospital, arriving at about 6.45 pm, he was five minutes too late. Peter had died of meningitis. This was a considerable shock. Peter was 36, full of life and good humour, and only the day before he had been laughing and joking with us while superintending the repair of all our sails. What was most shocking was the manner of his death. Had he been knocked down by a bus it would have been no less tragic, but less sinister. The idea of an airborne, water-droplet transmitted disease being passed on, possibly just by a sneeze, and killing someone within 24 hours seems the stuff of science fiction until it intrudes, obliquely, pointedly, and very finally into your life.

Rio was our last jumping off place before the really big adventure. Mythologically speaking this is the point at which a voyager receives a magic token, a blessing, or a special weapon to help him on his way. Sometimes he or she receives a test or a portent of things to come. We had had one flirtation with death; the plane on which Fernando had originally been booked to fly from Sao Paolo to Rio to meet us had crashed, killing everyone on board. Now, suddenly one of us was gone. 'We owe God a death ... He that dies this year is quit for the next.' I often recall those lines from *Henry IV*; and yet none of us can escape the feeling that each of us should take our proper turn.

In the midst of life, is death. And nowhere are you more in the midst of life than in Rio. There is virtually no topless sunbathing, and the reason is obvious; it is the cult of the bottom. Here in Rio, after all, the 'dental floss' bikini was invented, here in this world centre for health clubs and gymnastic centres (and of course a world centre for plastic surgery). Here women flock to the different professors, who run the exercise clinics, in the search for the perfect 'bunda' or behind. And although new announcements are frequently made amongst the cognoscenti that this professor or that professor absolutely has 'the secret', and although caprice dictates that no sooner does this one have it than he must lose his title again to another, the results are astounding. High, rounded, fulsome, brazen, an absolute, exuberant statement of female sexuality, the Rio bottom is a work of art and a deep joy to behold.

The Buzios party returned just after we had seen Mike Hutt and his wife Ann off on their way to the airport, and apart from Peter's death they were in good spirits. Ciara had decided to return to Buzios and spend a few more days there. Jo and Joe were off to visit one of the great sights of Brazil: the falls at Iguacu.

Not surprisingly, perhaps, the change in diet from dehydrated food to Brazilian cuisine had left some of us with some stomach problems, thus it was that Spike went with me one morning to obtain further supplies of Imodium. He had been into a pharmacy previously and asked for something, only to be told: 'No, No.' The pharmacist had indicated in a mixture of sign language and Portuguese that what he wanted was available on prescription only. 'That's all right, I'm a doctor,' Spike had explained, in English. 'Oh, OK,' said the pharmacist, 'No problem!' This time the pharmacist offered us a packet. Spike examined it. 'No, no,' he said, explaining to me, 'This is the opposite; this will make you go more!' He handed the packet back with a shake of the head and made a downward gesture from his bottom with one hand, whilst holding up the other and saying: 'Stop, stop.' 'Oh, sim,' the pharmacist nodded, picking up another package. He imitated Spike's downward gesture, still nodding, then held up his hand in a clenched fist – the internationally recognised symbol on yachts and boats for 'stop winching, stop hauling,' or whatever the case may be. 'Sim, stop,' he said with a big smile. We smiled back.

Shortly before we were all immersed in our final preparations for leaving I took a bus out to the Botanical Gardens with Helen, Jos and Fiona, the girls from *Nuclear Electric*, and Fiona's boyfriend Dave. To my great delight the Botanical Gardens included a Zen garden – a real life, honest to goodness, no nonsense Zen garden, with beautiful stones and raked white gravel. I paused and enjoyed a 'very important moment' before slightly reluctantly re-joining the others. A toucan flew between the trees, impossibly exotic, triumphantly ridiculous.

With one week to go our impending departure started to occupy all of us. We were back in the work programme, preparing the yacht for the next leg, and some of us were inside our minds, preparing ourselves. As at Southampton, I spent a great deal of this time sorting out the food for the leg with Joe, Ben and Judy, one of our two new 'leggers'. It was hard work, and made me wonder how many pounds of food we had moved over the course of doing this, since each box ended up being shifted *many* times. We had the merit of being a cheerful team, thank goodness, and we made it all a laugh and a joke, whistling and singing silly songs: passing them from one to another, until we had worn them out.

I was taking a last walk along the Avenida Atlantica when someone called to me: 'Hey, do you speak English?' 'I do,' I replied, turning round to show my face, 'and you caught me with that one the other week!' 'Oh, gee, I'm sorry,' he said as he came up to me, 'It was half true, I *had* walked a long way.' 'How much do you make?' I asked. 'About 200 *reals* a day in summer.' 'Nice work, and there for the asking,' I told him. He fell into step beside me and asked my name. I told him and asked his. 'Richard Simpson,' he said, 'and that's really funny because I'm Canadian and there's a store in Canada called Simpson-Sears. We'd make a good team.' He told me his story: he had been financially let down and was stuck in Rio wanting to get back to Canada. 'Surely not at 200 *reals* a day just for walking up and down the Avenida Atlantica,' I said, 'You'll spend the rest of your days here.' 'I am pretty well known,' he confessed with a sigh. 'Funnily enough most of my money comes from the locals, and they know me. I'm known everywhere around here as "Speak English?"'!

We were nearly at the end of our time in Rio. I had been up the Sugar Loaf mountain, ascended Corcovado, and been on the beach at Copacabana and Ipanema. I had drunk a beer in the bar where Vinicius de Moraies and Tom Jobim wrote the song (the 'Girl from Ipanema' was real; her name is Helo Pinheiro, she is a successful business woman in Sao Paolo and has two lovely daughters and a son) and I had been to the Emperor's summer retreat at Petropolis. The only thing I had not done was get a date with Glory! I telephoned again. 'You are leaving when?' she asked, 'Tomorrow? OK, let's go out for dinner.' Glory took me for a guided tour of Ipanema's best restaurants, and then we settled for a pizza, but a Brazilian one of course. We talked about Rio, and she told me about the spectacular New Year festival when everyone dresses in white and goes to the beach to make offerings to Yermanja, the goddess of the sea. 'I throw nice things, things that she will like, perfume and lipstick, Yermanja likes those,' she told me, 'You should take some lipstick with you when you go!' I found myself rather taken with pantheism. We had already established Huey the wind god on board, and now Yermanja, goddess of the sea. Departmentalising one's gods seems like a good system to me, rather like Hinduism, which does this on one level while maintaining the idea of one all-embracing whole behind the pantheon.

Then, as in all the best myths, Glory gave me a good luck charm. She had been talking about something that had happened in her life and she used the word *saudades*. My Brazilian friends tell me it is completely impossible to translate: it has to do with missing some-one, but more than just missing. It is not quite keening because it is not painful, and similarly it is not quite longing, but it is a kind of missing, and holding, for someone absent, with great affection. Glory wrote it on a piece of card so that I could see the spelling, then with a mischievous grin she signed it and handed the card to me. So in the last place before all the mortal dangers, someone did indeed give me words of wisdom and a good luck charm.

The following morning as I was about to step down into a dinghy to go out to *Toshiba* I heard someone call my name. It was Felicity, Chay's wife, to say, 'I just wanted to say good luck. See you in Wellington!' It is really impossible to explain how much such a simple action meant to me in view of what we were about to do.

5

Just a Bunch of Amateurs?

*'It's a wonderful experience, a long passage, with or
without a crew.'* Chay Blyth

Some adventures just happen; some you wish, at the time, were not
happening; and some you plan. Planning and preparation: our
last week in Rio was devoted to getting *Toshiba,* and ourselves,
ready to face the worst seas in the world. Six weeks: around Cape
Horn and across the Southern Ocean. SIX WEEKS! CAPE HORN!!
'Have I done this well enough? Will this stand the Southern Ocean?'
we constantly asked ourselves.

The tensions began to show, and I was vividly reminded of Arthur
Haynes, who sailed on *Heath Insured* in the British Steel Challenge,
saying after the event: 'I had all these visions of how it was going to
be, with us all working together as a team, and it just never happened!'

There was a sudden drama over the dehydrated food. Whilst each
yacht had ordered their required supplies of McDougall's separately,
the Challenge Business had collated the requirements, purchased the
food and had it shipped out by container. Whether something had
gone wrong with the order, or whether some crews, on being first to
the container, had taken off things they had not ordered, was a subject
of heated debate. We were left with some shortages, which we felt we
could rectify with diligent shopping, but *Motorola* were left, just
days before the start of a 40-day voyage, with hardly any food at all
and had to start provisioning almost from scratch.

Finally we went sailing. We checked our newly repaired spinnakers,
re-calibrated our instruments and blew away the cobwebs. The
difficulties of preparation disappeared on the water and whatever
apprehensions and doubts we may have been harbouring as we

69

sailed out round Guanabara bay, we certainly looked like one big happy family.

The beginning of a big adventure can be a testing time, and in many ways for all the crews in the BT Global Challenge, leaving Rio was really the beginning of our adventure. My apprehensions surfaced the day before the start. I woke up, in the by now familiar hotel room which I had shared with Geoff for nearly a month, feeling disquieted. Oddly, Geoff and I made good room mates. Oddly only in as much as Geoff is a lark, up with the dawn but no great stayer-out-late, while I am more of a night owl. 'Early to rise and early to bed makes a male healthy and wealthy and dead,' remarked James Thurber! Geoff was the quietest and most considerate of sharers, but he was usually up and gone by the time I rose. My disquiet stayed with me as I showered and went down to breakfast. It stayed, but I could not pin it down. Then, outside the hotel, stepping into the bright Brazilian sunshine, hit by the noise of the traffic going by, I got it. Did I *really* want to do this?

I thought about it for a moment. Then, with remarkable clarity, the answer popped into my mind. 'If you don't want to do it, Alan,' I told myself, 'all you have to do is find Simon, tell him you are not going to go on, and catch a plane home. You'll leave Si and the rest of the crew in a bit of a hole, but that will get you out of it.' And in that instant I knew that I absolutely did want to do the next leg. Without question. This was what we had come for.

Following Simon's crew debriefings and his own assessment of our first leg, we considered some changes to the watch system. After a conference lasting several hours, Simon, Ben and Mark announced that having tried every combination they could think of they were back where they had started, so we carried on as before! Sadly, we had had to say goodbye, at least for the time being, to Mike and Chris, but we were able to welcome Judy and Ange in their place. Ange is the daughter of a Brixham trawlerman, so we expected her to be as tough as they come, and were not disappointed. Ange has the most beautiful blue eyes in the world and a voice that would peel lemons at five hundred yards. She was tough, hardworking, and very determined – you don't get to be 'The Luckiest Legger of All' without! An outdoor pursuits instructor and lifeboat crew, Ange had only one problem on board *Toshiba*, she could not stand Earl Grey tea! Judy, a marine underwriter, faced an even trickier dietary challenge: she was a vegetarian. Take a pair of sparkling eyes, add a huge swathe of bubbly blonde hair and an ever present smile, and that was Judy. Alternatively, look for a bright yellow dry suit being buried under another ton of water by the low-side mast winch during a reef; that would be Judy too, still smiling, and probably still singing. The watches lined up as follows: Ben led Guy, Drew, Kobus, Ange and Woolly. Mark's team was Judy, Jo, Geoff, Spike, Ciara (whose family nick-name, Kiki, had been discovered, leading to a re-christening) and me.

Astute observers will have spotted that this arrangement left Ben's lot one short, as it did on the first leg. The reasoning was this: there is no specific role for a Mate in this type of race. Although someone had to be nominated to the position to take over if anything happened to the skipper, leaving that person out of the watch system was unnecessary. Better to have one watch of six and one of seven, with the skipper to back up the short-handed watch if needed. Similar reasoning lay behind our choice of two watches and not three. The idea of a 'mother watch' taking care of non-sailing chores can work very well, but it also means that sometimes the best sailors will be on watch, but below decks. With two watches, the on-deck work and the domestics can be balanced among the members of each watch. We also established proper rotas for the cleaning and cooking, which suited me; I spent a lot less time in the galley after we had done that!

The leg to Wellington started on 20 November and contrary to our usual practice we made a good start. And contrary to weather expectations in Rio it rained all day. It was raining when we left the hotel, kit bags loaded, it rained throughout the start, and it was still raining when night fell. If you are pragmatic you will say a weather front came through. If you are a romantic you will say Rio opened her arms to let us go and her skies flooded with tears. A lot of people were pleased to leave Rio and start sailing again, but I was sad to go. I had met people and made friends, and besides it is the kind of place that creeps in under your skin. Above all, though, I was sad at no longer being in touch with people at home.

There was very little wind at the start off Copacabana beach, just rain and a grey mist, so we 'shot the line', turning the engine off bang on the five-minute gun and squeezing through a tiny gap between *Save the Children* and the buoy marking the outside end of the line. We crossed the line in about tenth place, but farthest offshore, in clean air, and farthest from the big swells near the beach. In the pouring rain, with crews in full foul weather gear, the fleet trickled along with barely the length of a spinnaker pole separating each boat. It was like a slow-moving nautical traffic jam. Gradually, however, things began to shape up. *Group 4* had started towards the inshore end of the line and appeared to be suffering in the swell nearer the beach. *Concert*, who won the start, managed to hold their place and were first to swing round the Rio fairway buoy and head for the open sea. Our outside position paid off handsomely and we gradually overhauled *Save the Children* (most of whose male crew were sporting the Save the Children logo shaved on to their heads!) and *Motorola*, both sailing almost alongside us, to be second round the fairway buoy.

Some went for spinnakers, but we thought the genoa was working better and stuck with it. While most of the fleet headed straight towards Cape Horn, those flying kites had to make the best course they could. *Time & Tide*, seizing an opportunity, took a flyer and headed west.

There is nothing like the smell of success for defeating poor conditions, so although the rain persisted through the night we remained very cheerful. Fresh food for dinner helped mightily too, and morale was high in the morning as we held on to second place. By lunchtime on the following day the sun had come out and we were sailing on flat seas, running third to *Concert* and *Save the Children*.

By day 3 we were under spinnaker reaching down the coast of Brazil. The fleet developed an east-west split, and, although we led the eastern charge, the westerly boats, now led by *Time & Tide* and *Courtaulds*, had edged ahead. Odd though it may sound, we were thrilled to bits to see *Time & Tide* leading the race. Some of their detractors seemed to doubt their ability, as a disabled crew, to even sail their boat, yet here they were showing us the way down to Cape Horn. A real nip and tuck game followed, and, as the weather favoured first one side and then the other, we went from being third, to half way down the fleet, and then all the way back up again. Not that that was very far in distance. *Pause to Remember* and *Heath Insured*, the backmarkers, were in fact only 12 miles behind the leaders.

This constant changing of positions was often puzzling to friends and family following the race at home. 'We wondered what on earth you were doing!' was a comment I heard more than once. The answer was usually that it was the weather that influenced the boats' positions. In sheer boat speed, the difference between the fastest boat over a period of time and the slowest is not likely to be much more than about half a knot. Now that is a lot in racing terms, but it will only account for a difference of three miles between any two six-hourly position reports. So when greater gains or losses were recorded the answer was usually that it was the result of more, or less, wind. I do not mean by this that ocean racing is a complete lottery; the fastest boats will always win out in the end, but over a short period even the best crew cannot do much if their rivals, perhaps only 20 or 30 miles away, have more wind for a while. As a report sent from *Save the Children* at around this time said: 'This morning ... we went from first to middle in one easy move – I just wish someone would tell me how we did it!'

On moths and mayhem

Drifting along in these very variable and mostly very light winds, conversation turned to the williwaws. 'The what?' asked Guy. 'The williwaws. Chay told us to watch out for the williwaws.' Along this South American coast, particularly near the mouth of the River Plate, fierce squalls blow suddenly off the coast, frequently without warning. Sometimes, however, there is a warning, in the form of huge clouds of moths which, travelling in front of the wind, often alight on boats, covering the decks and rigging. Chay had experienced this phenomenon during his singlehanded voyage. His problem was that he had become intrigued by the invasion of moths and by the time he had remembered that, in this area at least, they are a certain warning of a bad squall, he had been hit by a 60 knot gust and *British Steel* was laid over on her beam ends! Hence his injunction to us at the crew briefing to 'watch out for the williwaws'.

We never did see any moths – the weather just came in. The wind rose from 8 to 30 knots very quickly. Down came the spinnaker. We went to change to a smaller headsail, but had only got as far as getting the No 1 down when the need to do more became urgent. We left ourselves without a headsail and put the first reef in the main – then followed it immediately with the second. Back on the foredeck the wind was too much for the No 2 even before we had hoisted it. We laboriously unhanked it, manhandled the No 3 on deck, and put that up instead. During all this, great sheets of water came surging over *Toshiba*'s bow every few seconds so that we were washed around the foredeck like billiard balls cannoning into each other. Simon was thrown hard along the deck, hurt his back and practically straightened out the heavy, right-angled stainless steel clasp that held his safety strop on to his lifejacket. On the next off-watch I got no sleep at all. We crashed over short, steep seas, pitching up and down and smashing off waves. The boat hook, a long aluminium pole secured in the companionway, rang, bell-like, at each crashing impact, sounding like a knell of doom! Later on in the trip we managed to stop this rather theatrical addition to the panoply of sounds that accompany a storm at sea.

In the middle of all this I used the heads (lavatory). Foolish, I hear you say, but regrettably necessary. For the only time in my sailing career I suffered what someone rather aptly described as 'toilet blow-back' – instead of pumping the debris away, the mechanism dumped a couple of gallons of raw sewage into the shower tray. There is, alas, no option. You have to clear it up. The smell would have made me gag on dry land. The pitching of the boat meant bracing oneself for dear life with legs, knees and one hand, whilst swabbing with the other. I lasted about 40 minutes and then finally, for the only time on the race, I was sick. It took me 12 hours to recover, with the aid of anti-nausea pills, sleep, no food, a little water, some TLC from Kiki, and an abating of the weather. This last cure always works. By 3 am the next day I felt fine and was much improved by Simon saying, 'That's really about as bad as it gets, mate.' As it turned out he was not wholly right about that, but at the time it cheered me up enormously!

Jo had worse problems. Washed down the foredeck in the middle of a sail change, she collided heavily with one of the stays and knocked her two front teeth out. Fortunately the teeth were a bridge and Ben was able to superglue them back into place, hilariously assisted by his newly appointed dental nurse, Ange. Ange's suggestion that Ben had in fact stuck them back in upside down caused a slight delay in the operation while everyone, including the patient, collapsed in a fit of the giggles. Only in the Southern Ocean could going to the dentist be this much fun.

The gale at least gave us the chance to try out our dry suits. 'Yellow fever' took hold, and while Guy insisted that he was only trying out the flap and zip system that lets the chaps, but not the girls, have a pee without taking the whole thing off, Judy was so enamoured with hers that she did not want to take it off. We began to wonder what she wore at home.

'Rio de la Plata to Cabo de Hornos' read the next chart, but we missed a break in the weather. The gale having subsided into very light winds, *Group 4* slipped away, followed by a chasing group, leaving us 10th or 11th on the water and losing us our overall second place. Ben remarked: 'Oh well, this is the true test of character,' but not the way you hear it said in the movies, all stiff upper lip and hearts of oak. We were in rather more of a mood to wonder what was coming next and how we would stand up to it.

The trip down the coast of South America was very changeable, from beautiful bright blue skies and flashing blue seas in the shining sun, to beating into 28 knots of wind in less than half a day. It did, however, get positively cooler. By day 11 Simon's noticeboard read:

'Water temperature = 8°C, survival time = not long, clunk-click every trip.' A salutary reminder to clip on all the time when on deck. Elsewhere, the rigours of the trip were beginning to tell. Kurt Kinast was taken off *Save the Children* by HMS *Lancaster*, en route from the Falkland Islands to Montevideo, with a suspected kidney stone, and Rhian Jenkins had to be airlifted from *Global Teamwork* by an RAF helicopter and taken to Port Stanley in the Falkland Islands suffering from a suspected duodenal ulcer.

Nobody said very much in the face of this news. In another two weeks we would be way beyond the reach of any helicopter and a long, long way from any of the world's shipping routes. Spike had said before the start that the emergency he most dreaded having to deal with was a fracture which exposed the broken bones. Kidney stones and ulcers were somehow slightly more insidious, but at the time our medical problems restricted themselves to bruises and sores. Mark had been bitten on the leg by some sort of demon insect just before leaving Rio and the bite, having become infected, had turned into a large painful boil. Spike operated with Kiki as assistant. Mark refused anaesthetic but sang throughout to ease the pain, causing Kiki to remark that she was glad to be a dentist – patients can't sing when you have your hands in their mouths! Spike was getting a bit of practice in this particular field because Geoff had had a similar problem during the stopover, which started when he walked into a fridge door! It persisted and left him *hors de combat* for the first part of the leg. My only problem at this stage was my back, which was always a weak spot for me, following an injury many years ago. Backache, as fellow-sufferers know, is very debilitating, and helming, especially under heavy reaching conditions, caused me a lot of discomfort and some distress from time to time.

The fleet also cleared the Falklands on day 11 with *Global Teamwork* at the front, ahead of *Save the Children*. From *Concert* in the west to *Save the Children* in the east, and *Teamwork* at the front to *Rover* at the back, we covered a box only about 75 miles by 130. We were about 250 miles from Cape Horn and had been racing within sight of each other almost all the way from Rio. We asked Simon whether he wanted to drop into the Falklands, and made him tell us again the story of how *Rhone Poulenc* suffered a mighty broach in the British Steel Challenge and had to put in there to effect repairs to the rig. It cost them 48 hours, destroying any chance they might have had in the race.

Simon gave us a Southern Ocean briefing. 'It won't be much colder than this,' he told us, 'and really it won't get much rougher.

We've been in short seas in a gale and that's about as bad as it gets. In the Southern Ocean the swells are bigger, but it's more long ups and downs.' Jo asked: 'What about 60 knot winds? We've only had 35 or 40 so far.' 'Fine,' replied Simon, 'We reef down, the boat doesn't heel any more than this, the galley is just like it is now, and I can go to bed – I love it!' 'What about the waves?' 'Oh, often there aren't any at 60 knots, the sea gets flattened by the wind and there's just loads of spray, it's quite exciting but it's really OK!' We believed him at the time.

Cape where?

I made an interesting discovery. Cape Horn is not where I thought it was. I had read all the books and knew all the place names, but I had never actually looked at the charts! The tip of South America curls away to the east and separated by a strip of water called the strait of Le Maire is Isla de los Estados, or Staten Island. The island is about 60 miles long, so going around it incurs an obvious distance penalty, but the strait, about 20 miles wide, is notorious for its strong tides, up to 6 knots, and conditions of wind over tide can render the passage dangerous even to a big ship. Having navigated your way around, or inside, Staten Island, you are still about 150 miles north-east of Cape Horn. The cape itself is the southernmost tip of a completely different island lying due south of the underside of Tierra del Fuego.

Coming down to Staten Island we had *Nuclear Electric* hot on our heels and a tricky decision to make about the timing and the tides. We focused harder than ever on boat speed, and here was a great example of making your own luck: we bent all our efforts and all our concentration to making the passage through the strait, and arrived just in time to do it. *'Nuke'* were too late, had to go around Staten Island; they never got on terms again.

The Le Maire strait was one of the absolute high spots of the trip for me. We passed between Cabo San Bartolomé on Staten Island and the wonderfully named Cabo Buen Suceso on Tierra del Fuego, with both clearly visible. The coast lines are tremendously rugged, like a cross between a volcanic landscape and a Scottish island. To our left it looked as though a maniac had been let loose with a fretsaw on a giant piece of black hardboard which had then been hammered into the horizon and topped with grey painted cotton wool. Ahead, looking over *Toshiba*'s bow, it looked just like the coast of Cornwall: a greeny-grey sea with white-capped waves. With the day sunny and bright, temperature about 7°C, this could have been a winter training sail heading back towards Plymouth!

Once through the strait we followed Chay's advice: 'Head south straight away and get out of the rough stuff.' Cape Horn is feared for its bad weather and big seas, and the reasons are geographical. The wind has the fetch of the entire Southern Ocean, endlessly circling the southern part of the globe, in which to whip up the sea. Cape Horn is the nearest land to Antarctica, causing a funneling effect and, as if that were not enough, the sea bed shelves dramatically from thousands of metres deep to a few hundreds. Why do waves break on a beach? Because the sea gets shallow there and it is exactly the same when the ocean bed shelves. The one thing a prudent mariner can do about it is to head south into deep water. Alas, this reduced the most romantic place in all sailing lore into a question of watching the longitude figure on the GPS! For the record, we rounded Cape Horn on Tuesday 3 December at 14.13 GMT, but we were a long way south of the actual headland, well out of sight. Nevertheless we were well and truly in the Southern Ocean and heading for our next waypoint, the Concert gate.

Being a good way south keeps you out of the rough stuff for which the Horn is notorious, and that meant for us just another sea with big waves in it. We were getting used to living this way, beating to windward at 8 knots. Imagine your kitchen tilted to 30 degrees and swinging from side to side, and that every 5 minutes someone picks your bed up 3 or 4 feet in the air and drops it, while hitting an oil drum with a sledge hammer next to your head, and you begin to have the idea. Imagine also that you weigh four times as much as you are used to and that gravity acts sideways so that you always have to brace yourself and move from handhold to handhold, making sure that your feet do not slither out violently from under you. This is life below decks. Down here it is warm or cool, depending on whether the heaters are working or not, and only wet on the walls and floors. Yet your world swings and jumps around in a crazy way; the floor lifts and falls as you try to walk on it, the walls veer away from you or rush up to meet you as you put out a hand to brace yourself. Forward of the dog-house and chart table area the banging and crashing is loud and furious. Often one almighty crash is followed by a whole sequence of slams and bangs – it's like facing an all-in wrestler three times your strength and weight; the first move is simply to break your grip and throw you off balance so that you have no defence against what follows. It's hard to believe that while all this mayhem ensues, someone still has to think about the catering.

Up on deck it is wet, cold and wild. The deck and cockpit hang in the air at crazy angles. Moving about is like mountaineering and yet, oddly, it all makes sense up here. Every pitch and twist of the boat relates directly to the wind and water tearing by, but here at least the motion is related to something, and from the cockpit, especially from the wheel, only the worst of the wave-jumping pancake landings actually sound an audible crash. The others register as dull thumps, seemingly of little consequence. It requires a shift of focus and imagination to think how it must feel down below. One boat, two worlds, and we alternated between them, governed only by the passing hours ticked off in the log.

Our passage across the Southern Ocean was measured out in 8-day blocks. This, of course, was because the food programme ran on an 8-day week. At the end of each period we cleared the galley, and moved the next 'week's' supplies in. Although it was a remarkably small volume of food for 14 people for 8 days, it is still quite a lot of weight when it came to moving it, without having the boat heaving and crashing at the same time. Like everything else, it simply had to be done whatever the weather.

As is so often the case, many of the things that I had worried about never materialised. I expected to be freezing cold and, apart from my hands, I stayed warm. I expected to be wet through and was never more than damp. I expected to be sick and (apart from the 'heads' incident) never even felt queasy, and above all I expected to be terrified and I was not even frightened. The Southern Ocean in a gale is an awesome sight, but the waves, huge though they are, roll by; the wind hums and howls, and generally we simply shortened sail and went on. In fact, once we had the boat correctly set up for the conditions in the force 8s and occasional 9s we experienced going to Wellington, things were fairly reasonable. Helming, however, was very hard work and it was easy to be caught off balance and thrown right off the wheel.

The nitty-gritty came as the conditions changed and the sail plan had to be changed accordingly. Commonly (but not always) the last sail change down to the No 3 yankee (the smallest headsail) or from the staysail down to the storm staysail, were the ones that tested the fibre, moral and physical. In gale or near gale force conditions, 9 or 10 metre high waves and sea temperatures just above freezing, this is the stuff that chills the blood as well as the fingers. Trying desperately to find the stability in which to work on a heaving, pitching foredeck canted at 30-40 degrees and never still; picking a moment to release your lifeline and transfer it clumsily with numb, unresponsive fingers to another safe point before the next wave sweeps across the deck with the power of a rip tide; clawing with broken fingernails at wet sailcloth and heaving packed sails the length and weight of medium-sized tree trunks may be character building stuff, but in my experience it does not necessarily bring out the best in people.

Weather systems, of course, come and go. When each new system was on its way, there was a certain sense of foreboding. Usually the weather deteriorated quite slowly, but there was a certain inevitability about it: you know that someone is going to have to make every one of the downward sail changes and reefs – will you bear the brunt of it, or will it fall to the other watch? Who is going to catch a packet this time? At its worst we went from No 1 yankee, staysail and full main to the No 3, storm staysail and all three reefs in one watch. This was continuous hard work, in freezing conditions on a pitching foredeck, being continually swept by icy waves for the whole of the four hours. The first time it happened Ben's lot drew the short straw. They looked gaunt and dead beat when we relieved them. Needless to say, much the same happened to us soon afterwards, but in between we had been back into light airs.

The biggest storm of the leg blew up in about 20 minutes (sometimes they do come quickly) and started as a series of squalls with wind speeds up to 30–35 knots and short lulls in between. Night saw the wind reach 40 knots but the main feature was the huge seas. Big waves, terrific drops and all very confused. Down below the crashes were louder than anything I had heard before. One thump in particular sounded as though we must have hit something solid, but it was only another wave. I felt slightly apprehensive getting up to go on watch in the night because, down below, it was so noisy and the movement so violent, but up on deck it seemed more reasonable, even though the seascape was awesome.

One of the waves I steered up not only seemed to carry on going up for ever, it seemed to get steeper and steeper as we reached the top until it appeared to hang vertically above us. I just kept telling myself: 'It must be all right,' and of course it was. *Toshiba* laboured her way up to the top, pivoted through the breaking crest and slid off down the other side, plunging into the next trough with mountains of white water burying the bow. I do not mean to sound sanguine or nonchalant about this; there were times when it seemed we couldn't possibly climb up waves so steep, or that a cross sea would inevitably knock us flat, but we always came through. Really I just had extreme faith in the boat – after all, unlike me, she had been round before!

Typically, a bad blow would last 48 hours or so before winding down and giving us a chance to recover, but the bad weather brought great camaraderie with it. Zipping each other into our canary yellow dry suits, pulling on our ice-climbing mitts and goggles, or the helmets provided for us by the RNLI for helming, was sometimes funny, sometimes grim. Sometimes it was downright painful as six or seven of us would be flung about bodily whilst trying to get our kit on. Then it would be time to open the hatch, stand on the companionway steps, reach out, clip on to the cockpit jackstay, sneak a glance round the corner to make sure the world's biggest wave was not about to engulf you, and out you go, into one of the wildest places on earth.

In spite of all this we had some fantastic sailing. The Southern Ocean really is very beautiful; it is rugged and imposing, like a mountain landscape, but the seascape is constantly changing. Just as a kaleidoscope makes endless different patterns from a few shards of coloured plastic, so the ocean performs protean miracles with blue water and white spray. The bigger waves were tremendous. When things were reasonably benign these waves would sweep up, like large, curious animals as if to see who and what these visiting strangers might be. They would hump us up on to their backs momentarily and then slide on remorselessly, indifferent to our slithering and crashing as we slipped, or slammed, down into the valleys they left behind. Not everyone enjoyed it, but those who dance are thought insane by those who do not hear the music.

By the half-way stage most of us were beginning to count the days. When Simon announced he was going to try to raise Wellington radio because 'After all, it's only 2500 miles away,' I replied: 'Yes, and so is almost anywhere else too!' It was not the remoteness, I think, which affected most people though, although it did make some a little nervous; it was mostly the time left to go. After three weeks at sea on a yacht 67 ft by 17 ft, another three weeks seems like a long time. We also spent a very long time in sixth place, which was difficult mentally. We didn't give up trying, but the more the leg seemed to be turning into something of a procession, the harder it became to keep everyone's spirits up and our attention focused on going fast. Which is odd because getting there as quickly as possible is the prime object of racing!

There was no shortage of incidents. Firstly, we had a call for all hands on deck. The top fixing holding the mainsail to the mast had come away in 35 knots of wind. Then, just as I was sliding out of my bunk, there was a squeal like a stuck pig from the galley, amidst a huge clattering of pots and pans that went on for so long that I

Above: The 'Wave Warriors' returned home. *Left to right back row:* Spike, Alan, Justin, Michael Buerk, Arnie, Mike Hutt, Chris, Guy, Drew. *Middle row:* Di, Holly, Kiki, Simon, Woolly, Jo, Ange. *Front row:* Geoff, Ben, Jack, Kobus, Roger, Judy, Mark. Haydon, alas, is not in the picture. PHOTO: SUSAN CONWAY

Food glorious food! Spike's flat becomes the quarter-master's stores for a week before the start. PHOTO: ALAN SEARS

Ready for the off. The fleet lined up in Ocean Village, Southampton. PHOTO: SIMON WALKER

Posing for the helicopter, just leaving Plymouth on our maiden voyage to Southampton. It looks like a nice day but ten seconds later we were all drenched when the bow submerged under a wave! PHOTO: MARK PEPPER/ND COMTEC ON-LINE SERVICES

Below One of the great sights of the race – *Group 4* astern! Our mascots, 'Larry the Lobster' and 'Sharky' are visible just in front of Spike, on the wheel surround. This is Mid-Atlantic after a week's racing. PHOTO: SIMON WALKER

Guilty? Horribly guilty. Justice being seen to be done in the court of King Neptune. Simon presides; Kiki administers the punishment; I am the victim; Mark, Drew and Jo get cleaned up; and the clerk of the court, Kobus, summons the next Defendant. PHOTO: ALAN SEARS

Left One leg done, five to go. Elation mingles with relief as we slip past the Sugar Loaf Mountain and the Statue of Christ on Corcovado just before the finish in Rio. PHOTO: SIMON WALKER

Blue sky, dark sea: more weather coming. Another day in the Southern Ocean. PHOTO: ALAN SEARS

A long way from anywhere on the chart, as Ben shows the broken D3 fitting that could have brought the mast down. Spike coolly checked the other one for damage before coming back to deck level! Note the salt water sores on Ben's right hand. PHOTO: ALAN SEARS

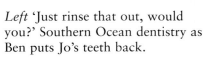

Left 'Just rinse that out, would you?' Southern Ocean dentistry as Ben puts Jo's teeth back.
PHOTO: ALAN SEARS

Right Spinnaker sewing circle in progress. Jo, Mark, Kobus and Geoff debate how best to put it back together this time. The white Dacron patches were ironed on using a hot kettle! PHOTO: ALAN SEARS

Simon with the 'Walker muglamp'. 'Do the best you can, with what you have, where you are!'
PHOTO: ALAN SEARS

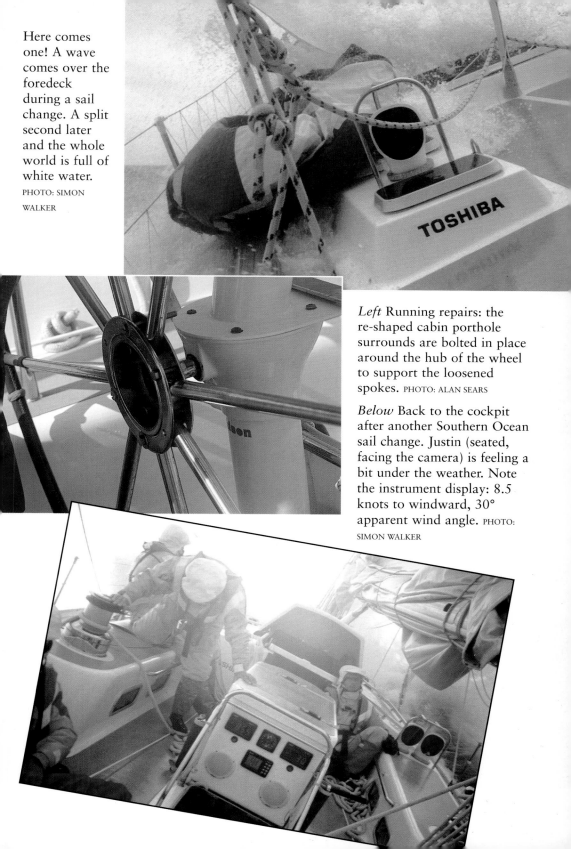

Here comes one! A wave comes over the foredeck during a sail change. A split second later and the whole world is full of white water. PHOTO: SIMON WALKER

Left Running repairs: the re-shaped cabin porthole surrounds are bolted in place around the hub of the wheel to support the loosened spokes. PHOTO: ALAN SEARS

Below Back to the cockpit after another Southern Ocean sail change. Justin (seated, facing the camera) is feeling a bit under the weather. Note the instrument display: 8.5 knots to windward, 30° apparent wind angle. PHOTO: SIMON WALKER

A sunny day in the windy city. The boats were stripped out in Wellington and every last piece of equipment checked. PHOTO: ALAN SEARS

Below 'Peeling the kite.' Mark and Guy haul the new spinnaker to the top of the mast while Ange tails the halyard at the winch and Spike sits atop the pole ready to 'trip' the old sail away – or that's the theory anyway!
PHOTO: SIMON WALKER

Safe haven in the Southern Ocean: Kobus wedges himself under the saloon table to drink a cup of tea in the middle of a big blow: PHOTO: SIMON WALKER

Below The Sun-God rises; a spectacular finish at Cape Town. Business as usual for the on-watch, however, weight forward and low. PHOTO: SIMON WALKER

Roger's 'big screen anagrams' and the 'Briggsamatic weather machine'. No shortage of weather faxes in the North Atlantic!

PHOTO: SIMON WALKER

Reunion! Mark hugs daughter Fay at the
finish in Southampton. PHOTO: MARK PEPPER/
ND COMTEC ON-LINE SERVICES

Done it! *Toshiba* returns to Ocean Village,
Southampton after 10 months and 30,000
miles around the world. PHOTO: MARK PEPPER/
ND COMTEC ON-LINE SERVICES

thought every last thing in the galley must be flying about, followed by one of the most heartfelt expletives I have ever heard. Drew came out, charging to his cabin in rage and fury. A pan of something hot had obviously spilt all over him; thankfully he had been wearing his dry suit and was not hurt, but all his frustration and disenchantment had boiled over. I felt he was living out the very nightmare I had dreaded, hating every minute of it, feeling unwell, driven to distraction by the lurching, crashing and banging and with no means of escape. On top of that there was the knowledge that he had to endure another three weeks of it, and even then his only way out would be to admit defeat and quit. There but for the grace of God ... I thought.

The mainsail repair was simpler to deal with. Once we'd got the sail down it just required a couple of hours' work at the mast in freezing temperatures drenched in cold water every few minutes. Our dry suits were fantastic, but you can't do this sort of work with gloves on, and the pain of extremely cold hands has to be endured to be believed.

When your hands get really cold, several things happen. At first you just feel cold, then you feel really cold and start rubbing your hands and blowing on fingers. Then your hands start to hurt, then they become painful and begin to go numb, not in the sense that the pain eases, just in the sense that your fingers go stiff and will not work very well. Then an odd thing happens. Your fingers stop hurting quite so much and seem to acquire a tolerance of the conditions. Then they *really* start to hurt. This is the agonising, hand shaking, face grimacing stage, but none of it helps. The only thing that works after this is to put your hands somewhere warm, where they are not doused in freezing cold seawater every few seconds.

Warm dry mitts are very good for cold hands, but unless you have just come on deck, cold wet mitts are likely to be your only choice. If you have just come on deck then your mitts, dried out against your body in your sleeping bag (unless you have been really lucky and the heaters have been working), will be cool, damp mitts by the time you put them on again. We could get away with wearing gloves for some jobs, but if we were to perform efficiently and safely even a numb and frozen bare hand beat a gloved one for much of what we had to do.

There may be trouble ahead ...

The first intimation that this might not be a straightforward passage came over the satcom in a chillingly formal message informing us that *3-Com* had lost their forestay. With the rig still standing they were effecting a makeshift stay using the spinnaker halyards. Checks on rigging wire led to reports from both *Save the Children* and *Global Teamwork* of broken strands in their backstays. In view of this, the race committee instructed the fleet to take 'course Wellington', to leave out waypoint Echo (situated to the south of New Zealand to make the course longer), and head directly for Wellington after passing through the Concert gate.

Two days later we had to effect a repair to strengthen the wheel: the spokes were beginning to move rather alarmingly in the hub. Simon's cold assessment: 'That won't stand 50 knots,' focused our attention on a solution. With great presence of mind Kobus, who was responsible for a number of clever solutions and suggestions during the trip, suggested we use two of the circular stainless steel plates which hold the cabin portholes in place, to go around the hub: one in front of the spokes and one behind; at which point we could bolt them together, providing a rigid centre to the structure. It took several days of filing to complete the job but the result turned out to be about the neatest solution anyone came up with to a problem that almost everyone in the fleet had to deal with.

On my birthday we changed the No 1 yankee down to the No 2. Routine, but including packing the No 1 away, it took one and a half wet, cold and exhausting hours. The sail was repeatedly washed away from us down the deck, the halyard caught round a hank on the stay-sail and in the end we had to lower that, free the halyard and re-hoist. Getting the No 1 down was like wrestling an angry elephant.

We finished half an hour late, and two hours' sleep did little for me. I spent the next watch in a state of exhaustion that I came to recognise. Whether it was tiredness, dehydration or something like low blood sugar I do not know. I am not talking about just being tired. This was mind-numbing, leaden-limbed, spaced out, can't act, can't talk exhaustion – and still we had to work.

At the same time I was being troubled by pins and needles in my hands and arms on waking up, a symptom also reported by Mark and Ben, and my fingernails had black flecks showing in the quick from being pulled when dragging sails down. I came to hate heavy weather sail changes and can still find nothing good to say about them. I didn't appreciate the challenge or find satisfaction in the job even when it went reasonably well (well, to be honest, a little satis-faction if we had done it *really* well). They were just a horrible, necessary evil. In good weather I relished the teamwork, but freezing cold seawater and being bashed about as a bit of wave fodder did more than just take the fun out of it.

Being bashed about was a constant hazard, but Jo took one of the worst knocks of the lot and hurt her forearm badly. She carried on gamely, but it was to have repercussions.

The real star for me was my cabin mate, Judy. We started referring to each other as 'flat-mate' quite early on, then we discussed whether our 'flat' would look better with Laura Ashley wallpaper or Regency stripe. We debated over who to invite to our next dinner party and whether to cook or to have something delivered, and ended by constructing a pair of characters and a script for ourselves that would have done credit to a TV sitcom. Judy was indefatigably cheerful and spent all her on-deck time singing, laughing or volunteering for the wettest jobs available. She kept me endlessly amused and I missed her sorely when we took our second foray into the Southern Ocean without her.

About half way from Cape Horn to Wellington we overtook *Motorola* and went up into fifth place, and then *Global Teamwork* reported five broken strands of wire in their forestay. As the old Chinese curse has it, may you live in interesting times! Two days later we passed *Concert* and were up in fourth place. Then came the high drama: *Concert* issued a message on the 'chat show' to say that they had 'dropped the rig over the side' – in layman's terms they had been dismasted. Amidst a great deal of wondering about the probable cause, listening to reports of damage to wire strands in the standing rigging of various other boats and thoughts of what might be happening over our heads, the framework of a rescue was put in place over the radio. *Concert* had dealt with their immediate problem by cutting away the mast before it punched a hole in the hull. With no other damage and no injuries to crew, they had only to consider where to make for and how much fuel they would need.

For some time it looked as though we would have to turn back and rendezvous to give them more fuel, but in the end the job fell to *Motorola*. I had the strong impression that Chris Tibbs, the skipper of *Concert*, was very reluctant to ask a yacht ahead of him to turn back, rather than one behind to come up, and I felt personally grateful to him. The following day, *Heath Insured* reported a failed rigging wire resulting in a two foot sideways bend in their mast. Only prompt action and expert seamanship from skipper Adrian Donovan and his crew averted a second dismasting.

The Inmarsat communications system was heavy with messages as skippers, crews and the Challenge Business tried to work out whether we were dealing with separate isolated incidents, or a common problem. The following night we charged through the wild blackness with winds over 40 knots and seas to match. Simon remarked: 'If the rig lasts the night it will see us into Wellington,' by now some 1500 miles away.

Thirty-six hours later, the weather had calmed down enough for us to make a rig check. We had already rigged rope lines to back up the wire in case of failure, and Spike went up to check everything for wear or damage. He had barely reached the second spreaders (the cross-pieces which sprout out sideways from the mast) when Simon, watching from the deck, yelled: 'We've got to tack – the D3's gone at the toggle!' The D3 is the same piece of wire that had broken on *Heath*'s rig and, we suspected at the time, might have been the seat of *Concert*'s disaster. A stainless steel fitting, essentially a U-bracket made of metal a quarter of an inch thick, had failed, leaving the wire slack and, potentially, one side of one section of the mast unsupported.

Spike traversed the spreader to check the equivalent fitting on the other side, which was both a wise thing to do and a piece of bravery verging on the foolhardy since the rig could have come down at any moment. Very fortunately, all this took place in relatively light airs and flat seas. The port fitting was OK. We tacked and set up a jury rig using ropes to bear the loads.

While one team were rigging arresters using our spectra spinnaker halyards, Simon was working out a way to cannibalise another part of the rig and thereby effect a proper repair to the D3. We managed to do that without any hitch other than having to 'heave-to' and make no progress for about three hours. After taking in the facts of the situation, my initial reaction was shock. I genuinely did not expect our race position on this leg to be compromised by a failure like this. That was followed by huge disappointment at the thought that we might end up limping into Wellington like a wounded animal, well down the field. Once I realised that the jury rig would be effected quite quickly, and that we would be back sailing in the right direction before too long, I returned to unquenchable optimism! Still, I certainly felt for a few moments a feeling of unjust fate which must have been magnified a hundred times on board *Concert* and *Heath Insured*.

Throughout most of this leg bad weather alternated with days of bright sunshine, usually very cold but providing wonderful sunrises and sunsets from time to time. In addition, we spent a fair amount of time reaching. This avoids the tremendous heaving up and down that is characteristic of beating, and usually when reaching one is actually heading in the desired direction. The only drawback is that the boat is often heeled over a lot, making things hard work down below – crossing the galley and saloon from side to side was like mountaineering!

Coming up to Christmas most of my thoughts were, regrettably, about getting the leg over and done with. Spike, quite rightly, kept urging everyone not to wish their lives away, but 'every minute Zen', that is to say living in the joy of the moment every moment, is quite hard under these circumstances. I ticked the days off every which way: eight-day food weeks, seven-day normal weeks, pairs of days in the watch system (our watch system gave a long working day followed by a shorter one), dates, numbers, anything I could think of to make it seem shorter. Usually this worked out quite well. Counting down the miles was another popular occupation. It is strange how much better 1580 nautical miles seemed than something still over 1600. Later when we were below 1000 miles to go, it felt as though we were practically there!

Christmas dinner, however, was a feast. I had found myself not really looking forward to Christmas as much as I had expected to, partly because it simply was not going to be the occasion it is at home. This feeling clearly was not shared by the whole crew, some of whom went to great lengths to make the saloon look remarkably festive with decorations, a miniature Christmas tree with lights – and, would you believe, Christmas stockings; Musto sailing socks decorated by Judy's family! Geoff and Spike cooked tinned turkey, tinned roast beef in gravy, real roast potatoes, tinned carrots, dried peas, chestnut stuffing, bread sauce, cranberry jelly and chipolatas, followed by Christmas pudding with custard and brandy butter; all accompanied by whisky, brandy, and an interesting fortified wine from Rio called simply 'Drink'! The whole thing went down riotously well which, since I had been in charge of the planning and purchasing, was very gratifying. The weather was light, bright and sunny – an enormous fillip for the festivities, but slow in terms of getting to Wellington.

The day after Boxing Day, with great presence of mind, Simon looked at the high pressure systems dominating the weather maps and had us lay out the spinnaker gear. By mid afternoon we were sailing downwind with our promotional spinnaker flying and life was a breeze, rather than a slog to windward. The drawback was that, as always under spinnaker, it meant hard and intense work, and we were not going fast – back down to 3½ knots or so, in fact. With just under 400 miles to go, and over 100 miles behind *Save the Children*, our second place overall was in jeopardy. Arrival times seemed to be going backwards. I was dead tired, not very thrilled with things, and because we had the kite up, all extra off-watches had been cancelled, just when I had one due.

By the following day I was really fed up. I was still very tired and our race position was steadily worsening. We were 217 miles behind *Group 4* and 160 miles behind *Save the Children*, going very slowly, with Wellington still looking a long time away. It was bad enough being behind, but being days behind really hurt, and even that would not have been so bad had we been second, but to lose to two other boats was real grief! Interestingly, Simon remarked: 'Part of racing is being fed up sometimes when you are not doing well,' which gave me food for thought about living in the moment and taking part joyously in life! The next weather reports told us that Cyclone Fergus was on its way with 70 knot winds and sea state predicted to be 'phenomenal'.

Now 'phenomenal' is the highest rating in the scale of sea states. The quoted probable wave height is 46 feet, but no maximum is given, so this news caused some anxious speculation! In fact the forecast was for the worst weather to hit the north of New Zealand, with about 40 knots and 'very rough' seas in the Cook Strait (that's the bit of sea between North Island and South Island) just about when we were due to get there.

We rattled on at 9–10 knots on an increasing breeze while, for the second time in two legs, *Group 4* found themselves stuck just off the finish with no wind. So we came in, unsure whether to expect a flat calm or 45 knots in Palliser Bay (the approach to Wellington harbour). In the end we ran through virtually every sail on the boat except the storm sails, and even had the anchor ready on deck to avoid being swept backwards by the tide when it looked as though the wind might fail us altogether. I asked Simon, 'Have you got any more toys you'd like to get out for us to play with?' We were not, as a lot of other yachts were, becalmed getting in, but it was a close run thing.

Wellington Harbour is spectacular. We were not able to see it properly until next morning, but coming in at night is always exciting, especially when the entrance is a narrow gap between wicked-looking clumps of rocks looming up out of the darkness. We navigated our way past the various buoys and lights and beacons until the glorious moment when we crossed the finish line. After 40 days at sea, we arrived at around 4 am on 31 December (having lost one calendar day by crossing the date line). Champagne, beer, congratulations and press interviews spread across the deck as we finally tied up and then, with great fortitude and very good grace, the staff members of Toshiba NZ sat down to dinner with us: huge steaks of roast lamb with fresh rosemary followed by wonderful strawberries and cream with ice cream; what a contrast to life at sea!

We were euphoric. We had arrived third in Wellington and any disappointment that we had not done better was shelved to make way for a flood of congratulations and good humour. And there were reunions: Mark's youngest daughter Fay led the charge, and Ben's girlfriend Becks was there (the waypoint closing velocity had been replaced by the BCV or Becks Closing Velocity in the latter stages of the run in), but Jo had to wait for her special moment. Ed Harrison, along with his *Concert* crew mates, had spent two weeks motoring to the Chatham Islands, where they re-fuelled, before making the last stretch of an interminably long passage to Wellington.

We had had our gruelling moments and I'm sure that most of us had times when we simply wanted to be somewhere else, anywhere rather than where we were. But for all that, this first Southern Ocean leg was, for me, a fantastic experience. The huge seascapes, so often under bright, sunny skies in sharply cold weather, brought with them a stupendous feeling of being really alive, right there all the time, which was unequalled by anything else I have ever done. Joseph Campbell, whom I regard as a sort of intellectual mentor, said that he thought what most people were really looking for was not the *meaning* of life, so much as the *experience* of being alive. On another occasion he quoted an Eskimo shaman who told European visitors that the only true wisdom 'lives far from mankind, out in the great loneliness, and can be reached only through suffering'. We had been out in the great loneliness and we had suffered to get there. Whether I acquired any wisdom I would not like to say, but I certainly got an experience of being alive.

Simon and I were last to collect our kit from the boat and walk up to the Park Royal Hotel. It was raining, we were still in our mid-layer sailing gear (salopettes and jackets, last washed 40 days ago) carrying two waterproof kit bags each. We strolled across the Park Royal's huge reception area to the desk, where no fewer than five uniformed staff stood in line and I said: 'I know this seems extremely unlikely, but we do have a reservation.'

6

Welcome to Aotearoa

'We saw a great land, uplifted high.' Abel Tasman

I took the lift to the third floor of the Park Royal Hotel, turned my key in the lock and opened the doors of heaven. How can I describe the infinite luxury of a bath after forty days at sea? The supreme comfort of a double bed after forty nights zipped into a sleeping bag? The wonder of a stable, non-moving toilet which flushes without pumping? Above all the sheer blessed peace of solitude ... Pascal said: 'All the ills of the world derive from man's inability to sit quietly in a room by himself.' It was all I wanted to do.

We had a day to recover before the New Year celebrations started, and to my great joy my brother Pete arrived with his partner Jackie, bearing presents from home. They had planned a holiday in New Zealand to coincide with our stopover and had just come up from South Island. We partied on the quayside, paused to cheer *Pause to Remember* in at about 3 am, then carried on until late. Wellington on New Year's Day is, thankfully, a quiet place.

With the boats due to come out of the water for inspection, we had our work cut out stripping everything off *Toshiba* that was not nailed down and preparing her to have the mast lifted out. This much was routine maintenance, but following the rigging problems throughout the fleet, the Challenge Business intended to replace all the standing rigging wire on every boat. For us, this meant that as soon as we had finished racing we simply became beasts of burden. Moving, fetching, carrying, heaving, lifting, pulling, pushing, on and on it went, two days' hard labour in the hot sun. When it was all done I waved Pete and Jackie off on the second half of their holiday and they left me a birthday present – *The Island of the Day Before* by Umberto Eco.

Moored alongside our row of Challenge yachts was *Phantom of the Straits*, the ex-*Lion, New Zealand*. As *Lion*, she had been Sir Peter Blake's boat in the 1985 Whitbread Race. She had been bought by Peter Brandels to use for adventure sailing trips around New Zealand and into the Southern Ocean, and he was kind enough to offer us a trip out into the bay to welcome in *Concert*. Chugging in under jury rig and engine, she looked like some strange form of dhow. We lined *Lion*'s bow with Toshiba red and gave them three cheers, but there was better yet to come. The tug *Kupe* came out with her water cannons blasting great fountains into the air in a spectacular welcome. Kupe was the name of the great Polynesian navigator credited with the discovery of, and thereby the populating of, New Zealand; the founding father of the Maori nation. Without exception, *Concert*'s crew were cheerful, philosophical and determined to make the best of their experience, which was highly commendable. No matter how much you joke about T-shirts saying 'We've seen the Chatham Islands', watching your hopes for the race disappear over the side in the middle of the Southern Ocean must be galling in the extreme.

To celebrate the end of work on the boat we went out for a team dinner, and by popular vote it was Christmas dinner! Included as team were three of our most fervent supporters for the whole race: Carmel, our 'boat buddy' for the stopover, and Lois and Justine from Toshiba NZ. Whilst attending to a call of nature during dinner I fell into conversation with a fellow user of the gents lavatory who was interested in the Challenge and who mentioned that he had crewed on a class-winning yacht in the last Sydney–Hobart race. 'If there's anything you need, call me,' he said, handing me a card. I glanced down at it and said: 'Nice to meet you, Rob. I met your son Boyd in Southampton!'

Toshiba had very generously arranged accommodation for us in appartments in Wellington, but sharing a two-bedroom appartment with four other people taxed my patience in ways which life on board did not. At sea we were there to do a job. It was difficult, the dog-house and galley were often crowded and there was no privacy, but it bore no relation to ordinary life. Everything was different and we all knew that in the end we just had to get on with it. The apartment was different. It had no real storage space, so kit littered the floor and over-flowed everywhere and we were still always on top of one another.

This crowded life had its funny moments, however. Geoff was woken one night by Spike yelling something unintelligible, then standing up on his bed, stepping across the intervening gap on to Geoff's bed – fortunately a double – lying down, snatching the pillow from under Geoff's head, putting it under his own and settling down – I cannot say 'to sleep' because, in the normal sense, Spike had not woken up throughout any of this. Two nights later Geoff had the measure of him. When Spike sat bolt upright in bed and yelled: 'Ease the ----ing kicker!' Geoff calmly told him: 'It's been done, mate,' and Spike subsided without another murmur.

There are about three million people in New Zealand, and one million of them live in Auckland. That makes Wellington just about the smallest capital city in the world, and one of the nicest. The city has a lightness and airiness which I think is partly due to its predominantly modern architecture and partly due to the fact that not only is it small (you can walk around most of Wellington very easily), but it is also well laid out. Only about 150 000 people live here, and quite a lot of them live out of town. This economy of population, coupled with the legendary Kiwi friendliness, makes the city an incredibly pleasant place to be. Nonetheless, the lure of travel and excitement took hold and most crews took off to explore the great outdoors.

New Zealand has it all. From live volcanoes to fjords, from hot springs to virgin rainforest, dramatic canyons to boiling rivers, snow capped peaks and underground caverns. Here are the highest mountains in Australasia, some of the most accessible glaciers in the world, the wonders of the Southern Alps, and the glory that is Milford Sound. If all that were not enough you can go tandem skydiving, white water rafting, black water rafting, rap jumping, jetboating, river surfing, abseiling, kayaking, bridgeswinging, and bungy jumping.

I nearly missed it all. I had come without a plan. By the time I got around to looking for someone to make a plan with nearly everyone had gone! I met Paul Stephens from *Ocean Rover*. 'I'm with the waifs and strays, Alan,' he told me, but even they had passed me by. I decided to start by visiting an old family friend, Maud Fraser, in Auckland. I flew up with Ligia Ripper from *Motorola* who was meeting her parents and some friends of theirs flying in from their home in Brazil. By the time we all met in Auckland I had an invitation to share their holiday, travelling through New Zealand and, as the only person in the party with previous experience of driving on the left, I became first call chauffeur as well as honorary Brazilian for two weeks. Two things convinced me that I was with the right people. We spent our first evening together discussing languages and *Macbeth*, whilst Ligia's father, José, and I demolished large amounts of his Johnny Walker Black Label. Then Ligia's mother, Afira, introduced me to Iris and André Vasarhelyi, explaining that Andre was the man I had heard about who, during his university days, was always to be seen with two books – one for reading whilst walking along the street and the other, a lighter volume, for reading whilst crossing the road!

We travelled through New Zealand, both North and South Islands, for two weeks being continually amazed. The extraordinary variety of physical geography on display, the sheer beauty of so much of the country, is incredible. The legendary friendliness and good humour of the Kiwis was proved to us time and time again. Best of all, though, was when we arrived in a tiny town, little more than a village, at about ten o'clock at night, found somewhere to stay, and then asked if there was a good restaurant in town. The motel proprietor looked thoughtful, then disappeared into a back room saying, 'Hang on a minute.' Minutes later he appeared, to report: 'There are two places you can eat round here and they're both closed, but I've given the better one a ring and they'll open up for you.' He gave us directions and off we went to an excellent meal accompanied, as always, by excellent New Zealand wine.

One other abiding memory is of a Maori taking my credit card for something and saying cheerfully: 'There we are, sir. Just sign away your land!' Whilst the larger, internationally-known cities have European sounding names, nearly all other place names are Maori, so it helps to become good at saying things like Whakareware-watangaoteopetauaawahiao (although this one is usually abbreviated to Whaka, with the 'wh' pronounced like 'f'). The Maori names provide a constant reminder that the first settlers of these islands arrived by canoe, and not in a ship of the line. Traditionally 12 canoes left Hawaiki, the homeland in the south Pacific islands, of which 7 survived the trip, thereby forming the 7 tribes of Maori, now divided into hundreds of sub-tribes. Kupe the great navigator is supposed to have made the trip previously, enabling him to instruct the 12 canoes in how to make the voyage to Te Aotearoa – The Land of the Long White Cloud.

Maori culture is alive and strong and non-Maoris will sometimes greet you with 'Kia ora' instead of 'Hi, how're yuh doin?' Perhaps that is because, as someone explained it to me: 'The Maori nation was still fighting tribe against tribe (losers go on the menu) when the Pakeha, the white men, arrived. They agreed to unite in peace and we now carry that banner forward as an example to others.' The government is, of course, and has been for some time, in the process of making reparations to the Maoris for the land taken from them, but New Zealand as a nation seemed to me very proud of its twin heritage, and justly so.

We walked through science fiction landscapes full of boiling mud and improbably coloured lakes, bubbling and steaming. We paddled and rafted through immense black caverns lit by the pin prick lights of tens of thousands of tiny glow worms. We went up Ruapehu whose snow white peak last erupted into giant clouds of dense black ash only two years ago and then we headed across to South Island, landing from the ferry at Picton. Heading west, the coast road was spectacular; bay after bay, the Tasman Sea sweeps on to rocky shores forming rank after rank of white horses stretching far out to sea. We passed through Hari Hari, which amused us greatly as we had earlier been through Rama Rama on North Island. 'Hare Krishna, Hare Rama...' We walked to the foot of the Franz Joseph glacier and gazed up at the enormous wall of ice rising up and backing off up the valley that it has been carving out for centuries. Then we arrived in Queenstown.

Flying the Pipeline

Back in Wellington, before travelling, one of the popular topics of conversation had been: 'Are you going to bungy?' I didn't think I was, then something came back to me. A comment by Sir Francis Chichester that I had written out and pinned to my noticeboard during training; 'I hate being frightened but, even more, I detest being prevented by fright.' That was meant for the Southern Ocean, but just like the Southern Ocean, I wanted to experience it, to find out what it was really like, and to do that I had to walk past the fear. So we booked it. The Pipeline Bungy – 102 metres, 340 feet, 40 stories down from the largest single span suspension bridge in the southern hemisphere into Skipper's canyon. The highest full-time land-based commercial bungy site in the world.

We arrived at the bridge and, lemming like, headed straight to the edge to peer down. Over 300 feet below us, the river rippled by: a foot or two of water flicking over the flat stony bottom. The bridge was a few feet wide, constructed of wire and wooden planks, it swayed slightly in the wind. We weighed in and walked out on to the bridge.

Into the chair goes number one to have the towel placed round her legs and the strapping wrapped around it. Carabinas clip the bungy on to the strap. With ankles bound together she hops out on to the small platform which projects from the side of the bridge. A smile, a wave for the camera, 5, 4, 3, 2, 1, GO!!! She jumps, forward, out into space and falls away beneath us, the wind swinging her back underneath the bridge. We step to the other side and peer down. Horrifying! She has already reached the bottom of the drop and is flying up towards us again, hanging by her ankles. At the top of her flight she is weightless for a split second, the bungy forming a huge white loop beneath her. Her head flies up past her feet, she rolls over in the air like a rag doll and falls away underneath us, back down towards the river. The wind whips along the canyon. She reaches the bottom of the fall for a second time and swings around wildly in the wind as she comes soaring back upwards again, arms akimbo. Another gyration at the top, another plunge. I stop watching and realise that on the bridge we are looking at each other with wild eyes and lop-sided grins. 'Oh my God!' says someone, voicing all our thoughts.

Kathy leaps into space. We have only known each other for an hour, but we are all friends now. Her boyfriend says over my shoulder: 'That's it, got to do it now!' A tiny Japanese girl produces a perfect swallow dive and, to admiring comments from the jump crew, holds it all the way down.

Ligia steps forward: towel, strapping, carabinas. The wind produces a ferocious gust – this is 60 knots at least. 'Too windy,' says the jump master, staring down the valley, but it is momentary; it drops back to just being very windy. Ligia ducks under the suspension wire of the bridge and shuffles to the edge. She grins, waves for the camera and looks out. We chant: 5, 4, 3, 2, 1, GO!!! She jumps out and away, folding her arms over her chest and falling away beneath us. I have her camera so I have to watch her heart-stopping rush back up towards us, the roll of her body at the top and her helpless plunge away from us as she falls again. I keep taking pictures, but my heart is in my mouth. I am prepared to go for the jump, but this is appalling! Two more commit the ritual and then a grinning face beckons me forwards. 'Okay, mate, just sit yourself down there.' It is probably an old chair from a barber's shop with a headrest for customers being shaved, but it looks morbidly like a dentist's chair. Just their sense of humour, I reflect. Towel, strapping, 'What's this yacht race all about, then?' I am asked, and they keep the questions coming. I talk about the race, about the route, they ask me about crossing the equator and I have to explain the court of King Neptune to them. One of them has heard something about it and wants to know what it is all about.

'Okay, mate, just get yourself over here.' Under the wire, hop, shuffle, legs locked together. The edge of the platform is two feet away. I shuffle out, holding on to the side of the bridge behind me and put the tips of my boots at the edge. A smile, a wave for the camera.

Oh God, how am I ever going to do this? Look up, look up, look at the top of the hill in front. 'Jump out,' they tell me, because of the wind. A gust almost carries the words away. 5, 4, 3, 2, 1; I can't be about to do this – it's not possible, GO!!! I jump as if to save my life, not end it, arms out into the swallow dive. For one split fraction of a microsecond it is okay, then I rotate and start falling. Whaaaaaaa ... Oh, God, this is what it's like to die, falling, falling, dropping like a stone, 340 feet to the river, one lurching second where every instinct for survival and self-preservation is in stomach-churning, mind-bending uproar, and then the great downward rush.

The sheer cliffs flash by in the edges of my vision, the river snaps outwards from a tiny thin line to fill the entire view between the grey walls and then suddenly, so gently that I am unaware when it began, I am slowing. The rush reduces, there is the river, there is the boat that will pick me up in just a few moments and there ...WOHHHHHH!! I am flying, it has all gone haywire, I am looking at the wall, not the river. Oh my God, where next? I have become the lash on the end of a giant whip; it is going to flick me round at the top. Stop the world, I want to get off! We don't flick. I fly round, gently, and fall away again. Oh yes, all right, this is okay. Enjoy, enjoy. I fall, I decelerate and swing in the wind. I am twisting, turning: where the hell are we going? Up again is the answer, but it doesn't feel like it. Submit, relax, go with it, I tell myself. I do it and the world goes calm again. Up we fly and down we fall and finally there I hang and this time the boat is coming in. I am being lowered gently down to a chap holding out a long pole. I grab the end, he pulls me in and folds me down on to the back seat of the boat. 'Okay, mate?' he asks – what else would he say?

So we have done it. We have flown the Pipeline. Was it worth it? A massive yes. Why did you want to do it? Because I was afraid of it!

We returned to Wellington for the prizegiving on the lawn of the governor's mansion, where I had a long conversation with the Prime Minister and his wife, the Governor and his wife, and Sir Peter Blake, who featured in Chay's introductory speech as 'Sir Peter Blake. I used to call him Peter,' a pause 'He used to call *me* Sir.' This does not usually happen to me at home! Brilliant sunshine, endless champagne; definitely my kind of event!

Ligia and I were not the only ones returning from a fantastic holiday. Jo came back, but with pains in her arm, and went to have it X-rayed. 'You've broken your ulna,' they told her, 'and it hasn't been mending properly because it has been moving. If it's not healing properly in six weeks' time it will need a plate. Don't get the plaster wet or you'll probably suffer a skin reaction.' How to say, 'I am going to sea, I will still be at sea in six weeks' time, and I already suffer a skin reaction to seawater without things getting any worse'? Jo put a brave face on it and went off to talk to Simon, but she was clearly very distressed. She didn't want to quit, but to sail with a broken arm ... Is that fair on your team mates? Is it even vaguely sensible? Time would tell.

7

The 'Wake Up' Leg

*'A chield's amang you taking notes, and, faith,
he'll prent it.'* Burns

It is about 1200 miles from Wellington to Sydney, about a week's sailing in a Challenge yacht, yet after what had gone before, we referred to it as 'just a short hop', a sprint across the Tasman Sea. We had two new 'leggers' to blood, Holly Day (it's true, I tell you!), whose husband Derek had started the race on *Nuclear Electric*, but had ended up going home from Rio, and our celebrity crew member, Michael Buerk of the BBC. Celebrity or journalist? Some boats carried fully-fledged correspondents, like Mike Calvin, sailing on *Motorola*, who had written so tellingly for the *Daily Telegraph* about the British Steel Challenge. *Ocean Rover* welcomed HRH Prince Michael of Kent on board, but what were they going to call him, we wondered.

Our Michael joined the port watch, had his name shortened to Mike, and took up residence in the port watch legger bunk, immediately below mine in the two-man cabin. Holly, enthusiasm undimmed by husband Derek's earlier defection, threw her gleeful efforts in with the starboard watch and smiled seraphically through everything, even seasickness. If it is possible to be too cheerful or too eager, Holly would qualify. For all that, it is no bad habit to have, and Holly pitched in determinedly – she was very determined, we found, to have the maximum value from her week on board. We also found out that those girl guide plaits concealed hidden depths: Holly was the only member of our crew to have driven a husky team inside the Arctic Circle. After further summit conferences about the watch system it was decided that Kobus would swap with Spike and Kiki with Woolly, so that Kobus and Woolly joined us while Spike and Kiki settled into the starboard watch.

It rained in Wellington on start day, so that maintained the race tradition, but the Kiwis still came out in force to see us off. The warship *Waikato* steamed-up at the quay, getting ready to go out and mark the start line for us, the rain dripped down, and there was hustle and bustle everywhere. I telephoned Pam from a call box; she had dinner guests and sounded very cheerful. On board we gave three heartfelt cheers for Wellington and motored off into the harbour, where 'Windy Wellington' was living up to its name.

As for the start, what can I say? Clean air, clear water – and near the back! In order to put on a show for the watching crowds the course took us from the start line, back in towards Wellington, round a couple of buoys and then off via a zigzag to the harbour mouth. Disappointingly we failed to make much ground during all of this. Simon watched *Nuclear Electric* hoist a kite and look rather fraught, so we stuck to the 'white sail reach' back across the harbour while some, though not all, went for their spinnakers. Andy Hindley on *Save the Children*, having won the start, held a kite up on the last short dog-leg, which was extremely brave, since there was nowhere to run to if you needed to get it down, except on to the rocks. Eventually we went for our flanker and for the *only* time in the entire race it went up with a twist in it. On the foredeck Spike and Mark thought the twist would come out; amidst growing confusion, Ben took a decision that it would not. We hauled it down again and hoisted the race spinnaker in its place, and almost immediately had too much wind to be flying that particular sail. The foredeck crew rushed to hoist a headsail before dropping the race spinnaker and, lo and behold, the headsail halyard was on the outside of the spinnaker pole. Put simply, that meant we could not hoist the headsail until we had got rid of the kite and lowered its pole to the deck. Only one thing to do: get the kite down NOW! Spike shinned up to the end of the pole in double quick time, the dropping party stood ready ... and the shackle holding the spinnaker would not release.

Now steering a yacht with a big spinnaker up in quite a lot of wind is rather like being on a bolting horse, and your options for controlling it are about as limited, especially if you don't have much searoom. Simon steered, Spike fought with the shackle, *Toshiba* surged on towards the none too distant shore, and then with a mighty cry of 'TRIPPED!' the end of the sail flew free – with great relief, we hauled it down. When we finally reached the Cook Straits only *Global Teamwork* and *Time & Tide* were behind us. I, for one, was very, very disappointed. I think we had all been hoping for a good start and, just for once, we had actually behaved like amateurs – in the pejorative sense of that much misused word.

With the wind blowing 30–35 knots in the Cook Straits and the tide running against us we started to get going. Time and time again this proved to be our kind of weather. Not, that is to say, that we necessarily enjoyed it or relished it, just that, comparatively, we went well when the wind got up. Life below decks returned to the usual battle to move around and the usual shipboard routines. Michael Buerk's comment on the first night's washing up was: 'I discovered on training that fear and exhaustion were usually followed by humiliation!' Fear and exhaustion referred to our first heavy weather sail change of the leg. Rather assuming that Mike, having reported from the war zones of the world before becoming a BBC newsreader, would find our kind of excitement rather tame, we cheerfully led him up on to the foredeck in a gale. The usual mayhem followed; it was like trying to do the job at the bottom of a swimming pool under a waterfall, but eventually we sorted everything out, and got the old sail down below. As we returned to the cockpit Mike stared around at us, shook his head and just said, very quietly, 'Good grief.' Mike really enlivened us with his presence and a wonderful fund of stories. He was very self effacing and it took us a little while to get him going, but he pitched in bravely with the work from day one.

The foredeck can be a very frightening place. The first time I was swept away down the deck, on a training sail, I was terrified. You are just picked up and carried away; in the worst of it you cannot even hold on. Unless you are physically braced against something fixed, the power of the waves will break your grip and send you hurtling back down the deck until you hit something hard, or you are brought up short at the length of your strop. And whilst your harness will save your life, that does not mean that it's a comfortable, or even a comforting, experience. Our lifejackets and harnesses were supplied by XM Yachting who put many hundreds of hours of development work into the project. They were first class pieces of equipment for which we all had reason to be deeply grateful.

On leg two, completing a sail change at a watch changeover, we had everyone in the cockpit when an enormous wave caught us practically beam-on. *Toshiba* heeled violently and Kiki was hurled full length across the cockpit. In front of her was nothing but white foam; the tops of the stanchions and the lifelines were under water, and she was simply falling into the sea. The snap as the strop on her harness went tight jerked all the breath from her body and left her gasping in pain where she had fallen, almost vertically, on to the primary winch on the far side of the cockpit. Not for nothing did we remind each other constantly to 'clip on'.

With hard work and concentrated effort, we moved ourselves up to fourth place by day three, with most of the fleet still in sight of one another, engaging in tacking battles. The notable exception was *Courtaulds International*. Boris Webber, *Courtaulds*' skipper, and his crew had endured two miserable legs. They had broken a spinnaker pole on leg one and finished in 13th place, and had improved on that by only one place to be 12th into Wellington. Boris, who is South African, had ambitions to be first into Cape Town, and to be the first South African to sail the 'wrong way' round the world. We were determined that Kobus would beat him on both counts. Off to a poor start, *Courtaulds* had no need to try to cover anyone else and Boris took off to the north in search of better winds and currents. Another boat with the same idea was *Save the Children* who went north and then had to hold their nerve as the rest of the fleet sailed away.

Meanwhile, *Ocean Rover* reported that Prince Michael was a good helmsman and a 'demon mainsheet trimmer', but what were they calling him? They were not letting on. On *Toshiba* Holly continued to astonish – how cheerful is it possible to be? – and Mike kept us all amused, chiefly through advance publicity for the article he was composing for the *Daily Telegraph*. His descriptions of the crew: Mark as having 'huge, capable hands', Ben as 'boyish, but sometimes mildly manic', were seized on with glee and continued to afford us enormous amusement long after Mike had left us in Sydney.

It must have been something I once read, by Joshua Slocum probably, but I had always imagined the Tasman Sea as a bright, glittering stretch of water, heavily populated with marine life. Grey and overcast by day and starless by night, it was not living up to my expectations. At last, however, after some very frustrating downwind work we had a moonlit night, and with 20–25 knots of wind, a superb run under the flanker. This was a tremendous, exhilarating, if rather wild ride. Every so often we would be turned up to windward by a big wave. With the helmsman hauling on the wheel *Toshiba* would roll hard, the end of the boom dipping wildly towards the waves. At this point, typically, all hell would break loose: the chapel watch would dump the kicker as the end of the boom crashed into the sea. With the flanker curling away at its leading edge, threatening imminent collapse, and the trimmer calling urgently for 'TRIM ON!' it was up to the winch grinder to fling his or her body over the winch and spin it for all he or she was worth. *Toshiba* would surf on and on, hanging on the top of the wave, amidst the rush and roar of the water, and then the moment would pass. As the helmsman let go of the wheel, which self-centres, the steering chains jangled cheerfully. In the relative hush that followed you would hear the sheet creaking on its winch as the trimmer eased it out again and, at the mast, the kicker rope squeaking over its turning blocks as the chapel watch ground it back on. It was fast, exciting and potentially lethal. At the watch change Simon came up to check that each of us knew what to do if it all went wrong. Not everyone liked these conditions, but to my mind it was what we were there for. The wind on deck was balmy, the night sky glinted above us and phosphorescence streamed in the wake, illuminating huge shoals of jelly fish. We were 300 miles from Sydney, going like a train. Then came our darkest hour.

The wind headed us and died. Now 120 miles from the finish at Sydney Opera House, we were five miles behind *Group 4* and three behind *Concert*, lying in third place. As the wind dropped, the fleet rapidly closed up until we could see the lights of other yachts all around. The next set of positions placed *3-Com*, who had been last, first; thus proving the truth of the Biblical adage! It was apparent that it had become something of a lottery, but dawn eventually brought home the appalling truth of the situation – we were practically last. We had known in the night that, with no wind to sail in, the adverse current had been sweeping us backwards, but we believed that the other yachts had been struggling just as badly. Yacht races are won and lost at night – *and in light airs*. It was a bitter and salutary lesson. Other crews had coped better with the difficult conditions and we had paid a painful price. To make matters worse, *Save the Children* and *Courtaulds* had been proved stunningly, jubilantly right. In six hours *Save* went from eleventh place to first! *Courtaulds*, flying up behind, came into second place, just a few miles astern. I am a high priest of the orthodoxy that it is the taking part that counts, and felt that particularly about this race, yet I hated it so much when we were doing badly that sometimes I could hardly believe it.

We fought back, regaining several places, and had a hard tussle with *Motorola* coming in towards Sydney Harbour. We overtook them, they re-passed us. We hoisted the flanker and took them again, only to have them hoist their flanker and regain the advantage. We won the flanker-dropping race, though. Knowing that whoever took the kite down first would lose ground rapidly made it a test of nerve as both yachts creamed in at night towards Sydney Harbour heads. We decided that discretion was the better part of valour and went for the drop. Seconds later *Motorola*'s flanker streamed out over her stern like a giant banner; it had blown before they could get it down. Amazingly it cost them almost no distance and they still led us going in to the harbour. 'They look very close inshore to me,' said Simon. 'Stay over that way a bit,' he told Spike, who was driving, pointing to the right with his forefinger. '*Motorola* have lost the wind,' someone sang out from the foredeck. '*Motorola have run aground!*' Simon corrected. We slid quietly by. They were only stuck for moments but we were past them and away.

At the last bend of the harbour, the Opera House swung into view, with the lights of Sydney blazing all around; the great towering arch of Sydney Harbour Bridge loomed up ahead of us. What a fantastic sight! For most of us this was the first glimpse of something we had been able to recognise from photographs since childhood; to see it first by sailing up to and under it was superb. It went some way to soothe the disappointment we all felt at our performance. It is always the case that at the end of a leg everyone has been up and working hard for a long time, so we were tired, but I felt so dejected I could scarcely raise a cheer as we sailed over the finish line.

Perhaps it was just as well that it took a while to organise all the boats, deal with the formalities of Customs and get tied up alongside. It gave a little time for reflection. Besides, one of the great things about the finish in Sydney was that because all the boats finished so close together we had a party on the quayside that included almost everyone. Beer, conversations, commiserations; it gradually started to feel a little better, especially when we worked out that only 40 minutes separated our tenth place from fourth place. Nonetheless *Group 4* had done it again: caught by the same weather system as everyone else they had managed to escape first, stealing second place from *Courtaulds*, who had to be content with third.

On the dockside, beer in hand, I bumped into Jon Hirsch and Hugh Fogerty from *Ocean Rover*. 'What we all want to know,' I told them, 'is what did you call him?' 'Oh, we called him "Sir",' said John, who had been Prince Michael's watch leader. 'What?' I asked, 'Even when it came to: "Ease the ----ing kicker, Sir!"?' 'Exactly that!' cried John with evident glee. But then sailing is a great leveller.

Not that we swore *at* each other on *Tosh*. Well, not often anyway. It was rather that swear words formed a standard part of everyone's vocabulary. They were part of the lingua franca. A great friend of mine, Ken Young, once remarked that he had noticed this phenomenon on yachts before: 'Everyone gets on board speaking perfect English and within half an hour they are all speaking basic Anglo-Saxon.' We lived in the world of the casual oath, so that no-one ever remarked: 'Heavens, I'm extremely tired,' or 'Good gracious me!' It was a source of great amusement to me to imagine those among the *Wave Warriors* whose careers grace the more formal professions, forgetting to switch back into English once returned to their everyday occupations, '... along that *far canal*,' as Ronnie Barker once sang.

Michael Buerk referred to us as having an apparent 'conspiracy not to get irritated' with each other. That's rather a nice idea and, although it was not quite like that, our new watches had worked well, Jo's arm had withstood a short passage at least, and after all we were in Sydney, half way round the world. Just one thing. We had been in third place 120 miles from home, and we had finished tenth. It was a shock, we had received a 'wake-up' call.

8

A Journey to the History of Time

*'The first question which a visitor to Sydney must
be prepared to answer is: "What do you think of
our harbour?"'* Adrian Seligman

Answering the above question Seligman said that you can reply
'with truth and conviction that you think it is one of the finest
in the world'. He then listed six other ports around the world, saying
that if you had never been to any of those then you could declare
Sydney to be the finest harbour you had ever seen! Whatever your
favourite, Sydney is magnificent, particularly since the redevelopment
of the Darling Harbour complex, where the Challenge yachts were
moored up. It made a cheering backdrop to our post-leg briefing.

The gist of Simon's message was: 'The weather made it a lottery –
that's yacht racing for you. Only 40 minutes separated us from fourth
place; the rig went out of tune early on, and that made the critical
difference to boat speed.' He added, perhaps most importantly, 'The
people who have beaten us are absolutely cock-a-hoop *because* they
have beaten *Toshiba*; we have the respect of the whole fleet, we
know we can do it!' It was good stuff.

The sad news was that Guy was leaving us, albeit with the possibility that he might re-join for the last leg. He felt that his motivation
had changed quite a lot from when he signed up, to when the race
started (he had considered dropping out before the start), and he had
done enough to satisfy himself. He did not, for instance, have a
particular goal to sail round the world. That really surprised me, but
on the same day I spoke to Christine Burge from *Motorola*, who was
also thinking about leaving, and her reasoning was much the same.
She said: 'I've sailed 40 days in the Southern Ocean, I've proved I can

do it, and I don't much feel like putting myself through that again.'
I sympathised – Christine had put herself through much more than I
had to get to the starting line. For one thing she was terrified of going
to the top of the mast, 79 feet above deck level, 85 feet above the sea,
and that was compulsory on training; but she had made it, with a
good deal of sympathetic encouragement from Pete Goss. I didn't
want to influence her, but my feeling was that finishing the race
would provide a sense of achievement not to be gained by doing half
of it, so I was very pleased when Christine, after long talks with her
skipper, Mark Lodge, decided to carry on.

Subsequently Drew made a decision to pull out of the next leg, and
re-join the boat in Cape Town. That did seem like a good decision.
Drew had not been enjoying himself, and his reasoning – that if he
went into the Southern Ocean again he would probably step off the
boat for ever in Cape Town – seemed sound. As it was, he went
travelling in the intervening period and came back with his enthusiasm renewed and his good humour back to the fore.

Taken overall, quite a lot of crew had quit in Rio, more in
Wellington and there were drop-outs again in Sydney. I kept thinking
of Jim Rohn's remark: 'You can do anything if you have enough
reasons', and was increasingly glad that I had given myself a lot of
reasons, not just to start the race, but to finish it. For me there was
never any question. I had signed on to race around the world, and
that meant completing the circumnavigation and returning to the
port from which we started. Sydney was simply half way round.

Joseph Campbell once remarked that you can tell where the heart
of a community or city lies by looking at its tallest buildings. He used
the example of Salt Lake City, pointing out that when it was built the
church was the tallest building. That was subsequently overshadowed
by the municipal buildings, and now the tallest buildings are all
commercial. Sydney's high-rise skyline is dominated by the names of
accountancy-based management consultancies. These organisations
are not about manufacturing anything, or creating wealth from
resources; they are just about how to run a business and, looking on
around the skyline, how to insure it and how best to invest the profits
in other enterprises. Nothing odd in that perhaps. Sydney City is
Australia's largest business centre, and Sydney North is its second
largest (Melbourne is third). So this is a centre of commerce, it is a
place largely devoted to making money out of money and, to some
extent, having a good time with it once you have done so.

At the Civic reception held for us in Sydney Town Hall, I met Di
Murphy, the Marketing Manager for Darling Harbour Development

Corporation, who asked what I planned to see in Sydney. 'Go to the Blue Mountains,' she advised. 'Stay at Lilianfels.' 'Where's that,' I asked, with great presence of mind, 'In Katoomba,' I was told.

Descending the Grand Staircase

So I teamed up with Peter Miles of *Motorola* and we caught a train. It was a very smooth, quiet train, which wound its way out of the suburbs of Sydney and up to Katoomba, some 40 miles away and 3336 feet above sea level. We stepped out into misty mountain rain, looked about and hailed a cab. 'Can you take us to Lilianfels?' we asked, without a clue where we were going. 'Sure thing, mate,' replied the driver coming round to open the boot, 'Sling your things in there.' It wasn't very far, as it turned out. Lilianfels, built originally as a country house, is now a small hotel of great style and enormous charm. We booked in.

Our inclination, backed up by the taxi driver's advice, was to explore while the going was good; and in a slight drizzle of rain, but with clearing skies, we set off to Echo Point to see the famous Three Sisters. The Blue Mountains are really a plateau, formed originally by deposits of sands and silts. Subsequent earth movements lifted this area up, whilst the coastal plain dropped, leaving the plateau exposed. Over millions of years, mountain streams cut through the upper layers of sandstone, following vertical fault lines, and leaving, in the case of the Three Sisters, dramatic rock towers standing out from the cliff edges. We walked out to the Sisters to see them close to and, on a whim, decided to descend the Grand Staircase – 900 steps down the cliff in a mixture of hewn rock and metal step-ladder. At the bottom (and 900 steps is more than you might imagine, even going down) we looked at the sign-posts on the Federal Pass Track. 'Always carry water on all walks,' admonished the sign for walkers. 'Carry warm waterproof clothing. Know your route.' All we had between us was a Lilianfels courtesy umbrella and a packet of post-cards purchased in true English fashion from the visitors' centre. We went anway.

'It can't be far,' said Peter, 'And there's a track.' It took us through wondrous rain forest, past staggering views of the cliffs and the valley floor below, to the spectacular Katoomba falls (which we viewed from three different heights) and a host of other scenic wonders. The Furber steps, our exit point from the valley, whilst easier than the Grand Staircase, were no sinecure after a brisk few hours stepping

106

out, but we marched to the top, pouring with sweat and shirts stuck to us front and back. A short walk took us back to the luxury of Lilianfels where we cooled off, still in our sweaty walking clothes, with cold beers served by a very smart waiter in a very elegant lounge.

The following morning saw Katoomba in the clouds so we went to the cinema. There is a giant screen cinema in Katoomba and the one item guaranteed to be showing at some point in the programme is a film called *The Edge*. John Weiley's film is a hymn of praise to this extraordinary landscape. Australia is the oldest land on earth: the oldest fossil evidence of life has been found here, along with human artefacts 22 000 years old, and the Blue Mountains are truly ancient. One of the advantages of looking at them on film is that you see all sorts of things which would probably escape you if you walked the paths and tracks for a year, but the biggest surprise of all is something that you would *never* see. For in 1994 a ranger called David Noble discovered, in a still-secret valley, a stand of Wollemi pine trees. Previously known only through fossil remains, Wollemi pines were thought to have been extinct for 60 million years. This is the stuff of Jurassic Park, the equivalent of live dinosaurs roaming the earth! The land that time forgot? And just an hour's journey from the heart of Sydney.

Suitably enthused, we made a second foray. Looking down into the valley from the cliff tops, all we could see was cloud. At its best, we discovered, the cloud rolls along the tops and then down into the valley giving the appearance of a giant waterfall and river, in fact photographs of the phenomenon have been known to fool people into thinking that they really are looking at water. In our borrowed 'Driza-Bone' jackets and akubra hats we descended once more and, wondrously, down below all was clear. The curtain of cloud hung above us sealing the eucalyptus groves off from the town above. So we walked and talked. Peter was wonderful company; he is a fellow enthusiast for things of the mind and the founder of The Partridge Club. The club, which boasts a list of eminent guest speakers over the years, meets in one of Peter's local pubs, the Pear Tree, and the two qualifications for membership are that you have to be prepared to talk about religion, and you have to enjoy drinking beer. Peter is, almost needless to say, an atheist with occasional slight doubts, and the local vicar is an enthusiastic club member.

Back in Sydney there was plenty to do and see, and a heavy load of corporate hospitality to be undertaken on the boat. Sydney was always billed as being a 'corporate stop-over' so we were warned, and while this was not a problem for us as a crew, it meant that

Simon and the other skippers had a fortnight's unremitting hard work immediately before taking off on the toughest leg of the race. That point was subsequently noted by Chay, but it did emphasise that a skipper's lot is not always a happy one.

Sydney was greatly enlivened for us by the local Toshiba staff: Annette, Barbara, Sue and Arno in particular, who, when not working or coming out sailing with us, showed us around, entertained us, helped us shop for supplies and supported us in a thousand little ways. Although we were only there two weeks, Sydney was a short but favourite stop-over. We flew up the coast by sea plane for a team dinner together, watched the gay Mardi Gras festival from various different vantage points, ate, drank and were merry. Sufficiently merry, in fact, that two of our number, having drunk themselves into oblivion, celebrated by having a beer or two in one of Sydney's ornamental fountains. Eventually, still unarrested, they found themselves unaccountably hungry, so they went for a Chinese meal. Amazingly, the restaurateur made no comment about their drip-dry apparel or about the large pools of water collecting on the floor.

It was great, and it was all over very quickly. Even while picking up my newly-ordered drysuit gloves (a desperate effort to counter the cold hands problem), the day before the start, the race felt a world away. Were we really off again across thousands of miles of empty ocean to battle with violent winds and huge seas? There was an air of unreality about it somehow, but it would seem real enough before too long.

9

I Can Tell You by Experience ...

*'There's a whisper on the night wind, there's a star
agleam to guide us, and the wild is calling, calling ...
let us go.'* Robert W Service

*'You know you are having a really big adventure when
you wish you were home in bed.'* Spalding Gray

'The challenge of a lifetime – the adventure of your life.' It was
written on the outside of the first mailing I ever received about
the race, and it conveyed *nothing* of the maelstrom we were about to
be pitched into as we headed into the Southern Ocean for a second
time. Nor did Sydney Harbour on a bright, sunny Sunday as we lined
the rail in our Toshiba headbands and gave our customary three
cheers. (The headbands, incidentally, originated with Ben, who had
produced one on a training sail, but had no idea what the message
emblazoned on it in Japanese characters actually said. Guy produced
a checked and certified script which translated into something like
'Easy, easy sailing', and we had a set made up with that on.)

We had resolved our crew problems in the best possible way. Chris
Gaskin and Ange, originally down for just one leg each, were re-
recruited in place of Guy and Drew, so we were bringing experience
back on board, and our two new leggers were keen and raring to go.
Haydon Edwards, our official RNLI legger, left his wife and family
behind as well as his business to make the trip, but since Haydon's
business is in heating we thought he might be particularly valuable
on this leg! A lesser man might have spent more time bemoaning his
fate as injury sidelined Haydon for much of his time on board, but a
dour northern sense of humour stood him in good stead, as did a lot

of very gritty determination. Completing the crew and taking up the spare berth in the port two-man cabin was Justin Hodges. Tall, good looking, ex-trainee fighter pilot, ex-model, city whizz-kid and heart-throb of the *Tosh* blondes, what chance did the rest of us have? A good dinghy sailor, Justin adapted to big boat sailing with great facility. Possessed of good humour and an easy natural charm, he fitted gracefully into life on board and his strength and vigour made him a tremendous asset when the going got tough, as it did for most of this leg of the race. After much deliberation, and with our unanimous approval, Jo swung her plaster cast on board and prepared to do battle, one-armed, with the Southern Ocean again. The 'wave warriors' were ready to go.

The start, on 2 March, thanks to a short starting line and a huge spectator fleet, was a mêlée. There was at least one collision, so our usual strategy vindicated itself this time as we stayed clear of trouble and managed to be about fifth coming out through Sydney Heads and leaving the city behind. As we headed offshore, the airwaves were thick with protests and counter-protests, and the real waves were dotted with yachts executing 720 degree penalty turns.

The first night was not auspicious. It was pitch black with continuous drenching rain. When it came in hard I could barely hold my face to it – even with the faceguard of my foul weather jacket pulled right up and the hood pulled right down – and I could not see a thing. There was no visible horizon, I could barely see the compass, or the instruments, for the water in my face and eyes, and, if that were not enough, we were reaching, and so needed to use torches and lights to trim the sails. Huge flashes of lightning acted like giant strobe-lamps, lighting up grotesque scenes of the crew momentarily frozen in action, and then leaving us all temporarily blinded. It was, as Simon said, 'Quite a testing little night!'

As if I needed any further omens, I felt quite ill towards the end of the night. One or two people were sick but I held on, although I had to give up cooking breakfast, and missed out on eating it, too. It was all pretty horrible and I went to my bunk questioning what on earth I was doing there and cursing myself for a fool.

The first few days of the leg covered the same course as the Sydney–Hobart race, and things improved as we headed down towards Tasmania. By the time we were passing the Bass Straits, which separate Tasmania from Australia, we were in the lead – for the first time since October!

The following day a wave filled the cockpit, found its way into the 'ready-use' locker by the companionway steps, and continued, by a devious route, under the headlining into the saloon, from where it poured down on to our two lap top computers. We got the weather-fax machine operating again fairly quickly, but the one which was used for all incoming and outgoing messages seemed to have died completely. Of the two, clearly the weatherfax machine was the more vital, but the prospect of being without communications and of having no contact with home for the whole of the leg was very daunting. It filled me with a certain foreboding. The same wave washed our 'Aldis lamp' over the side, which also seemed rather a disaster so early on. Although an Aldis lamp is really a piece of signalling apparatus, we used it as a very bright, hand-held spotlight, chiefly for checking sail trim at night; so its loss was significant.

It was a tribute to the hardiness of our sponsor's equipment – all the yachts were equipped with Toshiba lap top computers – that Spike finally got the second one working by taking it apart, washing the seawater off with clean water, drying every individual part and then re-assembling it. I don't think I would have dared to open the casing, but needs must when the devil drives! In a similar fashion, Simon came up with a brilliant solution to the Aldis lamp problem by inventing the 'Walker Muglamp'. Geoff rooted around in the spares and produced a spare sealed-bulb unit – originally intended for the deck lamp – so all we needed was something to mount it in. Ange proved that she is not the holder of a Blue Peter badge for nothing, by suggesting we use an insulated drinking mug from the galley. It proved to be the perfect size. The two parts were glued together at the chart table, the wires coming out at the back were sealed in place and, although it required some maintenance as we went along, it basically lasted the trip.

The weather went light off Tasmania, as it is prone to do, and we changed headsails surrounded by 30 or 40 dolphins, jumping 4 and 6 abreast in unison. They are a truly wonderful sight and most of us never tired of watching them. In contrast to all our weather fore-casts, local knowledge, predictions and updates, we then had a steadily rising breeze, and bowled along at 9 or 10 knots watching the coast slip by. Encouragingly, we seemed to take being first much more lightly than before. Previously the responsibility of trying to stay in first place, even if it was only a responsibility we felt towards each other, seemed to weigh rather heavily on us. Now we were enjoying it. The Tasmanian coast is spectacular and beautiful viewed from the sea, with craggy cliffs and headlands outlined against the pale sky. It made me want to get off and go exploring, but perhaps that was partly a reaction to thoughts of how long it would be before we would have our feet on dry land again.

All in all, this first week was good sailing. We had the occasional blow, the occasional bad night, but the moon and stars still came out some of the time, the sun still shone during the day, and generally everyone enjoyed themselves. By contrast I was a little unsettled. I thought I was just taking a while to get back in the swing of things but I found myself getting annoyed about little things. What is more, some of the little grievances stayed with me. I found myself frustrated when people didn't do the basic things we had all agreed to do – sit with our boots over the rail perhaps, when we needed to adjust the balance of the boat with our weight. In 'normal' life (whatever that may be) I have scant regard for rules, but a boat runs by rules, protocols and agreements to which we had all committed, and I found my ire raised considerably by people around me ignoring these things.

Most of the crew, however, were very happy. Haydon had settled in and was holding his own against the insults of his fellow 999ers on the starboard watch – so named because they consisted of three RNLI crew members, two dentists and a doctor! Ben's leadership style: a mixture of 'Come on, let's do it!' militarism and Goon Show humour, was working well; Ange was well up to form in complaining about the tea, and Chris was trading Scouse insults as always. Chris actually comes from the Wirral, but that was near enough Liverpool for the rest of us, especially when he would shrug his shoulders, put his head on one side and say: 'Don't blame me!'

On the port watch, heavy weather reduced us to six on deck. With the best will in the world there was no possibility of Jo performing her usual job of mastman, but the rest of us had never *ever* been so well looked after with hot drinks; in addition to which Jo did at least half the domestic chores, and monitored the navigation instruments and the radar. We had evolved a system of 'buddying' the new leggers, so I was teamed up with Justin, and for a solid week he asked me questions; and, in that week, he never asked the same question twice, or asked me to repeat an answer. By the end of the week he had practically taken charge of things!

Rounding Tasmania we knew there was a weather front coming, but it still looked as though we might make it through the first week in pretty pleasant conditions. It didn't last. As the front came in, we had 30 knots plus overnight; we reefed and tacked and tacked and reefed and changed headsails, and then in the morning it blew up to over 40 knots. We ended up with the No 3 yankee, the storm stay-sail and three reefs in the mainsail, meaning that we only had one possible sail change left: to hoist the trysail in place of the main. I banged my left thigh horribly on a hatch coaming whilst being washed down the foredeck, and then, during the same sail change, had an incredibly lucky escape. I was hit by a wave coming from behind me while I was kneeling. I was picked up, my feet washed straight out in front of me and then dropped, flat on my back, about two feet on to the deck. I was braced to cry out in the expectation of smashing down on to a winch or a cleat – there are so many solid things to hit when you are being knocked about like this – and yet by some miracle I landed on a flat piece of deck, unhurt. We were in foul weather gear, not dry suits (sometimes you just get caught out) and I have never come off deck so wet. As we came off watch back into the cockpit Justin, perched on the coaming, threw his arms up to the sky and yelled simply: 'I'm alive!' The motion down below was violent, with some huge crash landings shaking the boat and throwing us around like rag dolls. I was in a black mood. On the Cape Horn leg I had been in fairly good spirits a lot of the time, but here I was not enjoying anything very much. A week into the leg and there were no messages from home. I began to convince myself that something awful had happened to someone and no-one knew how to tell me.

The race positions were like snakes and ladders by now and I found myself going up and down with them, which was very silly. Ocean racing is a long hard game. Things change, you get different weather in different parts of the fleet, and tactical decisions play a big part in what happens in the short term. Nonetheless, I was not the only one. Kobus was the most fanatical of us all at watching and waiting for the six-hourly position reports. With the fleet being automatically polled, using satellite equipment, and the results sent back to each yacht from RHQ, we were virtually involved in four races every twenty-four hours. A mile gained, great joy; a mile lost, anguish!

Kobus had a mission in life to be first with the results and, having achieved that, he would relay them to the on-deck crew. Now, it is not always easy to remember a set of figures, and when you start to put in differentials, who has gained, who has lost, and by how many miles, the whole thing can become a bit tricky. Kobus became a legend in his own watch for statistics that did not quite add up. At every query he would be forced to disappear back down the companionway steps to re-check the figures and try again. And just when he had everything at his fingertips we would ask: 'What's the difference between first place and fourth, Kobie?' Which was all very amusing, but didn't always stop people's spirits rising and sinking with the figures.

We celebrated Justin's birthday, which was a slightly painful occasion for him. Nothing emotional, just the result of being hit hard by a big wave whilst standing with one leg on either side of the inner forestay. 'It seemed like a safe place until that happened,' he commented ruefully. Soon after that we had a proper Southern Ocean day. Ben's lot handed over to us with the No 3 yankee and the storm staysail up, and the third reef in. We had 30–35 knots of wind all day with bright sunshine and blue skies with lots of fluffy white cumulus clouds; typical 'behind the cold front' weather, and cold it was! We were standing our watches at four hours on and four off through the night, six on, six off through the day. Whilst there was no doubt that this worked better physically, because the longer periods off watch allowed us to get more sleep, nevertheless I found it very difficult psychologically. When the weather was cold or conditions were bad we would, in common with all the other boats, use a rotation system. Commonly when sailing to windward, with no trimming required, two people would stand a turn on deck, one driving, the other 'riding shotgun', for half an hour or forty minutes, then they would be relieved and go below to thaw out. Of course if anything else (a reef for instance) needed doing, then as many people as it took would be on deck. On this particular day every time Geoff and I finished a stint on deck and went down for a quick warm up we were called back for another tack or a reef. We had about half an hour not actually working on deck in a six-hour spell and were absolutely frozen when we finally came off watch.

The Ides of March?

It was then that we were hit by a real storm. Imagine that you have put on an airline eye mask. Now have someone bind a good width of black velvet around your head to hold it in place, pull a black mask over the lot, and that's how dark it is as you come up through the companionway hatch. The white of the cockpit coaming is the first thing you can make out, then more white, high up in the sky – blotches, and long streaks of pale greyish white. They look like clouds, and then you realise that these are the breaking tops of waves towering above the boat. As you inch your way along the gap between the side of the cockpit and the central deck locker (the 'coffee table' as it's nicknamed), which sits like an island in the middle of the forward part of the cockpit, the whole thing seems to have more in common with mountaineering than sailing – except that the mountain is bucking and jerking like a wild animal and the roar of the wind is like white noise – it deafens, and blankets all other sound.

I was steering, fighting really, thrown this way and that, struggling to hold *Toshiba* on some sort of heading, when I was hit. A massive blow to the chest left me hanging on to the wheel with all my might, and then came the deluge. It was like being hit by a fire hose – smashed by water. There was more water than I could imagine, and it just kept on and on coming down. I needed to breathe, I needed to get my head out of the water to gulp air – and I was still standing up. In an instant my hands were pulled off the wheel as the sea wrenched at the rudder. I was thrown the length of my safety strop, and swept over the cockpit coaming into the farthest corner of the side deck, where I washed up against the stainless steel legs of the pushpit (the metal frame around the stern of the boat) virtually underwater. Joe Watson was flung down into the well behind the wheel and yelled to me as she struggled up to grab it. 'Are you all right, Al?' 'No,' I shouted back, 'I've hurt my knee and can't get up.' It was an understatement. I could not move my left leg, which meant that not only could I not get up, but I was pinned by my own weight, held only by the safety strop at the very back corner of the boat, on the low side.

The side deck was almost continuously under water, and every few seconds I was washed under again by another wave smashing down on top of me. Joe yelled for Simon. 'The steering's gone – I can't move the wheel!' Simon appeared very rapidly from the companionway, grabbed the wheel and yelled to me: 'Are you all right, Al?' 'No,' I shouted back, 'I've hurt my knee and can't get up.' I was stranded in pain and shock. The next thing he yelled was, 'The trysail's gone,' and sure enough the trysail had torn away from the mast track. It was held only by the halyard at the top and another rope at the bottom. Simon wrenched at the wheel – and wrenched again. The steering was OK, but I had bent the wheel so far before I let go that it was jamming as he tried to turn it. 'Alan, can you recover the danbuoy?' he yelled (the danbuoy is a tall pole with a float attached, used to give an indication of position in the event of a man overboard). One of them had washed away and was trailing behind the boat, attached only by the line which holds it to a horseshoe-shaped lifebuoy.

Reluctantly, I supposed, the answer was yes. I managed to twist myself over and lie along the side deck, reaching out over the stern to pull in the danbuoy's rope. The pull on it was tremendous and the danbuoy itself is quite heavy, as well as being five or six feet long. In the end I got it back into the cockpit and managed to lever myself up, at which point Simon asked if I could take the wheel again so that he could help deal with the trysail. It was probably just adrenalin, but something made the pain in my knee abate a little. By hauling myself up by my safety strop I managed to heave myself back over the coaming and into the cockpit. My leg felt dead and useless, but I braced myself as best I could, and tried to steer so that the worst excesses of the sea would not cause us any more damage. Every time another huge wave tore across the deck, sweeping the people at the mast, all still trying to bring the trysail down, out of my sight, I cursed loudly; and every time the boat banged or rose and bucked and shuddered I winced at the pain in my knee. Worst of all, though, was the moment of uncertainty as each new wave poured down – a burned child dreads the fire and, already hurt and unable to balance myself properly, it took a considerable act of will to hold on to my nerve and keep fighting.

During the worst of this we had 65 knots of true wind. Wave heights are notoriously difficult to estimate, but the wave which trashed the trysail and swept me off the wheel was falling down on to us as it broke. The top of the trysail sits roughly half way up the mast, about 45 feet above the waterline, but the maximum probable wave height quoted for a force 11 is 52 feet. Force 11 tops out at 64 knots, and other yachts not far away recorded wind speeds up to 76 knots on this same night. This was a force 12, and no maximum wave heights are given. It is the raw, shocking, hard-edged reality, of actuality, of the fact that this is *happening* to me right now, that is so extreme, so horrifying. But it was happening and it was absolutely brutal. Every rope strained bar-tight, every fitting under extreme load; the wind itself would have blown us off the deck, but to be hit by these waves was like falling downstairs and having half a ton of bricks poured on to you at the bottom. And on it went. Again and again we were swept, foredeck to cockpit, by sheets of white water; every time I stared, dumbfounded, still to see a dozen figures in front of me, still working, hauling, heaving, winching our shattered trysail down. Unbidden, an icy, chilling thought rose into my mind: 'If it *was* all to go horribly, fatally, wrong, it would probably start like this ...'

We got the trysail down without injury or incident and sailed on under the No 3 and the storm staysail – and sailed into the lead! 'When the going gets tough ...' we told each other. Not long afterwards the headsail sheet gave up the ghost and, in spite of our having taken the precaution of cleating off the lazy sheet, so that there would be something to arrest the sail in the event of a breakage, the sail flogged itself half to death. So we were left, for the time being at least, with just our smallest sail, the bright orange storm staysail, flying. We made four knots, as best to windward as we could. Mark and I shared six hours' helming through the morning in 55 knot winds. It was cold, massively wet, with stinging spray and vast, confused seas throwing the boat this way and that. It was, in four words, horrible, ghastly, awful and hateful.

While all this had been going on, the galley seat had uprooted itself from the floor, spilling the contents of the food lockers underneath it everywhere. All the ropes on the leeward side at the mast had escaped their lashings and carried over the side, the gas bottles had displaced themselves, and a plastic 'gash' bag burst and filled the cockpit with old mayonnaise and detergent bottles. We were intrigued to discover, on checking the log, that this storm blew up at midnight, GMT, on 13 March. We thought at the time that this was the Ides of March and only discovered later that, for nine months of the year, the Ides is the 13th but the Ides of March is the 15th.

This was just one storm. Overall on this leg, the fleet experienced 12 days on which winds of over 60 knots were recorded. Winds of gale force or above blew on 28 days, the maximum recorded windspeed was 76 knots, and 6 boats were knocked flat at different times. Thankfully that did not happen to us.

Where danger is double and the pleasures are few

What did happen, of course, was that in spite of wearing dry suits on deck, we got incredibly wet. Eventually, it seemed, water permeated the outer layer of the suits at the protective knee patches and found its way between the inner and outer layers of the suit into our boots. Over time, due to constant immersion and constant hard work, the inner layer broke down, resulting in wet cold feet. Before the race, we had researched all the major manufacturers of suitable technical clothing and decided unreservedly to go with Musto. Personally I think their kit is superb, and although as a crew we did have some problems, the way in which the company dealt with them was exemplary. That notwithstanding, the clothing system which had worked so well on leg two was just not standing the pace here. Coming warm from my bunk, peeling off the warm, cosy, Trax boot liners I used as bed socks inside my sleeping bag and then pulling on cold wet sailing socks was beginning to get to me. The boat heaters were not working and with the air temperature below 5°C and the boat running with condensation, nothing would dry. Boots full of water and supposedly

117

waterproof socks wet through was utter misery. Most of us simply lived in our thermals, long johns and long sleeved T-shirts. I put my first set on when it first got cold and then simply added a second set when it got colder. The first set stayed on until we were near the African coast and things had warmed up considerably!

Wind and water were, however, not the only hazards we had to face. As the water temperature fell, ice became an increasing danger. Reports of iceberg sightings started to come in on the twice-daily 'chat show'. The real problem with ice is not the bits you can see, but the ones you cannot – the 'bergy-bits' and growlers that float just beneath the surface. This was the one part of this whole experience that was genuinely unnerving. The thought that a lump of ice about the size of a car could sink the yacht, and we might never even see it, was not one to dwell upon. As with everything, though, we had a plan. Simon's iceberg briefing left nothing to chance; at least if the worst happened we all knew what to do.

Shortly afterwards we saw our first ice. *Group 4* were about a mile and a half behind us and, while keeping a weather eye on them, we spotted a berg. No spectacular floating castle, this, just a thin white line on the horizon, lifting into view as we rose over the waves. This one, at least, was behind us, but where there is one there are usually many, and in all this we had not stopped racing, even for a moment. Sir Peter Blake used to say cheerfully that icebergs go to bed at night. Charging through the blackness, blinded by spray, with no possibility of seeing anything coming, I wondered. Even with a permanent radar watch and the on-deck crew keeping a constant lookout, you cannot escape the feeling that it is all in the lap of the gods. Sometimes the days were just as bad. Warm sector weather (and warm was a relative term) often brought fog, with visibility down to a hundred yards or so. Throughout all of this Simon exemplified Hemingway's wonderful definition of guts: 'grace under pressure'.

It is an oft-quoted fact that the average wind speed in the Southern Ocean is about 25 knots and, just as in any other ocean, the storms tend to be followed by calms. There is something particularly galling about this after a really bad blow. Instead of just moderating into reasonable sailing weather the worst gales often left us sloshing about for a day afterwards. One morning we registered a maximum wind speed of seven knots for the entire watch as we sat under sunless skies in the permanent Southern Ocean grey. With the moon usually hidden by veils of cloud at night and no sign of marine life or seabirds since leaving the coast of Tasmania behind, the sense of isolation hung heavily around us.

Of course, light airs means drying weather, but only if it is warm enough to dry anything. Despite sterling efforts from Haydon, Mark Spike and Geoff, sometimes in unison, sometimes in opposition, we could not get both heaters working for any length of time. So kit remained soaked through. My sleeping bag would have served as the fountainhead for a small stream – nothing too big, just a small Hampshire trout stream or a medium sized Scottish burn, but sleeping in it usually warmed it up a bit. In fact the only dry thing left on board was the sense of humour and even that failed from time to time.

Discomfort was small beer, though; injury was the real worry. The reports were coming in thick and fast from other boats, and we had our share. Chris had hit something very hard and broken a couple of ribs but was still working, albeit in great discomfort, while Haydon had pulled a muscle in his back and was confined, in great pain, to his bunk for a day or two. I had concluded that a yacht is no place for a twisted knee, having been reduced to dragging my bad leg behind me on deck and yelping like a wounded dog with each fresh jerk or twist. It looked very swollen but there was really nothing to be done except use a support bandage and take painkillers.

We were almost at the half way point for the passage when a perfectly reasonable day turned into a nightmare. We had to change down through every sail on the boat, and I was on the wheel. That, make no mistake about it, is the plum job, but you are then responsible to some extent for the safety of the crew on the foredeck, who are right in the firing line. Everything went as well as can be expected when a gale blows up very quickly, but by the time the wind was over 35 knots, Mark, Kobus and Justin were struggling with the storm staysail, with Geoff at the mast, when we ran up a very big wave. Now, protecting the foredeck crew means slowing the boat down and keeping things a little more level, both of which are achieved by sailing closer to the wind than normal. The difficulty in heavy seas is that the wind in the troughs between the waves is sometimes different in strength and direction to the wind on the tops. As we came up this particular wave I was just too close, the wind got behind the headsail and flicked it across – I had 'crash-tacked'. There is only one thing for it; put the wheel hard over, keep the boat turning with the pressure of wind on the headsail all the way round through 360 degrees, and then get back on course.

When we came down below, almost immediately afterwards, I was very annoyed with myself and rather upset about the whole thing. Mark gave me a big grin and said: 'What was the penalty turn for, mate?' which was quite funny, but unfortunately Kobus followed it with a remark which, whilst it may have been meant to be funny, made me see red, and I hit him! He was one short step away, coming up from the saloon into the dog-house, and I don't think he knew what was happening until after it was over. If I were a fighting man and not a failed pacifist I would probably have said that he got what he deserved. As it was I felt terrible, apologised, and asked him to shake hands. I wasn't surprised when he went to his bunk without saying a word. We never did refer to it again until we got back to Southampton, and then only rather obliquely, but Kobus's reaction to the situation did him great credit. We had a day or two of rather cool relations, after which it was as though nothing had ever happened. 'Circumstances do not make a man,' said James Allen, 'they reveal him.' I felt very humble when I found that remark in my log book, where I had written it, on the top of the page for this very day, a month before leaving Southampton.

Fly *Toshiba*, walk on water

Crew relations may have been back on an even keel, but the weather continued as before. On the wheel one day, it occurred to me that the wind had not dropped below 38 knots for the past hour. 'So it is a gale,' I thought, 'and we no longer think anything of it.' Ludicrously, we had reached the point where 40 knots seemed reasonably comfortable, just so long as we had approached it by coming down from 50! As night fell, this particular gale blew into a storm, with the wind running at a constant 45 knots, but with the sea relatively (and only relatively) flat for that amount of wind. This meant that *Toshiba* would crank right up to about 8½ knots, and then we would hit a 'backless wonder' or a real corkscrew. A wave with no back to it gives the boat nothing to slide down; you just take off from the crest and plunge way, way down into the trough beyond. One moment you're flying, the next the boat is practically submerged and you are walking on water. The corkscrews, on the other hand, pick the back of the boat up as they pass underneath, twist you round and throw you down into the trough – the effect is much the same.

I felt in imminent danger of serious personal injury for every minute I was on the helm during all this. All we could see, even granted an occasional flicker of moonlight between the sullen clouds, was a dark grey horizon with a black sea billowing beneath it. When the horizon rose up rapidly, so that most of what we were looking at turned black, we braced ourselves, gritted our teeth and hung on.

120

Half the time nothing happened. *Toshiba* would roll over the top of the wave, twist, and try to head off the wind. I would steer to correct that, there would be some spray, and we would slide down the other side, untroubled and unharmed. Then, every so often, we would be launched with enormous propulsion, like a powerful steeple-chaser taking off at a truly huge fence, and we would plunge down, free-falling, until *Tosh* buried her bows with an almighty crash. If steering, you would be flung against the wheel while, simultaneously, it would be wrenched round with more force than you could possibly hope to counteract. The instinctive reaction was to hang on for grim death – or should that be dear life? If you did that, the wheel swept your hand into the narrow gap where the wheel rim passes very close to the cockpit seat. At best that was very painful, at worst things got broken. Simultaneously a huge mass of water would slam into your head, shoulders and chest, knocking you backwards. It was blinding. Even with a helmet or goggles you cannot see through solid water. Walls of white foam rushing by above the sides of the cockpit would add to the flood swirling round your feet; there was just water everywhere. Half standing, re-bracing your legs, you would drag the wheel back because already the next black monster would be rushing towards you, climbing higher and higher on the bow. 'What a nightmare!' was Kobus's succinct summing up.

Spike was caught out helming in these conditions. He was knocked off the wheel by a particularly vicious wave and, as the wheel spun, his arm went between the spokes, one of which smashed into his elbow. Justin walked around for a week with the imprint of a steel rigging wire marked across his cheek and eyebrow. These were painful injuries but the worst was still to come.

The change down from staysail to storm staysail was one of the worst tasks. It always took place in fearsome conditions, and meant working in the middle of the foredeck, with very little around to hold on to. Struggling with the change one night, Ben's watch were practically swept off the deck by the biggest crash any of us ever heard on *Tosh*. Ange, Ben and Kiki all sustained minor injuries but Haydon, not long over his back problem, was in serious trouble. Unable to move, let alone get himself back to the relative safety of the cockpit, he was clearly in agony, and it looked as though Spike's worst medical nightmare had come true; we thought he had broken his leg.

The prospect of getting a badly injured person off the foredeck in these conditions does not really bear thinking about, but in fact we had thought about it, in advance. The first part of the plan – to run downwind, keeping the boat stable and the deck relatively flat – was easy. After that there was nothing for it except to drag Haydon back, as gently as possible, whilst trying to support his damaged leg. His trip down the companionway steps was a miracle of teamwork and compassion, and we finally laid him on a pair of coffin bunk mattresses on the floor by the chart table. 'Are you particularly attached to that dry suit?' asked Simon, preparing to cut the fabric away. 'I am, as it happens,' replied Haydon through rather gritted teeth. So we inched his boot off and painstakingly got him out of his dry suit, and slowly, piece by piece, removed enough of his kit so that Spike could examine his leg.

It didn't look good. A possible fracture of the shin bone was only half the story; it looked as though Haydon might have broken his femur as well. We managed, with the aid of painkillers and some improvised padding, to get Haydon secure in his bunk, and considered our options. There were not very many and, depending on Haydon's condition over the next 24 hours, pressing on was the only one immediately available.

'Serious physical injury' had always been my first reply to the question: 'What are you most afraid of?' and Haydon's accident really drove the point home. Grateful as I was to have escaped so lightly, that still did not ease the problem I had, that every time I went on to the foredeck, I hurt my knee badly again. It simply was not possible to stop yourself being flung around, and every wrench crippled me anew. I upped the painkillers and continued to swear, flatly, vehemently, viciously and repeatedly every time it happened. When we finally rounded the Kerguelen Islands waypoint after just 24 days at sea, everyone had really had enough. Even Spike remarked to me that he was counting down the days!

As if to herald the approach of better times we witnessed a superb sunrise. The sun lifted up, a pale gold disc with two fleeting banks of cloud trailing across. Then as it rose, brightened and deepened in colour, the cloud dispersed leaving the rising sun off our port quarter and the pale, mottled full moon hanging high in the sky over the starboard bow. Later that day the generator exhaust failed terminally. We had barely enough fuel to charge our flagging batteries and keep the water maker operational using the main engine, and there were still 2000 miles to go to Cape Town.

Nevertheless a certain euphoria set in. We all agreed that you should never predict your time of arrival, but most of the crew were cheerfully indulging in just that pastime. And things did gradually get better. We headed up north, on course for Cape Town, and sea and air temperatures rose from freezing to tolerable. The risks of icebergs receded. The wind no longer roared up above 50 knots with frightening regularity, and we began to look forward to some sunshine. Only a few days after his terrible accident Haydon struggled up and began making cups of tea and monitoring the chart table instruments, while still barely able to drag himself about the boat. By some miracle his injuries were restricted to a compression fracture of his shin bone, diagnosed in Cape Town, and a very nasty looking swelling the size of a large melon at the back and side of his thigh.

We were almost out of it, but not quite. The change to the storm staysail caught us once again, this time on our watch. Geoff banged a previously damaged arm and bruised himself badly being flung against the winch he was working, Mark's hand was dragged through the side netting, put in place to stop sails being swept overboard under the lifelines, and Justin banged his head. I was practically winded by a wave which hit me square on the back, and I hurt all the bits which hurt before plus a few new ones. More 60 knot gusts followed, and in one of them we achieved one of Simon's great ambitions: we broke the starboard head falling off a wave! A good two seconds 'air-time' was followed by an unbelievable rig-shaking, hull-quaking CRA-A-A-A-SH and the porcelain lavatory pan cracked wide open from base to rim. Kobus got a good joke out of this a few days later, on April Fool's day. Amidst a slew of reports from other yachts of mines spotted in rafts of kelp and new forms of marine life, he put a 'Do not use' notice on the port head, leaving no option but to 'bucket and chuck it'. Several of the new watch appeared on deck for a pee without saying anything, but the word was out before we really caught anyone.

Looking back we were able to pinpoint, to the day, our leaving the Southern Ocean behind. We looked behind us and saw the lowering clouds of the last of those massive weather systems, and from that day on things became reasonable again. Now we were left with the small matter of trying to win a yacht race. The generator exhaust was still proving an on-off affair as Geoff and Haydon, working in spite of his leg, struggled to bond bits of old tin can and anything else they could find around the offending junction. That meant saving on electricity by being mean with the lights, as well as using as little water as possible. The deck light had given up, the Walker Muglamp was on its last available bulb, and we were nearly out of torch batteries. We had no sugar, and were low on cheese, butter and bread mix. Toilet paper was being strictly rationed, and breakfast was reduced to cereals only, but we were still able to put together a respectable chilli and rice followed by apple crumble and custard for supper.

Still a week away from Cape Town we sailed in under the centre of a high pressure zone and stuck, perhaps not quite as 'idle as a painted ship upon a painted ocean', but at one knot it was hard to tell the difference. Even the compensations of warm sunshine and a dry airy boat did not immediately remove the tetchiness that built up as we slowed down, and the prospect that we might run out of food didn't exactly improve matters. 'Oh well,' Simon said cheerfully at the prospect, 'it was bound to happen on one leg!'

It didn't happen, of course. The wind filled in, and once again we gave chase to *Concert* and *Group 4*, whose battle for the lead was, to our chagrin, taking place a few miles ahead of us. At one point Simon managed a top boat speed of 21.5 knots under a poled out No 1 yankee, and then, before anyone else could threaten that speed, decided that we needed to change down! Kobus then proceeded to clock 18.3 knots with the No 2 yankee up, the staysail and the first reef in the main, which must be some sort of fleet record.

The much written about Agulhas current, which we expected to sweep us around the tip of Africa in majestic style, failed to materialise, but just after 9 am on Tuesday 8 April, after 37 days at sea, a distant smudge on the horizon brought a cry of 'Land Ho!' from on deck, and we charged up to gaze at a tiny uneven blur at the distant edge of the sea. 'Is that all?' someone said jocularly. 'That's Africa,' I said, 'and it's the first time I've ever seen it.'

10

Under African Skies

'We ask ourselves, who am I to be brilliant, gorgeous, talented and fabulous? Actually, who are you not to be?'
Nelson Mandela

'Welcome to the parking lot,' Simon called out as the wind died. *Toshiba* drifted on in a desultory fashion, and the sails hung down like curtains. The 'parking lot' is really the wind shadow caused by Table Mountain and, like anything else in nature, it cares not a jot for how far you have come, or what you have been through to get there. Cape Town is often called the most beautiful city in the world, which is ridiculous, but it is probably the most beautifully *sited* city in the world. With the morning sun rising spectacularly ahead of us, and the city nestling ribbon-like at the foot of its flat-topped mountain, it was the gateway to a new continent, and all we wanted to do was get there!

Group 4 finished, with *Concert*, who had fought so hard and so determinedly to win a leg, an agonising 0.9 of a mile behind. With the last remnants of the dying wind, and just about enough boat speed to steer, we headed offshore. It was a pre-determined strategy and, once again, it paid handsome dividends. It was slow, pain-staking work, but we avoided coming to a complete standstill, and finally drifted across the finish line under lightweight spinnaker at 7.20 am, accompanied by a South African lifeboat bearing Lou, Kobus's wife Debbie and Justin's girlfriend Vicki among a crowd of supporters. The on-deck party was followed by breakfast at Bayfront Blu's, the restaurant having adopted us for the duration of the stop-over! Chris, Mark, Justin and I ordered steak, eggs, sausages and bacon, with mushrooms and tomatoes, ate the lot, and promptly

125

ordered it all again. It was just as good the second time around.

Later on I tried to work out how I really felt about having finished this leg, and the answer was mostly a very deep-seated sense of relief that it was finally over – a kind of very slow relaxing, like trying to let the muscles go in a place where you have become used to bracing an old, but still painful, injury. Any sense of achievement was much slower in coming through, but by now I was becoming used to that. It took some time for it to sink in that we had sailed from Australia to Africa, through some of the worst weather in the Southern Ocean, and that it was something that everyone who had taken part could feel equally proud of. My hands were still very stiff and sore, I couldn't close up my fingers to make a fist with either hand, my knee was still very wobbly, and my elbow, which I had banged very painfully against a winch, ached most of the time. On the quayside, bandages and strappings were much in evidence, and the gaunt, if smiling, faces and the belts pulled in several notches tighter all told a story.

After two days' work on the boat I took leave of absence and, in very high spirits, called a taxi and had Fahmi drive me to the airport to meet Pam. Fahmi was a Cape Muslim and a fervent Manchester United supporter whose name, if correctly pronounced, sounds exactly like a very rude exclamation of surprise in English (or perhaps I mean Anglo-Saxon). Reunited after six long months, Pam and I spent our first few days in and around Cape Town together, and then set off along the 'Garden Route' towards Port Elizabeth and the Shamwari game reserve.

Big game experience

We travelled up the N2 and then down the dirt roads to Shamwari. At the main reception lodge we discovered that there were a further 30 kilometres to go to Shamwari Lodge itself. The rain had turned the roads into a mud bath, which was not so bad on the wider, flatter parts, but the last few kilometres 'once you leave the main road', as it was rather charmingly described to us, were very hairy: slithering and sliding around at only a few miles an hour. Years of driving in good old British snow and ice definitely paid off as we opposite-locked our way out of one or two nasty slides and ground our way up slopes running with liquid mud; snaking from side to side.

We were met at the lodge by Lucky the chief ranger, treated to gin and tonics, and had an hour or so to chat about the reserve and its animals before the next guests arrived. Shamwari is the creation of

Adrian Gardener, a Zimbabwean businessman, who originally bought the lodge and some surrounding land as a retreat from city life. Over a period of years he set about buying up the adjoining land from local farmers, who were largely happy to sell, in order to create a private game reserve. Although nearly all the animals here have been brought to Shamwari (it means 'friend'), they were all originally indigenous, having been hunted out of the area by the farmers. One of the extraordinary things about Shamwari is the profusion of game and the ease with which it can be found. This sort of experience can lead people to decry the setting as 'not real', but what you actually have here is a return to the conditions you would have encountered before most of these animals were hunted down to their present minimal populations.

The lodge, although only some 10 or 15 years old, is built in the style of an African home. The parents' room would be a building on its own; the children had completely separate accommodation, with girls on the left and boys on the right as you entered the compound. The *lapa*, our barbeque area, would have been the main meeting place for the family to discuss important news, and the modern dining room and lounge would have been the communal area. I imagine that the original version came without our swimming pool and its outdoor bar!

Lunch revealed that everybody staying there was connected to the Challenge in one way or another! Kate was organising a photoshoot for Debenhams, who were a business club member on *Rover*, and her mother, Caroline, was travelling with her. Mike and Anne had a daughter, Rachel, sailing a leg on *Rover*, and Anne's brother Tony and his wife June were travelling with them.

At around 4 pm four of us piled into Lucky's open top Land Rover and set off to encounter elephant, impala, bush buck, plesbuck, springbok, hartebeest, eland, wildebeest, black rhino and giraffe – all in four hours!

Driving up a steep track winding away from the buildings we spotted a small group of elephants down below us, near the track on which we had come in the day before. Lucky drove us down to the nearest vantage point and, as the elephants started to move on through the bush, steered a precipitous path down off the road to keep them in sight. There is something magnificent in seeing these huge mammals twisting branches off the trees with their trunks and munching their way through the foliage; yet elephants are hugely destructive feeders, demolishing trees and bushes and laying waste to vegetation. Someone rather aptly described them as bulldozers that eat and drink – and they do drink: about 160 litres of water a day. Not that we were worried about any of that, we were all in raptures, cameras clicking and oohing and aahing to one another.

As we drove on, Lucky picked out one variety of antelope after another, teaching us to recognise different markings and shapes of horns. Suddenly Lucky pointed: 'There!' We were off the track, rumbling slowly through grassy clearings between large thickets of trees and bushes. He cut the engine. 'Black rhino,' he whispered, and half hidden, about 30 yards away, stood a full-grown male. Head down, horns in profile, he shuffled forward into the open and crossed in front of us. Lucky emitted a curious shooshing noise and kept repeating it. The rhino turned his head, paused and walked on. Lucky continued, the rhino swung his head ponderously and looked, turned his enormous shoulders, and took a step towards us. Then on he came, head up, straight towards the headlamps of the Land Rover with the dusk around us. At a distance of 8 to 10 yards he stopped. No-one moved. Then in an instant he snorted, waved his head, lifted one foreleg; someone in the Land Rover gasped, Lucky turned the ignition key, and the whole world hung before us in an instant of expectation. A black rhino typically weighs about 800–1000 kilograms. It can run at up to 36 mph and it can accelerate much more quickly than you would believe possible, so 8 to 10 yards is nothing on this scale. How long do you want to live?

The engine fired instantly, and the sound was enough. Our rhino threw his head round to his right and lumbered away into the gloom. All about us in the rapidly cooling night air, the nearness of the moment hung quietly around our outbreak of excited chatter. We drove slowly away in a babble of conversation. Lucky grinned broadly and said, 'He was as frightened of us as we were of him.' That may have been so, but he left us with a legacy of wild excitement which lasted right through our coffee and Amarhula under the southern stars.

Back in Cape Town we went to dinner with friends of friends. The conversation turned, as it always did no matter who we spoke to, to the political situation or, more accurately, the social situation. Hilary runs a lymphodoema clinic and a bed and breakfast business from a charming house in Cape Town's Pinelands suburb, her husband Ian is a civil engineer. Pinelands is beautiful, with tree-lined streets, grass verges ... and high security gates. Ian's work as President of the Civil Engineering Institute takes him frequently to Johannesburg. Hilary confirmed the rumours; the last time she was there with Ian everyone at dinner had a hijacking story to tell. 'Cape Town is not like that,' she reassured us, 'although obviously there are parts you shouldn't go into, especially at night; and I wouldn't wear a gold necklace in the city,' she added. Pam's hand rose to the gold and silver chain around her neck which she never takes off. I wondered about the two diamond studs that Spike wears in his left ear, the propensity of muggers in Rio for using knives, and the fact that Spike still has two ears to go with his studs. Pam, of course, still has her necklace.

But what do any of us expect? It seems that everywhere in the world half, or usually less than half, the population lives in gentility and affluence in a Pinelands or a St Margarets, where I live, while the other half lives in the poverty of a Rio Favela, a Crossroads township or a run-down British council housing estate. But in Rio and Cape Town, and across Africa and the East, it is not just poverty that grinds away at people. It is the very basics of health care, sanitation and quality of life. I wondered what Nelson Mandela, surely one of the most compassionate of world leaders, thinks when he considers the townships, and the problems of poverty and rising crime. Does he have a plan? A way forward? Does anyone?

11

Paradise Lost

'... *as they say, God is always on the side of the big
battalions.*' Voltaire

'*When it's hit the fan, there's nothing left to do except
sweep it up, package it and sell it as fertiliser.*' Heinlein

The day before the start of each leg was always a slightly odd
time, and leaving Cape Town was no exception. In part I was sad
to be leaving and yet I also wanted to be away. We had enjoyed a
wonderful reception in Cape Town, particularly from everyone at
VTC Toshiba and the NSRI, the South African equivalent of the
RNLI; and we were particularly sad to leave the Hotel Graeme
where Maud, Graeme and their staff had not just looked after us but
had been so enthusiastic about what we were doing. Chay had told
us this was the 'paradise leg' – dolphins, porpoises, whales, gin and
tonics; and at the start it looked as though he might be right.

It was what Capetonians call a 'champagne day': bright sunshine,
blue skies and a 'table cloth' of white cloud capping the mountain.
Before the start, Archbishop Desmond Tutu spoke of the changes
since 'the bad old days when you would not have caught me dead at
a ceremony like this,' and of the good that sporting events like the
BT Global Challenge do in uniting people. He gave us, 'Those that
go down to the sea in ships,' followed by a blessing, 'in my home
language,' his wonderfully sonorous voice rolling around the bay,
and sent us on our way across the Atlantic for the second time. The
fleet left to a tremendous send-off, huge crowds waving goodbye and
cheering, a jazz band playing and a host of spectator vessels bobbing
in the bay.

We had a plan for the start. We were to reach to the first mark (a buoy we had to leave to port), turn almost back the way we had come, sail until we could use a spinnaker to sail to the second mark, and from there go straight to Boston, avoiding running into Robben Island. It worked, but not as we had envisaged. We made a good start and were in third place at the first mark, but as we tried to gybe we fell into the wind shadow of Table Mountain, as did all the other boats as they each rounded the buoy. For five agonising minutes we could barely sail, being flatly becalmed, with the fleet all around like stranded leviathans, sails flapping and hulls swinging. This meant frantic crew activity, of course, as we tried to get going – first one way, then another – until finally we found a breath of wind and got moving again, in last place and in a different direction to everyone else. But our scheme worked: we picked up the edge of the fresh wind and passed the next mark second only to *Heath Insured II*, who had taken it very wide, out of our sight behind the huge spectator fleet.

The down side

The 'Paradise leg'? On the first night we blew our brand new race spinnaker to pieces, lost about five square metres of material and were unable to repair it or use it again. It was a bitter blow, and even when we heard that at least half the fleet had also damaged spinnakers you could see the anxiety behind even the most philosophical faces on board. Nonetheless, we were going downwind, and what a contrast it was too! Downwind we could stand up, walk along the deck or down below, hear each other, cook without fear of being hit by flying pots or scalded by boiling water, we could use the heads without having to be acrobats, clean our teeth without hanging on for dear life, or even for grim death, and we could sleep! Sleep, the great balm which washes away the sailor's cares, and 'knits up the ravelled sleeve of time', was ours. We were lulled by gentle rocking and soothed by the gurglings and swooshings of the South Atlantic as we headed to Boston, 7000 miles away, at 10–12 knots.

What is more, we were dry, at least most of the time. I say most of the time because we were drenched by the most monumental wave on our first night out. According to the experts, about one wave in every 300 000 can reach up to four times the height of its brethren, and in an average wave height of three or four feet, this one broke over my head while I was at the helm! I lost my balance, the wave bashed the stern round, and I really thought we were going to broach. We didn't, but it was a hell of a shock. Unfortunately we had some galley hatches open and water flooded the saloon, but at least in the warm weather it dried out again fairly quickly.

By day two things were settling down, but with a certain air of predictability – *Group 4, Concert, Commercial Union* and ourselves setting the pace. In fact we four made a definite break, with *CU* giving *Group 4* the best run for their money. We raced in sight of each other, with yellow mainsails and billowing spinnakers visible by day, the boats turning to small dots of light through the night. 'That's *Concert,* that's *CU* and *Group 4* are over there,' became a regular part of the watch handover; but nothing lasts long at sea. We made a decision based on our weather information and gybed away from the others. Usually I liked it when we were alone on our own in the ocean, but this time I felt worried that we might miss the cut and thrust of close-quarter racing and consequently slow down. As it turned out, we did come to question our decision, but for different reasons, and of course hindsight is a very precise science.

The first week passed under cloudy skies, giving temperate days and black nights. As we passed into our second week at sea, the weather became more typical of the trade winds with blue skies, hot sun and starry nights. The wind, which had been very fickle across the fleet, had improved, and although the positions had stretched out, leaving us in fourth place 45 miles or so behind *Group 4,* spirits stayed mostly high – so much so that at one watch change when we went on deck, Kiki had retreated (but in good humour) to the galley to avoid another onslaught of schoolboy humour from Ben and Spike, which had left everyone on deck speechless. All I could hear when I came up was choked breathing interspersed with snorts and hoots of merriment. They had passed beyond plain laughter! 'Childish, isn't it?' said Ben in between howls of mirth, and perhaps it was, but it was no less funny for that. By contrast, we were tending to concentrate grimly on performance, which was fast, but almost dull; just mechanical steering and trimming. The sheer number of days at sea was beginning to tell on me. On leg 1 the simple act of getting up and going on watch had generated great enthusiasm in me. No longer, I discovered.

In fact Ben's watch seemed to be having rather more fun than we were. Perhaps it was having Ange, our 'mega-legger', back for a third time, this time replacing Guy. We began to wonder who Ange was going to try to 'nobble' in Boston to ensure she had a place on the last leg! Or possibly it was the addition of Woolly's brother Arnie (Keith really, but Arnie suited him better), trying to stage a Watson family takeover of the *Toshiba* crew. Either way, not to be outdone, the port watch had recruited Di Hemming. Now Di shares her name with a famous yachtswoman, apart from being one herself, so when the lists of leggers were published we made sure to mention that Di Hemming was joining us for leg five. '*The* Di Hemming?' '*The* Di Hemming,' we would affirm, and *The* Di Hemming she remained.

Di was delightful company, a little unsure of herself when she joined us, but quick to feel at home and settle in. Her one great desire was to see lots of wildlife and in that, sadly, she was thwarted. It was all on leg six, not leg five. As for Arnie, named for that upper-body-build, Arnie found the sailing too easy and took to doing press ups on the foredeck. The Watson family penchant for riding easily through life and enjoying nearly all of it found expression in Arnie every bit as much as in his sister Joe. A big wide smile and willing attitude made him popular from the start.

We celebrated Mark's birthday. Woolly having by now passed on the secret of making birthday trifle on board, birthday treats were de rigueur and this one was well up to standard: rice with tuna and cheese sauce, trifle and peach schnapps! We presented Mark with a gold plated teaspoon bearing a South African badge, ostensibly for being such a 'stirrer', which was, of course, a joke since Mark is one of the least contentious men you could ever hope to meet; and then discovered that he is the proud possessor of a teaspoon collection, inherited from a distant relation!

We had known from before the start that this leg represented our last real chance to take the overall race lead. *Group 4* were just less than a day ahead of us on combined times, not an unreasonable target in an ocean crossing of nearly 7000 miles. On the other hand we knew that simply sailing the same route as they took was unlikely to yield such a margin. In fact, based on all previous experience, although we felt we had improved our downwind and light airs skills a lot, it would be very difficult for us to beat them by just match racing in the same part of the ocean, let alone gain any significant margin. The tactics therefore came out looking like this: the conventional wisdom was 'go west, young man'. There was likely to be more wind to the west as the fleet headed up to the doldrums, we would take our chances with the ITCZ and hope to compensate for sailing slightly further by picking up good winds and favourable currents on the far side. But we needed to gain a day. How could we do that? 'Risk, risk anything!' said Katherine Mansfield, so we risked the easterly route. On average, the ITCZ has wind speeds two knots higher in the west than in the east, but also to the east there is usually

either no wind, or more wind than there would be in the west. We
had been heading east, convincing ourselves that this was the right
choice, when things came to a rather crucial juncture. We had separated ourselves from *Group 4* and *Save the Children*, who had come
flying up once again, and now the wind was most unfavourable for
us to try to gain westing and close on them. We were committed, but
unresolved, and it caused some problems.

Any simmering tensions were kept down by the joy of being on
deck in shorts or swimming costumes and by our commitment to sail
to the best of our ability. We had reduced the personal kit list yet
again in Cape Town in an effort to keep the weight down, and with
an almost continuous round of spinnaker peels and gybes on deck
there was plenty of opportunity to keep our skills sharp. We also had
some great racing: duels with *Concert* and *CU* keeping us on our
toes. Passing St Helena provided a diversion too. There was a rush
for the pilot books and we all became temporary experts on the
island of Napoleon's exile and death. *Heath Insured II* unfortunately
had to make more of a diversion. They dropped off crew member
Andy Pilkington who needed medical attention for a kidney stone.
The fact that it was not, as had been thought, appendicitis, was
probably very little consolation to Andy or to the rest of his crew.

Our frustration increased as the weather faxes continued to show
the more westerly route as favoured, and Huey the wind god continued to send breezes which kept us to the east. The pessimists began
to mutter darkly, the optimists to talk about better wind angles to the
north of the doldrums, and the sybarites worked on their suntans.
Kiki, rising sleepily to go on watch and asking, 'What's everyone
wearing on deck?' was told by Mark: 'Shorts, factor 25 suncream
and a variety of Australian hats!' On the other hand a commitment
to racing all the way detracts mightily from the usual pleasures of
this sort of fine weather sailing: sitting around on deck with a drink
in one hand and a good book in the other for instance.

Di joined the birthday club and we celebrated with a bottle of
Bacardi, our one concession to weight being a bottle for each birthday. More significantly perhaps, the day was marked by a fantastic
shooting star early in the morning. Low on the horizon and bright as
a flare, but not lasting long enough to be one, it was quite amazing.
In keeping with the mood of celebration, 'Sharky', our plastic mascot,
was taped near the wheel, and from then on ritually squeaked at
watch changes and other exciting moments. Geoff began to teach
Woolly and Di to sing: 'My father was the keeper of the Eddystone
light, and he slept with a mermaid one fine night ...' amidst great

hilarity. To temper all this we had a very polite call in the small hours of one morning saying: 'Could we have some people on deck please, we've blown the kite!' The promo had split right across just under the word 'Toshiba', but miraculously had only torn apart for a few feet down one tape, meaning a reasonably quick repair.

Drew was having a wonderful leg. He had obviously made good use of his time away and had come back in good humour, making light of waking up and still feeling sleepy, getting to grips with the fact that the food was as it was, and generally being good fun. Jo seemed to be having trouble with it all, though, as always, she worked hard and in particular led the spinnaker repair team by example, but she seemed to have lost the fun of the whole thing. Perhaps it was because we were not doing well. *Save the Children* had passed us as we finally set about making some westing, and we were down to fifth place, 76 miles behind *Group 4*. Nonetheless Jo surprised us over dinner when she asked whether we would condone dumping our 'gash' plastics overboard if it would make the difference between first and second place. Not that she was proposing this; it would actually make no difference and was simply a hypothetical question. Geoff, Mark, Woolly, Di and I all instantly said absolutely not. Jo then asked whether we would run without water in the tanks. This was a trickier question because it would confer a weight advantage, but the rules stated that yachts should run with the tanks full, 'if possible', which seemed reasonably clear. Slightly frustrated, Jo asked us: 'So you're all happy to finish second and have everyone say, "Oh well, *Tosh* could only manage second, but they're a nice bunch of people"?' And we all said, 'Yes!' In fact one of our crew protocols, right from the beginning, was to be 'squeaky clean' with regard to the rules, in letter and in spirit. It seemed that on the British Steel Challenge there had been rather loose interpretations of some points and *Rhone Poulenc*, Simon's yacht, had been among the freer spirits in this respect. Anxious that we should not for a moment be tarred with the same brush, Simon set out to impose and maintain the highest standards.

As ever, this was probably just an example of competitive spirit and frustration at being behind, but we managed to put it all behind us temporarily while crossing the equator on Jo's birthday. The court of King Neptune duly sat for the second time on the voyage, and found all who crossed the line for the first time horribly guilty of a huge variety of crimes, in order that the usual punishments could be administered. Arnie, it was stated, had too many names, regularly ate leftover food when asked to throw it overboard, and had been caught working out enthusiastically on the foredeck. Di had not only left her husband for the first time in nine years of marriage, but had immediately removed her wedding ring and shacked up with another man (yours truly!) in the port two-man cabin. If all that were not enough, she had also been discovered in possession of pornographic literature: a Jilly Cooper novel, which she had failed to share with the rest of the crew. Ange set a record for the longest list of crimes ever assembled, chief of which were hanging around ports of call repeatedly until invited to do the next leg, and failing to catch any fish in spite of claiming descent from a Brixham trawlerman. In addition, Drew received a saltwater soaking for having the temerity to suggest that we might all take saltwater showers on deck on this leg, after he had missed all the saltwater showers of leg four, and Kobus was punished all over again for failing to provide any evidence that he had been tried and found guilty on a previous crossing!

Stung by the slur on her family's skills, and a message from *Motorola* saying that they had enjoyed fresh squid for breakfast, Ange went into action. Not that we were going to be trailing any lines – this was to be fishing at racing speeds. We enquired of *Motorola* the most effective method in their opinion. 'Take down all sail,' they responded, 'Point a light at the water, squid will rise to surface.' Having already found one minute baby squid on the foredeck very close to the 'luff light' we had arranged in order to illuminate one edge of the spinnaker at night. Ange detected a method. A suitably positioned torch, and a bucket to catch them in; simple really. We sent a further message to *Motorola*: 'Have reduced sail (we had in fact taken the spinnaker down and were under headsails) but still no luck. Is ten and a half knots too fast for squid?' We got our come-uppance the next day when they were going well and we were not. A message came in: 'Eleven knots under spinnaker, decks awash with squid.' Ange did however gut and cook several flying fish which landed on deck and, to my great surprise, they were absolutely delicious.

We had some running repairs to do, inevitable on a long passage, but having the main sheet traveller car threatening to pull off its track did look rather serious. If this had actually broken we would have had no means of pulling the end of the boom down or trimming the mainsail. In fact sailing would have been pretty well impossible, let alone racing. An engineering committee rapidly convened. The major problem was that of access to the underside of the assembly. Kobus suggested drilling a hand-sized hole in the deck, Simon paled visibly under his suntan, Geoff brought forth the tool box. In the end, as with virtually everything we had to repair, an ingenious solution (removing one of the bolts which held the track to the deck *just* gave access for a socket to be used) yielded a neat and wholly effective repair, and a few laughs on the way.

As it turned out, we passed through the doldrums relatively unscathed, but while we tried to dodge the rain clouds and find the breeze, the westerly boats were charging on at 10 knots in plenty of wind. Disappointingly for us, the leaders all seemed to get through with relatively little trouble too. That might not seem very fair-minded or charitable, but the one advantage of our position was that we had managed to choose a narrow band of ITCZ to pass through, at a point where its northern boundary was very low (the whole thing moves about all the time), and had hoped to recoup some miles once we popped out at the top. In fact we did start to make sizeable gains, but not before we had joined the '200 club' – 200 miles behind leaders *Group 4* that is – and descended to eleventh place. Simon gave us a pep talk on keeping our spirits up when the position is not good and, even more importantly, keeping our *team* spirit up ...!

One day after clearing the ITCZ we crossed our outward track. We had sailed 23 109 miles and spent 117 days 12 hours 4 mins at sea since we had last been at this position (9° 19' N 25° 30' W for those who like to know this sort of thing) on 13 October – we had officially sailed round the world. The evening sky turned pastel: pale blues and soft pinks surrounded us. As we glided through the quiet night the Plough was visible, pointers down towards the horizon on our starboard side, and behind us the Southern Cross with its two bright pointers was still clearly in sight. For those of us who had not been in the southern hemisphere before, the Southern Cross had in many ways become a great symbol of the whole adventure, and I felt slightly sad to think that it would soon drop out of sight altogether. But what a thrill to be back in the northern hemisphere, with the familiar constellations of home waters above us! The Pole star sat winking low on the horizon, beckoning us north, to higher latitudes and to home.

As the last of the fleet made their way through the doldrums, two things became clear: firstly, that our easterly route had not paid off in getting to the ITCZ quickly, we had gained no advantage over our immediate rivals while crossing it and were not favoured by better winds once through it; and secondly that things were settling down into something of a procession, with everyone making similar progress. Our much-vaunted ability to 'nibble away' at the opposition seemed to have deserted us. In the west, *Motorola*, who had staked everything on a bold westward move right from the start, swept imperiously through into second place. *Nuclear Electric* who followed *Group 4* through the doldrums at exactly the same latitude but 24 hours later, lost huge numbers of miles, which made it look rather as though, had the race started a day later, our easterly route would have been favoured. What wonderful things ifs and buts are.

As if all this were not enough we had run out of pasta, except for lasagne, which did not, alas, work so well for other dishes and Geoff had a bit of trouble making lunch. In the end the result, with a little help from Woolly, was perfectly fine, but Geoff was very defensive at first. It was amazing how cooking set up this defensiveness in some of us, including me. People began to think they would come in for criticism if the meal was not brilliant, and would start to get worked up before anything was said. I often felt that, had everyone followed Simon's example of eating everything and declaring it all good, the problem would never have arisen.

Nearly everyone in the crew had suffered from some mystery 'bug' in Cape Town and although most people had recovered completely, Jo and I were still in trouble. My 'glands' (they are lymph nodes really) were up, my stomach would not behave properly without Imodium and my tongue was horribly green and furry! Spike prescribed some antibiotics. They made things worse in the short term, as he said they might, so I was taken off them again and was left feeling quite rough and very washed out. In fact I felt so 'done in' that I came straight off deck feeling terrible, skipped breakfast (the first time I had not eaten a meal that I could remember), went straight to my bunk and almost straight to sleep. I didn't feel much better after that and Spike recommended that I stand down for the 10.00 to 02.00 watch, thereby spending the whole night in my bunk which, reluctantly, I did. I got a reasonable amount of sleep although I had to take painkillers for backache at around midnight. Our bunks were not good for more than about six hours. I got up feeling rather woozy, with my bowels normal for the first time in a fort-night, but feeling generally flu-like: weak and shivery. Spike's treat-ment, consisting of no treatment for the next 24 hours or so, in the best traditions of doctoring, especially at sea, produced an improve-ment. In the meantime the weather was beautiful, sunny, with the wind around 20 knots, and the boat going well.

We had a sudden explosion of interest in navigation on this leg. The sextant came out, and Mark, Kiki, Woolly, Ange and Jo all had their eyes on the rational horizon and were deep in the almanac muttering about calculated zenith distances and the like. Under

Simon's patient tutelage we all learned more stars, and on a good night could spot Alkaid, Alioth, Merik, Dubhe, Polaris, Sheddar, Arcturus, Spica, Vega, Deneb and Altair. Of the constellations Orion and Pegasus were not visible, but Scorpio was very clear behind us.

Somewhere around this time I began to feel I had been away from home for long enough. There had been too many days at sea for this leg – too many days to be going slowly at any rate. For the first time since we left Southampton I started to chafe at the confining space of 67 feet by 17 feet. There are too many good things in life that you can't do at sea, and after a while the fun and excitement of a long passage ceases to compensate for them. I cooked dinner with Woolly and during a pause we sat down for a chat. I started to tell her I was a bit fed up and, to my great surprise, articulating this suddenly brought it all home and I felt completely miserable! Fortunately I cheered up as we served supper – and Woolly was so sweet and so much fun it was hard not to be cheerful when she was around. At her instigation we all had a drink and I felt much better.

My feelings about rules and protocols were not improved when, for the second time on this leg, with 23 000 miles of sailing behind us, it became necessary to post notices asking (telling, really) everyone to flush the heads properly! Back in the race we were out of the 200 club, and up to seventh place, having caught up a little. After one or two watches in moderate winds I felt much better – in fact very cheerful. Then something rather unfortunate happened.

We were in very light conditions, with four to five knots of wind and the promo up. It was painfully slow, but an otherwise beautiful day. Having been so miserable the day before I had cheered up dramatically overnight, almost as if I had snapped myself out of it. I got up feeling fine, washed up breakfast and went on deck. Simon asked for 'weight forward and low' and Woolly, Geoff and I obliged. Woolly asked me to put some sun cream on her back and I was doing that, and rubbing her shoulders, when Simon asked someone to call the trim. So I got up, went forward and checked the genoa, returning to my seat on the rail and Woolly's back. A few minutes later there was a very irate call from the cockpit to 'stop messing about and call some trim', except that 'messing' was not the word used! I stood up and called back, rather tetchily, 'All right, all right, I didn't know you wanted somebody to stay on the bow.' 'Well it's very frustrating,' came the reply, 'when we're back here trying to make the boat go fast and people are messing about giving people massages!' I was out-raged – and this wasn't helped when I went forward again, signalled the trim, and nothing happened. I had to storm back to the mast to yell, 'if you want me to trim the thing you might pay attention to the signals!' and I was tempted to lard that sentence with very rude words.

I was livid, and I stayed livid for a good few hours, raging against the injustice of being told off for 'messing around' when my understanding was that we were supposed to be on the rail. There had been plenty of opportunity for someone to ask me to stay calling the trim, but no-one had, and above all I was livid because I do not mess about on watch. Woolly was convinced that the criticism had been aimed at her, but I didn't take it that way. So, instead of letting it go, I harboured it, nursed it, resented it and worked myself up into a dire state of anger and potential retribution. This is the kind of attitude which gets people into fights in bars and it showed me once again how close to the surface my emotions were from time to time. It also made me aware of how closely I could be in touch with that dark side.

So there I was, very upset, a lovely morning put thoroughly out of kilter for want of a tiny bit of co-operation over some sail trim, but that's yacht racing for you. I was also very upset because it was literally the first time that Simon and I had been at odds since I had known him. I hoped he might apologise, but deep down I knew that it had been a momentary criticism, born out of frustration, and that, unlike me, he had forgotten it had happened five minutes later.

Not long after this I felt ill again with a very sore stomach. Spike ruminated about appendix and gall bladder, but seemed reassured by the answers I gave to his questions. Just as well, since Simon had pointed out just the day before: 'We are 2000 miles from anywhere again,' adding that no-one should break a leg or develop appendicitis! It didn't feel like 2000 miles from anywhere this time, perhaps because we were seeing so many floating objects: a jerry can, a fishing buoy, a plastic safety hat, and a quantity of plastic bottles had all floated by. The detritus of the seas, and nearly all plastic, of course.

We had a sudden burst of euphoria with an improvement in both wind and boat speed, and a growing conviction that we could get up to fourth place, leading the eastern side of the fleet. Woolly pointed out that my morale was probably a function of my physical well-being as much as anything else, to which I replied, 'Then thank God I'm feeling a bit better!' But there really ought to be a sailing proverb along the lines of the old military dictum that, 'If your advance is going well you are probably walking into an ambush.' We blew the promo right on the 2200 watch change – it tore from side to side, right across one of our previous repairs. Drastic illnesses need drastic solutions and, after two and a half hours of decision making, Simon opted to cut a panel out right the way across, and join the two good edges together. Incredibly, the edges came back together without distorting, meaning that we were able to avoid any penalty for irreparable damage, even if our spinnaker was now rather smaller than originally designed! We had moved up to fifth place and were only two miles off fourth.

In spite of feeling generally better I was suffering from more stomach pains, and in the course of his researches into my condition Spike took my temperature again. This time he did it while I was helming, amid endless insults and many jokes that he had found a way to shut me up at last. I should explain that I have in the past volunteered myself as Honorary Secretary of the Hind Leg Off a Donkey Club, and that Mrs Patrick Campbell could have been talking about me, rather than George Bernard Shaw, when she said: 'It's too late to do anything but accept you and love you – but when you were quite a little boy somebody ought to have said "hush" just once!' My temperature was predictably normal. Whether it was our performance, the fact that we had got some wind, the knowledge that we could not be much more than a week from Boston, a change in my physical condition, or just my determination that I had been miserable long enough, I did not know – but I made an improvement.

The champagne leg

The moon rose at dawn! The thinnest slither of a pale golden crescent rose up against a background of translucent orange which, fading into a paler blue, in turn darkened to the last moments of the still night sky, with the last stars fading overhead. Sailing, or at least being at sea, was the best possible lesson in the solar system and the patterns of the Earth. As the sun and moon rose and set, Venus and Jupiter crossed the night sky and the constellations revolved (or more accurately, appeared to revolve) overhead, it became much easier to make sense of simple astronomy. On the other hand, it served only to deepen the metaphysical mysteries. Even an understanding of DNA and how we came to evolve, coupled with modern theories of cosmology, does not quite deal with the mystery of life on earth, because it does not deal with the transcendent mystery of the universe. So we are left with the age old choice – to worry or to wonder.

This leg was unusual because we actually made contact with yachts outside the fleet. We spotted one yacht and called them on the

VHF radio. They identified themselves as *Low Profile*, a Moody 47, skipper Hamish, crew Sue and Margaret, 12 days out of Antigua bound for the Azores. They were on a year's cruise, they told us, and had been to the US and the Caribbean. Their biggest problem was that their fridge had broken and they had no means of chilling the champagne! Immediately after this we were called by another yacht and a voice said: 'Hello Simon, this is Susannah from Oslo, we met last year!' Much hilarity all round! Susannah was sailing on *Wind Hook*, a 30-year-old Hallberg Rassy on delivery from St Martin to the Azores. We saw her about 20 minutes later, a fine-looking ketch with mizzen, main and a big genoa up. Both yachts asked for weather information and that made me realise how lucky we were. We may have been a little short of champagne, but both these yachts had heard reports of impending 50 knot winds in the Azores and had no detailed information on which to base decisions. Simon pulled out sheaves of printed weather faxes and satellite pictures as he gave them a complete rundown of the forecasts, and I began to re-evaluate my definitions of travelling in luxury. It was somewhere around this stage in the race, while we were discussing Simon's background in yacht deliveries and his previous racing experience, that he happened to mention that our Fastnet Race had been his first ever race as a skipper! That put the classic *Toshiba* start routine into perspective.

So this was Chay's 'champagne leg' without the champagne. Fabulous weather, bright sunshine, brilliant blue seas and starry, moonlit nights, but a poor performance and the usual privations of 14 people in a small space, very little personal kit and, in spite of Woolly's stunning efforts, a food programme we were beginning to have had enough of. Not that the menu had not evolved on the way round. As well as trifle we had produced birthday cake, which you make with McDougall's chocolate sponge mix coated with a topping of hot chocolate, butter and golden syrup, decorated with jelly tots – or at least, that was how Kiki did it. As if that were not enough, pizza made a regular appearance (bread mix, tomato purée, dried onions, cheese, and anything you could find in the 'goody' locker), as did cheese and onion pie, although this always appeared as constituent parts – base and topping served separately, after one of those disasters you can only have with an un-gimballed (not swinging) oven at sea.

Speaking of disasters, we had been avoiding any blocked toilets by the simple expedient of not putting any loo paper down them. This did have the slight drawback that we would each have to carry our small parcel, or large football, depending on who we are talking about, of loo paper along the companionway and throw it overboard after each visit, preferably missing all members of the on-deck watch and avoiding wrapping it, streamer-like, around the mainsheet. Have you ever set out to do something, found yourself distracted and forgotten the original objective? Woolly and I found Kiki by the chart table, in the middle of a watch, looking around worriedly, obviously concerned about something. 'What's the matter?' we asked. 'I think I've put my loo paper down somewhere,' she replied! We decided fairly rapidly that she must in fact have thrown it overboard, to the great relief of all concerned.

So this leg of strange contrasts continued, with much hilarity off-setting a deep disquiet rumbling under the surface. At the darkest moment, when it had looked as though we might finish well down the order, Kobus had declared that he had wasted three years of his life, Spike had wanted to take over the navigation and weather routeing and an air of dejection had permeated the boat. But then we had begun what, in my opinion, was actually our best performance of the race.

Storming down to Boston

There is only one thing to do in a yacht race when things are not going well, and that is to do, as Franklin D Roosevelt said, 'The best you can, with what you have, where you are,' in other words to keep sailing to the best of your abilities and keep going as fast as you know how; and that is what we did, and it paid off. We had started to improve our position against the other easterly boats and, as our self confidence returned and our morale rose again, a funny thing happened: it blew a gale. In fact it blew into a full-on North Atlantic gale overnight. Our 1800 to 2200 off watch was full of the flap and groan of sheets and halyards on winches and the flogging of sails as Ben's lot got down to yankee 3, staysail and main with three reefs! We then had four hours bashing into it as we reached down the dark night like a demented express train, running into walls of water and flinging out spray instead of smoke.

Gales at sea are never exactly pleasant, but this one had the very great merit of being a warm water gale. The usual drenching cascades flooded down the decks, but it was like taking a dip in a warm bath, and in fact the wind wasn't cold either. I found the water warming my hands up when it hit, instead of freezing fingers to the bone and robbing them of all sensation except pain. In addition, we were reaching not beating, so that as *Toshiba* thundered on into each fresh curling wave, the great gusts of spray, flying up to half the height of the mast, were whipped away sideways forming a sheet of mist that at times stretched 20 or 30 yards from the bow. We had seen it coming on the weather charts and were not unprepared, but it still seemed slightly surreal to be flying through the dark night with the storm sails set. 'Are you sure we didn't turn left instead of right when we left Cape Town?' Ange asked, as the wind gusted up to 48 knots, 'This is like being back in the Southern Ocean.'

In some ways it was. Some of the cabin hatches were leaking badly and my bunk was a river – thankfully we were on starboard tack so we were sleeping on the other side. But this really was our kind of weather, and we used it to our fullest advantage. We imposed a lead on *Save the Children*, left *Commercial Union*, with whom we had been battling neck and neck, 60 miles behind us, and caught and passed *Global Teamwork*, thereby securing Geoff's £10 bet with Kiki's mum about whether Kiki or her father John would be in Boston first. To our great delight we also passed the third of the boats on the more westerly course, *Courtaulds International*. We converted a deficit of 60 miles with 1000 miles to go, to a lead of 22 miles over them shortly before the finish, and although *Motorola* and *Group 4* were out of our grasp, we were, nonetheless, in what I considered to be a very meritorious third place.

As we closed on the coast of America, *Group 4* finished, leaving us something like 150 miles adrift. *Motorola* had slowed down considerably, we presumed due to little wind off Boston. We charged past the George's shoal, parts of which are very shallow, without the anticipated heavy seas, but punching the tides all the way down to Cape Cod, with the fear that those coming up astern might catch the favourable tide behind us. The sea turned green, and the temperature dropped; it was only 60°F in Boston and it was freezing on deck! I had my full three layers on and was very grateful for them. *Motorola* had stopped, they reported on the chat show: no wind, sails flapping – would it be our fate too?

It was our fate! We were only about 20 miles off, but at one point we went backwards 0.6 miles in about half an hour. So for the fourth time out of five it looked like a no-wind finish. So near and yet so far, once again. *Motorola* finished, and the only good news was that while we had been going nowhere (and backwards) we had taken three miles out of *Courtaulds*! This time the wind was not long in coming back, and we made a great finish coming into the harbour under spinnaker. *Toshiba II*, on promotional duties in the States, came out to see us, and commented later that at one point they couldn't keep up with us under engine while we slipped along at 10 knots under the lightweight kite. They were joined by *Group 4*, and in front of this rather select audience we peeled and gybed our way in like true professionals. At one point, spotting a small hole in the lightweight kite, we collapsed it, patched the hole and rehoisted it without missing a beat. So we stormed down a gloriously sunlit Boston Harbour with the airport on one side and the city on the other looking spectacular, and finished to a great quayside welcome from *Group 4*, and most of the *Motorola* crew, still celebrating their second place on the leg.

Group 4 gave the fleet a spectacular drubbing and in doing so virtually assured themselves of overall victory. By the same token, although no-one, not even a crew which included a South African poultry farmer, should count their chickens, our second place overall looked fairly certain. In spite of my mid-leg blues and the discontent caused by our choice of route we had had a fantastic run from Cape Town.

We had learned the names of a whole host of new stars, seen the 'green flash' of the tropical sunsets, watched the comet Hale-Bopp creep across the night sky, taken sun sights and chatted to various cruising yachts, and had arrived in Boston at the end of our second Transatlantic crossing, having become circumnavigators in the process.

We had sailed a route south of the great Capes, in excess of 21 600 miles, passing all the lines of longitude and crossing our outward track in the northern hemisphere, and that is that, by all definitions. It had already been a journey of incredible contrasts, and a phenom-enal challenge both physically and mentally. An experience which, for me, had encompassed all human emotion: joy, sadness, passion, resignation, love, hate, rage, serenity, excitement and fear, and above all it had been a great adventure, of a kind that is perhaps not so easy to come by these days. A real experience of the fullness of being, a levelling, a grounding in what is important in life and what is not. It had been a journey, the purpose of which was to look life squarely in the face and say, 'Yes, I'm on for this, I want an experience of life, take me.' Now all we had to do was to sail back to Southampton to complete a truly astonishing voyage.

12

How Much Do They Pay You?

'And this is good old Boston, The home of the bean and the cod, Where the Lowells talk only to Cabots, And the Cabots talk only to God.' John Collins Bossidy

I woke early and looked out of my hotel room window. The street was strangely full of European-looking cars. Where were the Chevrolets of my dreams? The Dearborn Fords, the Cadillacs, the Oldsmobiles? The only sign that I was in the USA was the trucks. Nowhere else in the world has trucks like this: big trucks, proud trucks, *American* trucks, with huge chrome grills and long bonnets – none of your flat fronted Skandias here – a Mack truck has an ego and knows its place in life.

I walked out of the hotel and across the street. A very tall, very languid, black traffic cop in a dark blue-black uniform criss-crossed with day-glo orange webbing, wearing a peaked US military-style hat and an impenetrable pair of dark glasses, ambled towards me. He pointed a thumb over his shoulder with a lift of his elbow and a flick of his wrist. 'You drivin' that thing, ma-a-a-a-n?' he asked archly, the thumb indicating a van parked obliquely on a corner. I looked blankly through his opaque black sunglasses, shrugged, and walked on. I hoped that I conveyed an equally languid, 'Would I be driving *that*?' but I fear the necessary cool was probably beyond me.

Toshiba had, as at all our stopovers, arranged accommodation for us, but this time I was after privacy. I had booked into the Marriott, called Pam, woken her up (I had forgotten it would be 3 am in the UK), and we had chatted for a couple of hours. I also managed to persuade her to come out to Boston. I said: 'Why don't you fly out for the weekend?' and she replied, 'I was thinking about doing that.' Easy, really!

Our work programme was shorter in Boston, the rigours of the Atlantic crossing being nothing compared to the pounding everything had taken in the Southern Ocean, but the temperature at Rowes Wharf, where we were moored up, was in the nineties, so we sweltered while we worked. What a setting, though.

There is a classic view of modern Boston from across the harbour, looking at the skyscrapers of the financial district. In the centre of this view is an enormous archway, capped by a dome. Underneath the archway sat our fleet of Challenge yachts. Because of the proximity of a conglomeration of offices and apartments we had a constant, fascinated audience. The braver souls wandered down on to the pontoons and engaged us in conversation. This being America, the most frequently asked question was: 'How much do they pay you?' The idea that we had paid to do it was greeted with varying amounts of incredulity. Not by Ed and Jarvis however.

I met Ed Berger and Jarvis Cribb exactly like that, just a passing chat on the pontoon. Except that they then invited me to lunch, and while we were at lunch they invited me to a barbeque that evening with their wives and various other couples. Ed duly met me, took me out on the 'T' (the underground) to 'the last parking space in Boston' and from there drove me to his home in Beverley Farms to meet his wife Lindy. We went on to the barbeque, on a grassy slope overlooking the local yacht club, to join up with Jarvis and Barbara and the rest of the Beverley Farms Summer Wednesdays dining club. I ate like a king and, after whisky in liberal measure at their home, Jarvis drove me the half-hour journey back into Boston, dropped me off and then set out to return home. Now *that* was hospitality!

Pam arrived, we booked into the Bostonian, and went sightseeing. Boston is the birthplace of American independence, and the politics and characters of this birth of a nation are complex and fascinating. One of the great Boston landmarks, Faneuil Hall, 'The Cradle of Liberty', and the meeting hall where 'No taxation without representation' was first mooted (although not quite in those words) bears a plaque. It reads: 'This is Faneuil Hall built and given to the town of Boston by Peter Faneuil, 1742. Still used by a free people 1930.' What a wonderful comment! Of course, you could argue that in Britain nobody would need to add such an observation to a historical plaque, but that argument is probably churlish as well as arrogant.

Boston is crammed full of good places to eat so, being spoiled for choice, one night we took a short walk to the North End, the Italian district. Strolling down one street of wall-to-wall restaurants and comparing menus, we passed a fellow in a rather dubious suit: long, draped, unvented jacket, wide pants, a black silk shirt buttoned to the neck, a Hollywood mahogany tan, black hair slicked down to the nines, and a single very large gold earring. He was talking to a very big T-shirted man leaning against a car about things you can do with a baseball bat, but that do not involve hitting a baseball. We walked on by. Having investigated every restaurant in the street, we returned to the one with the gangster outside. A group of people were peering at the menu on display outside; it looked crowded inside. We dashed for the door, and were headed off by the gangster. 'Can I help you folks?' he asked. I was slightly taken by surprise, but reacted like a chess master to an unconventional opening: 'Yes, do you have a table for two?' 'Two. Yeah, okay,' he responded.

We had the last table for two, and took our waiter's recommendation for a starter. It was extraordinary. Supposedly, wild mushrooms baked in a brick oven with prosciutto and cheese, and served on a raw spinach salad; it had the exotic pungency of some fantastically rare truffle, whilst managing to seem almost like finest fillet steak. The salad contained all sorts of hidden delights and the whole thing was stupendous. We were enjoying ourselves. So was our waiter. 'So who is the guy in the suit?' I asked, 'Is he the owner?' 'The owner is away at present,' I was told, 'that is his brother.' 'Oh, I see,' I responded carefully, 'that is the owner's brother.' 'Yeah.' 'So it's kind of "in the family"?' 'Oh, no,' he laughed, 'It's not like that any more.' 'So how is it now?' I asked. He shrugged, grinned, and spread out his hands, palms up. 'Well,' he lifted his hands slightly, 'We all know each other.' 'So it *is* still like that?' 'No, not really. All the mobsters have been sent to gaol.' 'So it is still like that?' 'Well,' a pause, 'not really.' 'But you all know each other?' 'Yeah,' another big grin, 'we all still know each other.' We laughed, we left, we tipped well; but the food was fantastic.

We crossed the river to Cambridge and walked around Harvard in glorious sunshine on a beautiful day. The massive steps and soaring columns of the Widener library would satisfy the most ardent of bibliophiles, and while other American universities have to make do with campuses, Harvard Yard is a glorious setting of grass, paths and mature trees that does more than justice to America's oldest seat of learning. The statue of John Harvard sits here. It is known jocularly as the statue of three lies because of its inscription, which reads: 'John Harvard, Founder, 1638'. Harvard in fact left half his estate, including his library of 320 books, to the divinity school which had been founded in 1636. Furthermore, the sculptor Daniel Chester French, coming on the scene 200 years later and, very reasonably, having no idea what Harvard looked like, modelled his likeness on a member of the class of 1882. So the statue is not of Harvard, he was not the founder, nor was the original college founded in 1638. None of this has stopped the bronze 'Harvard' from having the toe of his left shoe rubbed to a shiny brightness by the countless thousands of visitors who, in posing beside him, raise their right hands and caress his protruding brass bound toes as their partners' cameras click to record another 'I've been there'.

Boston may be the cradle of liberty, but to me Harvard has always been the cradle of free and positive thinkers. Franklin left Boston because it was too conservative, but in later years Harvard nurtured the likes of William James, adding experimentation with mind altering drugs to seminal American philosophy, Ralph Waldo Emerson, and his great pupil Henry Thoreau. Not to mention Buckminster Fuller (who was thrown out twice) and the late, great and much lamented Tom Lehrer. Which free thinking led me back to Boston itself, where the statue of General Hooker stands beside the State House. There are no statues, alas, of his female followers, the original 'Hookers'.

We walked down to the Charles River. A sign on the Amex Travel Office said: 'Please go away often.' An ambulance came by, all flashing lights and wailing sirens – and they do know about sirens in America. The lettering on the side read: 'Professional Ambulance'. After everything that had been thrown at us in the course of the race would anyone, I wondered, really want an amateur one? The Charles River was absolutely beautiful and, best of all, looked exactly like the Thames at Richmond – more blade skaters and fewer dog walkers, but just the same feeling. It was almost as good as being back home. I took Pam back to the airport for another goodbye, but this time only for a month.

For services to yachting ...

If you were to write the words 'For services to yachting' on a piece of paper I cannot think of a more appropriate name to follow them than Chay Blyth. Chay completed one of the truly heroic voyages in the very early days of singlehanded circumnavigations by sailing round the world against the prevailing winds and currents. He took line honours in the very first round the world race with a boat not named after a commercial concern but called *Great Britain II* and, with his crew of paratroopers, showed that his leadership could make non-sailors into seamen in a short space of time. He went on to an illustrious career: racing and setting records; and then created a race in which ordinary men and women could share the experience of taking on the oceans of the world, with all the challenge and the personal development which that entails. While we were in Boston, this record of outstanding achievement was rewarded, and Chay received a knighthood. Of course, it can be quite funny when someone you know is honoured in this way and much fun was had at the crew party as various new forms of address were tried out.

The other notably public event in Boston was that Mark Lodge, skipper of *Motorola*, and a graduate of Sir Chay's round the world school of yachting, married his long-standing girlfriend Michelle. It would be difficult to imagine a more popular couple than Mark and Michelle, and it would be impossible to imagine a group of people more willing to celebrate a great occasion in style than the crews of the BT Global Challenge, so it would be fair to say that this was another day on which a good time was had by all.

The real Holy Grail of my first trip to the States was still calling me – a visit to the ball game. Most of our *Toshiba* crew had watched a game on the night I took Pam back to the airport. Their verdict was that next time they would spend the evening watching paint dry – it would be more interesting. Perhaps, I ventured to suggest, they had not really understood what was going on. Oh, no, no problem there, they had had expert guidance in the game, not only from Drew but from another home town supporter. The subsequent discussion confirmed my suspicions. Not only had one or two rather fundamental points been overlooked, but so had the very essence of the game. Baseball is essentially a 'mano a mano' combat between the pitcher and the batter – the rest of it is all secondary to that duel of egos. I fell in love with baseball when I was nine years old, inspired by pictures in an American encyclopedia. No-one in Britain had the faintest idea what I was talking about, and I still regard my finest feat of leadership as the time I managed to put together a team of 13-year-old cricketers, footballers and rugby players to go out and 'play ball'. We only lasted one game, but I could barely believe I had carried them with me that far.

Fenway Park, home of the Boston Red Sox, is only a few stops from the centre of town on the T, and on the platform I met two *3-Com* crew members, Kath and Alan. The Challenge was a bit like that, you were always bumping into new friends. When we stepped out at street level again it was into the most torrential downpour. On the basis that we would dry out eventually, we took seats under cover and settled down. The game was delayed by the rain but eventually, after several futile attempts, the covers were rolled back. 'Ladies and gentlemen, Mr John Kelly will sing the national anthem,' said the announcer, and a young black man in an open necked shirt walked out on to the pitch carrying a hand-held microphone. He hit *The Star Spangled Banner* without accompaniment, but with obvious relish, and a great deal of soul. We had been treated to a few trills and adornments on the way, but when he got to 'the home of the brave', and held on to it in a manner worthy of Otis Redding or James Brown, the crowd went wild. We had about a minute of cheering, yelling, whistling and applause before things quietened down enough for him to sing, 'and the land of the free'. You can't do that with *God Save the Queen*, more's the pity. It was tremendously moving and a hugely enjoyable performance in its own right. The game was fantastic, and the Red Sox won; my night was complete.

There was more to come. On the last weekend before we left, I took a flight to New Jersey to visit one of my old guitar students. Since Stewart was only ten, visiting was a family affair with Stewart's parents, Frank and Monique Hendricks and his brother Adam. Even though Boston had been tremendous fun, a family weekend came as the most wonderful treat. Basketball in the yard, evening barbeques, bagels for breakfast, Stewart's new guitar, Adam playing the piano; it would all have been wonderful if they had not taken me to New York, but they did. I had not intended to go; you see, neither Pam nor I had been to New York and we were going to go together sometime; but when your friends invite you ...

Back in Boston I had one last job to do, to send home some of my increasing souvenir mountain. You could miss the post office in Post Office Square because you might not expect it to be a vast, imposing, stone-clad building that rises up to surmount its doorways with huge columns and goes on upwards, producing an edifice which would please any captain of industry. Nor, necessarily, would you expect it to occupy the whole of one side of a large square, even when that square is called Post Office Square. Nor might you expect a full blown security check after you pass through the outer revolving door. But this is not only the post office, it is also the court room. So as you proceed you may have cause to wonder whether the marble steps have been worn down into hollow scoops by generations of eager correspondents, or by fugitives from justice and attorneys at law. The US Marshals' '15 Most Wanted Fugitives' are in fact displayed on the wall, wild west style, on 'Wanted' posters with descriptions and photographs. Most are considered 'likely to be armed and dangerous', nearly all are or have been involved in narcotics. My pick of the bunch was a drug dealer called Hemp (although the joke seemed lost on the Marshals) who was wanted for 'continuing criminal enterprise'. I have often thought that many criminals show considerable enterprise, and that if they put the same effort into a legitimate career as a criminal one they would do very well.

Just before we left for our final all-out race back to England, the Boston Globe revealed a tale of great skullduggery. It seemed that the FBI informer who had helped jail a number of local Mafiosi a little while ago had been set up by two other local hoodlums, themselves FBI informers, to take out their opposition. Everyone involved in the case had an appropriate name: there was Stephen 'The Rifleman' Flemmi and his partner James J 'Whitey' Bulger, leaders of the Winter Hill Gang. Angelo 'Sonny' Mercurio was the informant they co-opted, and the reputed Mafia boss jailed along with various supposed henchmen was Francis P Salemme – 'Cadillac Frank'. So it's not like that any more, it is just that we all know each other.

13

I Know a Man Who's Rowed It!

'There must be a beginning of any great matter but the continuing on unto the end until it be thoroughly finished yields the true glory.' Sir Francis Drake

'Here's tae us, wha's like us? Guy few, an' they're a' deid!' Traditional

For most of us, sailing across the Atlantic would qualify as a fairly major experience. Indeed, Simon pointed out to us in our final briefing that it was not many years since he had set out on the adventure of his life, to do just that. Yet without taking it lightly, leg six was being referred to as 'a short sprint' even before Sir Chay said, 'This is nothing to you lot, I know a man who's rowed it, for God's sake!' What struck all of us was the ease with which we could say, 'We're only going to be out there two weeks, I won't need this,' as another piece of kit was put aside.

Mark, Geoff, Ben and I packed up our things together with No 1 *Toshiba* supporter and veteran of the Hobart to Cape Town leg in the British Steel Challenge, Roger Peek. Roger had been sending us a set of cards with stunning photographs and inspirational messages to keep us focused as the race progressed, now we had the man himself signed up to the starboard watch for the last leg. Always keen, and with a terrific sense of humour, it was great to have him with us in the flesh, having had him with us in the spirit all the way round. His nickname from the first race, 'Sexual', was rapidly changed to 'Past his' (spelled 'Pastis') by the Tosh Blondes!

Taking up cudgels for the port side was Jack Goldie. Jack is a game-keeper, a water bailiff, a martial arts expert and oriental philosopher.

He has been shot twice in the course of his work and stabbed more times than he can remember. He also knows more ways to disable a man than you or I have had hot dinners. I resolved not to fall out with him. Jack was brought up in a tough part of Scotland and had the misfortune, under those circumstances, to be a wee fellow. He responded to adversity, and to being bullied, by learning how to look after himself, and mastery of a number of martial arts took him into eastern languages and culture. He was the only one of the Wave Warriors who could speak Japanese! A fisherman among other things, Jack held more superstitions than most of us. He was very concerned that the Challenge Business changes the names of its yachts on a whim (or at least on the offer of a new sponsor), and chided me gently from time to time for whistling on board. Migraine headaches had the better of him once or twice during the leg, but he battled through and worked hard.

The final leg! It was hot and sunny in Boston, and with a jazz band playing and huge numbers of well-wishers crowding the quays and pontoons it was all rather reminiscent of Cape Town. Father Paul of the church of Our Lady of Good Voyages (!) performed a blessing for the fleet, and *Group 4* gave us three very rousing cheers as we slipped our moorings alongside them. There was very little wind as we motored out to the start line and discussed our tactics, but what there was meant a downwind start – head to the line and up with the kite – always an exciting prospect, and never more so than with very little wind and 14 large boats in a confined space. Who would be a skipper?

The start itself was absolutely frantic – all the boats were on top of each other, all going very slowly, the air thick with yells: 'Gybe! No, don't gybe! Pole forwards! No – that pole!' On and on it went. It became an hour of the most intense and frenetic sailing we had ever done, all the way down the harbour, gybing this way and that. We were about twelfth going over the line; at one point we were practically in the lead, five minutes later at the back again. There would be a gust here and a hole there, and yachts would come flying by with spinnakers pulling hard while others only yards away sat with flapping sails and collapsed kites. *Rover* got very close to the wall at one point, there were lots of cries of 'Starboard!' and 'Mast abeam!' and when the dust settled we were doing quite well. We were so close to *CU* at one point that we could have shaken hands with Syd on their bow, but at a crucial moment we pulled a 'John O'Driscoll' on them – we simply swung the boom across, gybing the main and putting ourselves on to the starboard gybe with rights of way over them! At more than one point we witnessed two yachts running parallel, side by side, on opposite gybes. The first race poll at 5 pm local time put us second to *Save the Children*, with *3-Com* third and all of us on the same 'distance to finish'!

As if to celebrate we saw a whale blow, hump his back, sound, and flip up his flukes for us just astern. Later on I saw the best dolphin leap I have ever witnessed – a glorious flight clean out of the water in a huge flashing silver arc.

The fleet started to split, some boats heading straight for the way-point, some, including *Toshiba*, heading south – a tactical move which meant going slightly further and thereby dropping some places, in search of better currents. Interestingly this group included *Group 4*, *Save the Children*, *Concert* and *Motorola*, all the top boats. So we enjoyed a fabulous first day, with fresh food to boot: cold roast chicken, potatoes and coleslaw.

The fog was not long in coming. The Grand Banks are notorious for it and although our route had been set, by means of a waypoint, to keep us south of the banks and below the ice line, that made no difference to the fog, or to the ice come to that! The day we left, the ice report had bergs south of our waypoint. It goes without saying that fog and icebergs are not a good combination for any sort of boat, and if we needed reminding Spike pointed out that we passed very near to where the *Titanic* had sunk!

Things became complicated tactically as we raced through the fog. We were going for boat speed and found ourselves passing through the fleet, which seemed like a good idea at the time. When we finally reviewed the night's work, however, it didn't seem so clever. We had gone from being the most southerly boat to the most northerly, and had run out of wind. One compensation was that with the north-south spread being only about twelve miles, everyone was in much the same weather; another was a beautiful red sunset over a flat calm oily sea, reflecting pinks and purples everywhere. We found a knot or two of boat speed and ghosted on, *Motorola* in sight behind, *Nuke* ahead. *3-Com* led the field.

More whales! First we saw one spouting off to port; it obligingly arched its back and flicked its flukes for us, then Simon spotted one spouting ahead and coming straight for us. It was fine on the port bow and crossed just ahead of us to swim so closely along the starboard side that we could have stepped off and on to its back. Moving past the stern he pushed the whole of his head up out of the water, then arched his back and went on his way. When later another spouted off to starboard, enabling me to achieve a life-long ambition by shouting, authentically, 'Thar she blows!' Whales were followed by dolphin and tuna leaping about and we even managed a solitary flying fish, so Jack managed all his wildlife sightings in one day.

The following night, ghosting along on glassy seas in fog and very wet, cold air, we saw a large blip on the radar dead ahead. Visibility was about fifty yards. We had just about convinced ourselves that it must be an iceberg when we made out the glimmerings of a light. The fog cleared a little and a very large ship came across us from right to left, made a very sharp turn to port and steered between ourselves and *Courtaulds*, who were off on our port side, before disappearing into the night. It was a little too close for comfort really.

Our great cheerfulness, and we had been in very good spirits as a crew, was tempered a little by being stuck in the longest patch of light airs we had experienced during the entire race. As for me, I had 'channel fever' anyway; I was dying to get home and see Pam. Kobus rescued a bird which had flown into the mainsail and, against much opposition, determinedly made a place for it to rest overnight, saying he would release it in the morning. He didn't escape a good ribbing about the 10 000 chickens slaughtered every day on his farm, but it was hard to say much the following morning when his rescued bird took to the wing again and flew off.

The wildlife display continued, as it was to do until we reached the coast of Cornwall. We had more whales, we saw dolphins every day and, biggest surprise of all, a lone turtle which came swimming by one day looking completely ridiculous and quite improbable, but there he was. All of this made our diligent trimming and helming easier to bear and we were finally rewarded when, for the first time since Tasmania, we took the lead, albeit temporarily. Sunny days gave way to grey, and with the rain coming down and the wind coming up, the North Atlantic began to take on the air of the Southern Ocean.

Infuriatingly I had started to feel unwell again, in spite of a thorough medical check-up in Boston. It transpired that the doctor Jo had seen suggested that we might have a particular bug which does not readily show up in tests, so we were on a course of treatment for that. My feelings were improved, however, by messages from home. Pam, having sent the first message we had received on board for this leg, was definitely in my good books, and there was good news from Mother as well. All I needed was a satmail from Joe, the dog, and life would have been complete. Kobus asked me the longitude of Britain and when I said 'zero' he didn't believe me! In fairness, he meant Land's End, or the Scilly Isles, but I still had to bring Simon in to persuade him that they are both 'a bit west of zero'.

As we closed in on the waypoint with *3-Com* leading *Group 4*, *Nuke*, and then us, it became a beat into the rain and fog. As the wind freed us, we headed more directly into the waves, making the pitching and pounding worse, and Jack, who suffers from migraines, was feeling far from well. *3-Com* had apparently utilised Bob Rice's weather information for the first time, and looked as though they were making better use of it than we were. There were mutterings in the cockpit: 'Our trouble is that we won't stick to a long term plan if it looks bad in the short term.' Was that a valid criticism? I don't know. My only thought was that nobody seemed any happier when we did take a loss in order to play a tactical game. Who would be a skipper?

In the end the wind freed us enough to get a kite up before rounding the waypoint. We squeaked by with 19 seconds of longitude and 9 seconds of latitude to spare – well, why go out of your way? Running downwind with the race spinnaker up at 10 knots made 1800 miles to go to the Scillies look very reasonable indeed.

'Arise and shine, for a new day is born,' runs the old hymn. In our case this meant that the black disorientating fog of night turned into dark grey fog, and then finally became an impenetrable light grey fog. RHQ's weather forecast, issued every day to all yachts, rather remarkably included some advice: 'You need to head north as quickly as possible to find the strongest winds at around 51 degrees north.' They had decided to weather-route the fleet in an effort to get us all to Southampton in time for the end of race party!

Jo was outraged. 'We paid $600 for that information,' she fumed, 'It makes a mockery of the whole race.' Others were more sanguine, and the divergence of opinion led to a discussion about the importance of winning. Jo's comment that 'I'm a very competitive person,' did not seem to be an answer, but 'It makes me feel good,' did. Jo also said that she, like Guy, hadn't had a goal to sail round the world, and that she would have got off the boat in Rio had we not been doing well. Geoff pointed out that since we had no control over who our skipper would be, or our crew mates, any of us might have ended up on *Group 4*; or on *Heath* or *Courtaulds*, who were the back markers, come to that. I bet Jo that we would finish the leg first or second.

Everybody settled into the watch system and the routine of being back at sea almost immediately on this leg. I was certainly there from the word go, but there was one disadvantage to this. It seemed as though we had been at sea for a week or more, when in reality it had only been a few days. By the time a week really had gone by I was beginning to feel like blues singer Willie Brown, who sang: 'The minutes seem like hours, the hours seem like days.'

We passed an 'Open 60' from Nova Scotia bound for Copenhagen. They had no SSB radio, they told us, a broken batten in the mainsail, and no spinnakers left, but since it was a delivery trip they were plugging on. The boat had been a would-be entry in the Vendée Globe challenge, but had sunk on its way to the start and had been worked on ever since. It sounded as though it might need a little more work. Our SSB radio was working. You could tell that by the ecstatic grin on Simon's face as *The Archers* theme tune rum-ti-tummed its way around the boat. Almost home, back to Lou and the children for Simon; Pam, Mum and Joe the dog for me, not to mention Sunday lunch, walks in the park, English beer ...

In keeping with the spirit of things the sun came out. I had begun to think I was suffering from some form of Seasonal Affective Disorder, it is remarkable how depressing no sunlight can be. There is an old Zen saying: 'Mount Fuji, good in fine weather, good in the rain,' but it is nice to have some of each.

We had another whale come right up to us. He came in at about 60 degrees to our course, looking as though he was going to ram us amidships, and then dived under our stern. He was so close we thought he might have done us a favour by scraping some barnacles off with his fin. The race situation looked slightly familiar: *Group 4* leading, *Tosh* second. Chris Tibbs was interviewed over the radio from *Concert* and said that he had no idea before the start that there would be such intense, concentrated racing all the time – this from a man who had completed two Whitbread races!

We watched a superb sunset; after the sun dipped below the horizon, a great arc of about 60 degrees was still lit by a huge swathe of orange and red, while over it the thinnest sliver of a crescent moon turned its back on a single bright white spot – Jupiter. As if that were not enough, the following morning was one of those when I was forced to agree with Spike (I usually argued vehemently about this) that one should 'Rise early, for the hours between dawn and sunrise are the most beautiful of the day'. 'In the desert, where that saying comes from, maybe,' I used to say to him, 'but not in Richmond.' On this day, though, it was true at sea. Fabulous red skies gradually turned into blue, showing almost every type of cloud in the weather book. What was more, we were enjoying some brilliant downwind sailing in 20–25 knots of wind with boat speeds of 10 or 12 knots.

July 9 was Kiki's birthday, and one of the great days in round the world yachting – it was the day we had 'Blighty' back on the chart. Within ten minutes a small arrow pointing somewhere in the region of Pontefract was marked 'Geoff lives here'. It was followed, inevitably, by everything up to and including 'Uncle Tom Cobley and all' somewhere in the region of Widecombe. A xenophobic demography of Europe soon followed, and that brought out some serious jingoism headed by Ben (Lt-Cmdr Pearson) who noted '*Bismarck* torpedoed and sunk by gallant British Navy.' Trafalgar was soon marked up as 'Site of another damn good thrashing!' and on it went. I was more taken with nostalgia for the Bishop Rock, the Wolf Rock and the good old Eddystone Light, all the familiar landmarks of our training sails, from what seemed like a long time ago. What a wonderful feeling it was, just to see those names on the chart as we raced back towards the toe of England; to think back to those training sails, of all the lessons we had learned and put to use, and most of all to think that we had very nearly done it. Four years of my life had been taken up with the dream of racing round the world, and we were within a week of achieving that goal.

Geoff said he was fed up, he wanted to go round again. Kobus, like me, was wishing the days away, no doubt wanting to be with Debbie in Southampton. Woolly was sad it was coming to an end, and Kiki said she didn't know quite how she felt but was sure she would be very emotional!

With under 1000 miles to go the leg looked very like a microcosm of the race itself. *Group 4* led, we were second at 11 miles, carrying a reasonable margin of about 40 miles over *Concert* and 90 over *Save the Children*. A well established second, but could we catch *Group 4*? In many ways this leg contained for me our most disappointing racing experience. A few days earlier we had duelled with *Group 4* on level terms. They had come up to us, passed astern and sat above us to port about a quarter of a mile away. We gybed, they gybed, and managed to sail over us and get ahead. Having held their race spinnaker up in about 24 knots of wind (its stated top limit is not much above 20), they had peeled to their flanker. Now, in an effort to capitalise, they went back to their race kite; we gained on them as they changed it. A short while later they either decided it was not in fact faster, or that discretion was the better part of valour, and went back to the flanker. We gained once more until this time we were alongside, and there we raced right through one afternoon and on into the night. By the changeover for the second night watch, however, they were ahead by a hundred yards or so. At the end of that watch, four hours later, it was two hundred, and over the next eight hours they crept inexorably away. It is an old maxim of yacht racing that the rich get richer. They had stretched their lead to perhaps a mile when they picked up the edge of a cloud, with its associated localised wind effect and, as so often happens, the 'elastic' holding us to them finally snapped. We were never so close again.

The weather continued to play a decisive role as a secondary low pressure system began to affect things. 'By dint of brilliant strategy, careful planning and the fruits of my experience,' said Simon, with eyes and eyebrows raised, 'we are in the bit between the high pressure to the north and the low to the south, and have wind where others do not.' It must be said that we had planned to be there, and we had worked for it. It was just that when we made the plan the weather patterns had been predicted rather differently. The Atlantic settled down to seven- or eight-eighths cloud cover and looked much more as we had expected it to, though we had one squall which went up to about 35 knots and made things look rather like a quiet day in the Southern Ocean; it was quite nostalgic in a strange sort of way. Forty-eight hours later, on Geoff's birthday, with enough weather information coming in to sink a battleship, we found ourselves in a hole in the wind! Was it shown on any of our myriad weather faxes? Was it ever. Instant dejection followed, split roughly half and half between those bothered about the arrival time, and those upset about the possibility of being overtaken. Our misery was compounded by a message from RHQ saying: 'You are only doing two knots on the 12.00 poll, is everything all right?'

As we finally made it back into our old stamping ground we could have been on a training sail, and a pleasant summer one at that, making eight or nine knots under spinnaker on flat seas with the moon just visible on an otherwise overcast night. No magic, just another ordinary night at sea. As if for old time's sake we blew the race spinnaker just before we got to Land's End, so up went our poor battered promo. The 'TOSHIBA' logo had become rather flat-bottomed and actually read 'TOSHIB-DELTA', the legs of the 'A' having been lost so that we had a triangular Greek letter delta at the end, but it still flew! I sent a message to John Burnie to come and share the champagne and we headed on down for the Needles. We came up the Channel in fog again, with the weather all coming in from the west and the tides to deal with as well, and spent a lot of time metaphorically looking over our shoulders for *Concert* behind us. Given that they were about 12 or 13 miles behind, it did seem like a rather bad case of the jitters, when someone excitedly reported that they could see a yacht with a spinnaker up behind us. It turned out to be Her Majesty's Frigate *Edinburgh* manoeuvring in the distance, but it served to keep us on our toes.

We were beginning to wonder whether we would see anything

before the Needles when, after nine months away and 30 000 miles at sea, we sighted Anvil Point light. It might have been an emotional moment but there was too much of a party atmosphere for that. We passed the lights of Bournemouth with the Needles light squarely ahead and the ebb tide running against us. For all that, we had an uneventful passage through the Needles channel and an enjoyable night sail up the Solent. Round Calshot Spit buoy and into Southampton water the RNLI were first out to greet us (apart from the anonymous fan who blew a hooter for us as we passed Hurst Point – which was very much appreciated) followed a few minutes later by a gathering flotilla of support vessels. Friends, families, all our friends from Toshiba – more and more boats kept appearing through the gloom, but they were all outdone by St Lucia's school, otherwise known as the Ben Pearson fan club. Their allegiance to *Toshiba* was so great that they had a side show at their school fete called 'Sink *Group 4*'! They rent the night air chanting in unison, shouting and waving, it was a fantastic reception.

Then the great moment; we had practised it, in fact we used to rehearse it at the end of our Southampton-based training sails, we had imagined it, we had dreamed about it. The gun went off – we had finished. Of course in our practice and our dreams we had always finished first. When it came to it we had to be content with second place, but we had been beaten fair and square by a crew which had consistently sailed faster whatever the conditions. We all had good friends on board *Group 4*, so there were certainly no hard feelings to spoil the celebrations. Sails down, we motored in to a rapturous reception in Ocean Village. Four o'clock in the morning it may have been but that did not stop a great crowd being there to greet us. I suppose each of us had our own feelings in those last few moments. Certainly most of us had eyes only for certain people. For me, Pam was right at the front of the pontoon, wearing a jacket I had bought for her in Cape Town. Mum was right behind her, having stayed up all night for the first time in her life! Pete and Jackie were there, and the rest of the crowd was a blur.

How was it to be back? Fantastic!

BT had laid on a barbeque which ran through the night and on through the next day as yachts continued to arrive. *Concert* followed us in, adding another to the string of great performances which perhaps went some way to make up for that terrible day on leg 2 when their chances had gone over the side along with their mast. Next came *Save the Children* and another reunion for me. I had worked together with Di Garside in a previous existence, and the first that either of us knew about the other taking part in the Challenge had been when I wrote to Di asking her to sponsor me. Her telephone reply of, 'I'm doing it too,' had come as something of a surprise. Di had actually sailed round the world before but her comment on that had been, 'Well, I didn't really do anything that time, Alan; Mike sailed the boat and I cooked and looked after the kids!' Di and I had shared our big adventure round the world, and now she was off to help Mike prepare for his solo circumnavigation in the 'Around Alone' race. You can't keep some people down!

Toshiba took us all to dinner on what turned out to be a very emotional evening. John Hill, whose superb backup and heartfelt enthusiasm for the project (and for us all as individuals) had been an inspiration to us, made a fantastic speech welcoming us back. John Farnhill of the RNLI brought with him the news that Toshiba's campaign to fund a new lifeboat had been so successful that the RNLI would not only be able to commission a new Atlantic class lifeboat, but would have enough left over to sponsor and pay for two training units for a year. Finally Simon rose to his feet to say a few words on behalf of himself and the crew. Normally an articulate and highly entertaining speaker, he was completely overcome by the moment. Struggling with a flood of overwhelming feelings he finally managed to choke out what we all felt about Toshiba as a sponsor. He told us, 'All I ever heard from John was: "You're doing great. Do you need anything? Come back safely."' By this time we were all either in tears or swallowing them back hard. There was only one thing to do – we had a party.

As Richard Slogrove, Director of Marketing for BT, had reminded us in every port of call, 'We do know how to organise a party.' We were superbly treated throughout the entire race by our title holding sponsor, and the crew parties BT put on for us were at least as memorable as the Southern Ocean. In Southampton they outdid themselves. Aerobatic displays, skydivers, fireworks, live bands, food and drink; it wasn't Rio, but it had a carnival atmosphere as great as anywhere we had been. That's because it's the people who make a good party and all the right people were there. Notably Sir Chay, of course, whose announcement at the prizegiving earlier in the day – 'If you want to get any sense out of me, talk to me now, because the party starts at eight o'clock and I'm going to get p----d!' – was a model of leadership from the front. It was a great extravaganza to end a great adventure.

14

Holding for the Void

'*Round the world! There is much in that sound to inspire proud feelings; but whereto does all this circumnavigation conduct? Only through numberless perils to the very point where those that we left behind secure, were all the time before us.*' Herman Melville

'*To be what we are and to become what we are capable of is the only end in life.*' Robert Louis Stevenson

Whereto does all this circumnavigation conduct? For some of us I think it has enabled us to be what we are. The palm, of course, must go to the crew of *Time & Tide* for what is surely one of the most extraordinary feats of human endeavour in any field. What of the 'Wave Warriors', though? Simon, re-unuited with his family, is thinking about a secure financial footing for his children, but still has a list of adventures as long as his arm to complete (and some of us are hoping to be invited along!). Is Ben off to private practice in dentistry, or to the Antarctic? Will Woolly settle down and grow lilacs, or will she cook her way around the world on a maxi yacht? Guy and Justin are back in the City, Mike Hutt is running his business, but he has plans ... For Roger, Jack and Haydon the end of their legs signified a return to business as usual; for Arnie, Chris and Ange perhaps a doorway to something new. Holly and her husband Derek can compare their different experiences, while Di's husband Tony is thinking about the next race, and Judy looks wistful whenever the crew are together. Mark is back with his family, growing more trees ('That's the thing about trees,' he told us, 'they just ... grow') and Kobus, after an English holiday in the West Country, is back running his farm with Debbie. Geoff was offered a job by the Challenge Business but, keeping his options open, has returned, for the time being, to his native Yorkshire. Jo has returned to the bank, at least in the short term, and Kiki is off to study facio-maxilliary surgery. Drew is staying aboard *Toshiba* for the summer corporate season, before packing his camera and heading back to Rhode Island, while Spike ('It's a problem that I like sailing so much, because I like doctoring too') is back saving lives, but *may* be available for another round the world race soon! Michael Buerk was interviewed shortly after getting back and confessed to a certain nostalgia for his life in the war zones. Whether that included the foredeck of the *Wave Warrior* he did not say.

Six months earlier as we came in to Sydney Harbour, half way round the world, someone had remarked, 'Imagine what it will be like coming in to Southampton – all this and a thousand other boats around' (needless to say – it was not like that!). Kiki remarked 'Sad day that'll be,' and I asked, 'Why?' 'Nineteen grand blown,' she replied, 'and that'll be it.' We were laughing, but it made me think about getting back, and I had already done quite a lot of thinking about it. It had occurred to me that for people going back to office jobs and the like, there would be plenty of bustle and business, not to mention people wanting to talk about the race, to make up for the loss of the personal contact and relationships that the Challenge engenders. By contrast my previously acceptable, but rather solitary, life began to look a little lonely as a return prospect.

In fact getting back was not like that at all. I had a continual stream of friends, well-wishers and supporters to welcome me home over the next few weeks; and in many ways, Pete Goss, with his injunction to 'share the race with those that are *not* going', was once again the man I had to thank. My efforts to raise sponsorship and to keep those who were supporting me in touch with what was going on were rewarded a thousand fold in the interest and the kindness I received when I returned. That injunction to share the race also brought me another huge reward. When I came home, thanks to Gavia Wilkinson-Cox, who had forwarded each of my newsletters as she received them to Janet Murphy at Adlard Coles Nautical, I had a book to write.

After that, who knows? Chay has often remarked that most people come out of their 'ordinary' lives to compete in the Challenge, do it, and then go back to their previous way of life. But my previous way of life was a succession of new beginnings; in fact I have become rather good at them. So much so that, although I knew it was important to hold a clear vision of what I wanted after the race, I did not want to formulate a plan so precise that it would shut out other possibilities. I wanted to create a vision of my life as it pleased me to live it, while leaving space in that vision for whatever might come along. I called this process 'holding for the void', and I used some of my race experiences to help me do it. I shall travel and I shall write, but some of what I have seen already I will not forget.

Two of my most vivid memories of the entire adventure are of the night sky near the equator, with its panoply of glowing stars covering the whole of the velvet black night sky, and of the Southern Ocean in a big blow, all huge waves and crashing water, flying spray and leaden grey skies. And what, I asked myself, do these represent of the inner journey? Clarity, came back the answer for the equatorial sky. Clarity of vision, clarity of purpose, and a sense of wonder and awe that things can be thus. And the Southern Ocean? Exultation in the face of fear. The sheer untrammelled joy of being alive in all that, of being open to such a wild experience of nature, of being and acting straight from oneself, freed of the chains of self doubt, just *there*. Rabbi Zusya said: 'In the world to come they will not ask me, "Why were you not Moses?" but "Why were you not Zusya?"' Besides, I have always liked the advice reputedly given to certain young American Indians facing their initiation ceremony: 'As you go the way of life you will see a great chasm. Jump. It is not as wide as you think.'

APPENDIX I

The Challenge Class One Design – Yacht Specifications

Rig:	Bermudian cutter
LOA:	67ft (20.42m)
LWL:	55ft (17.76m)
Beam:	17ft 3in (5.26m)
Draught:	9ft 6in (2.82m)
Displacement:	37 tons at half load
Ballast:	12 tons
Sail area:	1,932sq ft (179.49m^2)
Mast & spars:	Atlantic Spars Ltd
Winches:	Harken USA (2 x 32 CSTs, 2 x 53 CSTs, 7 x 56 CSTs, 2 x 66 CSTs)
Deck gear:	Atlantic Spars Ltd & Lewmar Marine Ltd
Rigging screws & terminals:	Sta-Lok Terminals Ltd
Standing rigging:	Dyform & 1 x 19 stainless steel wire
Running rigging:	Liros polyester & Dyneema sheets & guys; Liros polyester & 7 x 19 wire halyards and Dyneema spinnaker halyards
Engine:	130hp Perkins 130C
Generator:	27hp Perkins 100 series
Fuel:	385 gallons
Water:	242 gallons
Water maker:	Aquafresh 800ED
Heating:	2 x Eberspacher D3LC
Hull construction:	50B steel
Deck:	316 stainless steel
Concept designer:	David Thomas
Working drawings:	Thanos Condylis (C & S Yacht Designs)
Builder:	Devonport Management Ltd

Accommodation
14 x Berths (in 6 cabins)
2 x Heads & showers
1 x Saloon

1 x Galley (including 4 burner gas hob and oven)
1 x Drying/oilskin room
1 x Chartroom/deckhouse
1 x Sailroom

Sail inventory
Mainsail, Genoa, No 1 Yankee, No 2 Yankee, No 3 Yankee, Staysail, Storm Staysail, Storm Trysail, Spinnakers.

Navigation & communication equipment
Brookes & Gatehouse Hydra System
2 x Magnavox MX100 GPS
1 x Thrane & Thrane Inmarsat Standard C
1 x Skanti 300 VHF radio
1 x Skanti TRP 8400 long range HF radio
1 x Raytheon 40XX radar
1 x Heart Interface Link 200 battery monitoring system

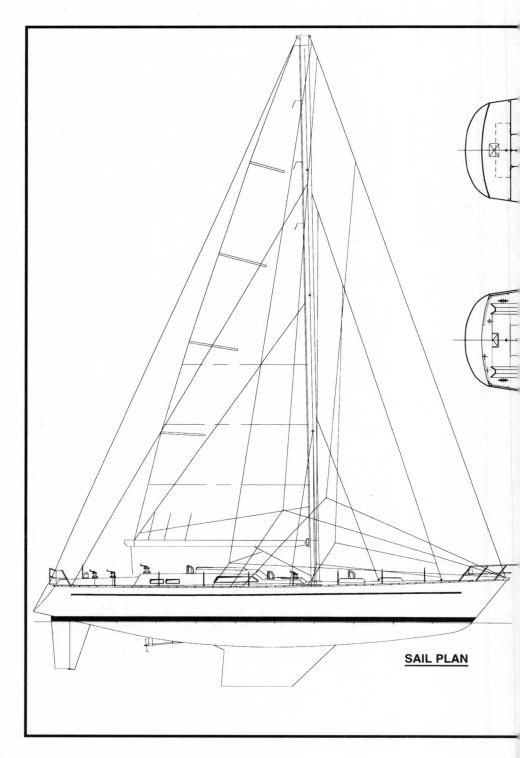

SAIL PLAN

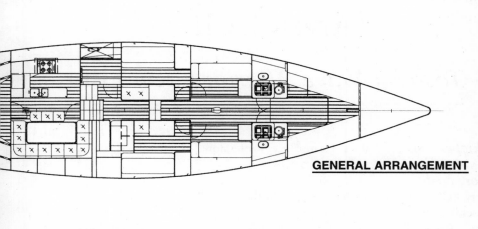

GENERAL ARRANGEMENT

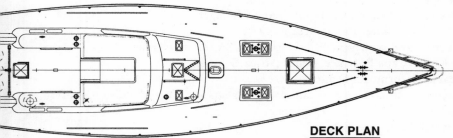

DECK PLAN

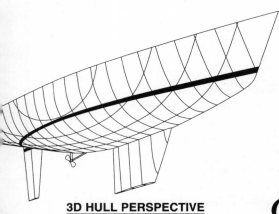

3D HULL PERSPECTIVE

BT

Global Challenge

thanos Condylis
C & S yacht designs
Naval Architects. Yacht Designers.Consultants
Shamrock Quay,Williams Street Tel: (0703) 639919
Southampton,SO1 1QL,England   Fax: (0703) 336377

APPENDIX II

Toshiba Wave Warrior Crew List

Skipper   **Simon Walker** Hampshire. Professional skipper.

Core crew
Guy Bell London. Financial analyst in the City. (We all think Guy is a stockbroker, but he says he's not!)
Spike Briggs Hampshire. Hospital doctor.
Jo Dawson Hampshire. Corporate Bank Manager.
Mark Earle Cheshire. Runs a tree nursery.
Drew Fernandez Newport, Rhode Island, USA. Photographer.
Kobus Kotze Cape Province, South Africa. Farmer.
Ben Pearson Cornwall. Dentist.
Ciara Scott Bristol. Dentist. (Ciara was still a student when the race began.)
Alan Sears Middlesex. Guitar teacher.
Geoff Ward Yorkshire. Salesman.
Joe Watson London. Accountant.

Leggers
Michael Buerk Surrey. Television journalist and newsreader.
Judy Crick London. Marine underwriter.
Holly Day Surrey. Chartered building surveyor and builder.
Haydon Edwards Northumberland. Runs a heating business.
Chris Gaskin Merseyside. Science teacher (although I do not believe Chris has ever actually worked as a teacher!).
Jack Goldie Ayrshire. Water bailiff and game keeper.
Di Hemming Avon. Admin Manager.
Justin Hodges London. Works in corporate banking in the City.
Mike Hutt Hampshire. Runs an electrical business.
Ange Morris Devon. Outdoor pursuits instructor.
Roger Peek West Sussex. MD, Iron Trades Insurance Co Ltd.
Keith ('Arnie') Watson Tyneside. Financial analyst in the City.

With the exception of Ciara and Chris, as noted above, this is what everyone was more or less doing when the race started; it is not necessarily what everyone is doing now!

APPENDIX III

Race Results

LEG 1 – Southampton to Rio de Janeiro

Start   Sunday 29 September 1996   Local time: 1205   5000 miles

Placing	Yacht	Arrival time (GMT)	Leg time D H M S	Penalty/redress +/- DD:HH:MM
01	Group 4 (01)	25 Oct 14:52:15	26 03 47 15	–
02	Toshiba Wave Warrior (02)	25 Oct 17:01:11	26 05 56 11	–
03	Concert (03)	26 Oct 01:57:23	26 14 52 23	–
04	Save the Children (04)	26 Oct 09:10:39	26 22 05 39	–
05	Commercial Union (05)	26 Oct 18:03:49	27 06 58 49	–
06	3-Com (06)	26 Oct 20:39:38	27 09 34 38	–
07	Motorola (07)	27 Oct 01:35:55	27 14 30 55	–
08	Heath Insured II (08)	27 Oct 03:37:03	27 16 32 03	–
09	Ocean Rover (09)	27 Oct 05:34:48	27 18 29 48	–
10	Nuclear Electric (10)	27 Oct 07:35:15	27 20 30 15	–
11	Global Teamwork (11)	28 Oct 06:48:23	28 19 43 23	–
12	Pause to Remember (12)	28 Oct 21:41:10	29 10 36 10	–
13	Courtaulds International (13)	29 Oct 08:19:58	29 21 14 58	–
14	Time & Tide (14)	29 Oct 10:45:33	29 23 40 33	–

LEG 2 – Rio de Janeiro to Wellington

Restart   Wednesday 20 November 1996   Local time: 1500   6600 miles

Placing	Yacht	Arrival time (GMT)	Leg time D H M S	Penalty/redress +/- DD:HH:MM
01	Group 4 (01)	30 Dec 00:16:30	39 07 16 30	–
02	Save the Children (03)	30 Dec 03:08:13	39 10 08 13	–
03	Motorola (04)	30 Dec 23:06:08	39 21 07 08	–00:08:59
04	Toshiba Wave Warrior (02)	30 Dec 14:27:23	39 21 27 23	–
05	Global Teamwork (07)	31 Dec 08:05:24	40 15 05 24	–
06	Commercial Union (05)	31 Dec 08:15:32	40 15 15 32	–
07	Pause to Remember (10)	31 Dec 13:23:30	40 20 23 30	–
08	Nuclear Electric (06)	31 Dec 20:50:37	41 03 55 37	+00:00:05
09	Ocean Rover (09)	01 Jan 16:05:12	41 23 05 12	–
10	Time & Tide (12)	02 Jan 06:16:18	42 06 42 18	–00:06:34
11	3-Com (08)	02 Jan 05:46:43	42 07 42 43	–00:05:04
12	Courtaulds International (13)	02 Jan 06:49:56	42 11 54 56	–00:01:55
13	Heath Insured II (11)	03 Jan 16:29:06	43 23 29 06	–
14	Concert (14)	10 Jan 06:48:00	50 13 48 00	–

LEG 3 – Wellington to Sydney

Restart   Sunday 9 February 1997   Local time: 1300   1230 miles

Placing	Yacht	Arrival time (GMT)	Leg time D H M S	Penalty/redress +/- DD:HH:MM
01	Save the Children (03)	16 Feb 07:32:58	07 07 32 58	–
02	Group 4 (01)	16 Feb 09:50:44	07 09 50 44	–
03	Courtaulds International (13)	16 Feb 10:51:45	07 10 51 45	–
04	Global Teamwork (07)	16 Feb 11:05:03	07 11 05 03	–
05	Pause to Remember (10)	16 Feb 11:17:41	07 11 17 41	–
06	Concert (14)	16 Feb 11:18:32	07 11 18 32	–
07	3-Com (08)	16 Feb 11:19:05	07 11 19 05	–
08	Ocean Rover (09)	16 Feb 11:33:47	07 11 33 47	–
09	Nuclear Electric (06)	16 Feb 11:35:34	07 11 35 34	–
10	Toshiba Wave Warrior (02)	16 Feb 11:39:30	07 11 39 30	–
11	Motorola (04)	16 Feb 11:41:44	07 11 41 44	–
12	Heath Insured II (11)	16 Feb 12:01:01	07 12 01 01	–
13	Commercial Union (05)	16 Feb 12:55:11	07 12 55 11	–
14	Time & Tide (12)	16 Feb 13:13:48	07 13 13 48	–

LEG 4 – Sydney to Cape Town

Restart   Sunday 2 March 1997   Local time: 1330   6200 miles

Placing	Yacht	Arrival time (GMT)	Leg time D H M S	Penalty/redress +/- DD:HH:MM
01	Group 4 (01)	09 Apr 01:35:05	37 23 05 05	–
02	Concert (14)	09 Apr 01:55:26	37 23 25 26	–
03	Toshiba Wave Warrior (02)	09 Apr 05:41:30	38 03 11 30	–
04	Commercial Union (05)	09 Apr 21:19:23	38 18 49 23	–
05	Motorola (04)	10 Apr 05:55:27	39 03 25 27	–
06	Save the Children (03)	10 Apr 09:53:39	39 07 23 39	–
07	3-Com (07)	10 Apr 16:13:30	39 13 43 30	–
08	Global Teamwork (06)	10 Apr 16:48:51	39 14 18 51	–
09	Ocean Rover (08)	11 Apr 07:45:43	40 05 15 43	–
10	Time & Tide (12)	11 Apr 22:07:29	40 19 37 29	–
11	Nuclear Electric (09)	12 Apr 08:07:24	41 05 37 24	–
12	Courtaulds International (13)	12 Apr 11:43:30	41 09 13 30	–
13	Pause to Remember (10)	12 Apr 12:33:33	41 10 03 33	–
14	Heath Insured II (11)	12 Apr 12:55:48	41 10 25 48	–

LEG 5 – Cape Town to Boston

Restart   Sunday 4 May 1997   Local time: 1330   7000 miles

Placing	Yacht	Arrival time (GMT)	Leg time D H M S	Penalty/redress +/- DD:HH:MM
01	Group 4 (*01*)	07 Jun 13:18:46	34 01 48 46	–
02	Motorola (*03*)	08 Jun 05:42:16	34 18 12 16	–
03	Toshiba Wave Warrior (*02*)	08 Jun 19:20:14	35 07 50 14	–
04	Courtaulds International (*11*)	09 Jun 00:01:05	35 12 31 05	–
05	Concert (*13*)	09 Jun 07:04:27	35 19 34 27	–
06	Save the Children (*04*)	09 Jun 09:02:54	36 00 37 54	+00:03:05
07	Commercial Union (*05*)	09 Jun 16:28:38	36 04 58 38	–
08	Nuclear Electric (*07*)	09 Jun 19:58:59	36 07 08 59	–00:01:20
09	Global Teamwork (*06*)	09 Jun 18:45:58	36 07 15 58	–
10	Pause to Remember (*10*)	10 Jun 00:37:07	36 13 07 07	–
11	Heath Insured II (*12*)	10 Jun 05:59:43	36 17 59 43	–00:00:30
12	Ocean Rover (*09*)	10 Jun 11:27:35	36 23 57 35	–
13	3-Com (*08*)	11 Jun 03:27:39	37 15 57 39	–
14	Time & Tide (*14*)	11 Jun 23:20:58	38 15 50 58	+00:04:00

LEG 6 – Boston to Southampton

Restart   Sunday 29 June 1997   Local time: 1330   3000 miles

Placing	Yacht	Arrival time (GMT)	Leg time D H M S	Penalty/redress +/- DD:HH:MM
01	Group 4	16 Jul 01:06:58	16 07 36 58	–
02	Toshiba Wave Warrior	16 Jul 02:39:46	16 09 09 46	–
03	Concert	16 Jul 04:07:41	16 10 37 41	–
04	Save the Children	16 Jul 14:32:23	16 21 02 23	–
05	Commercial Union	16 Jul 14:33:59	16 21 03 59	–
06	Nuclear Electric	16 Jul 18:11:21	17 00 41 21	–
07	Global Teamwork	16 Jul 18:29:17	17 00 59 17	–
08	Ocean Rover	16 Jul 18:54:29	17 01 24 29	–
09	Heath Insured II	16 Jul 19:06:06	17 01 36 06	–
10	3-Com	16 Jul 19:09:55	17 01 39 55	–
11	Courtaulds International	16 Jul 19:09:58	17 01 39 58	–
12	Motorola	16 Jul 19:13:24	17 01 43 24	–
13	Pause to Remember	16 Jul 19:15:27	17 01 45 27	–
14	Time & Tide	17 Jul 08:34:49	17 11 04 49	–

FINAL RESULTS

Placing	Yacht	Combined times							
		D	H	M	S	D	H	M	S
01	Group 4	161	05	25	18				
02	Toshiba Wave Warrior	163	11	14	34	+ 02	05	49	16
03	Save the Children	165	20	50	46	+ 04	15	25	28
04	Motorola	165	22	40	54	+ 04	17	15	36
05	Commercial Union	167	08	01	32	+ 06	02	36	14
06	Global Teamwork	169	20	27	56	+ 08	15	02	38
07	Nuclear Electric	171	01	29	10	+ 09	20	03	52
08	Ocean Rover	171	11	46	34	+ 10	06	21	16
09	3-Com	171	11	57	30	+ 10	06	32	12
10	Pause to Remember	172	19	13	28	+ 11	13	48	10
11	Courtaulds International	173	19	26	12	+ 12	14	00	54
12	Heath Insured II	174	10	03	47	+ 13	04	38	29
13	Concert	174	21	36	29	+ 13	16	11	11
14	Time & Tide	176	18	09	55	+ 15	12	44	37

APPENDIX IV

8 Day Menu Plan – Leg 4

MENU PLAN LEG 4 – SYDNEY TO CAPE TOWN								
	DAY 1	DAY 2	DAY 3	DAY 4	DAY 5	DAY 6	DAY 7	DAY 8
BREAKFAST	Scrambled eggs	Bacon & beans	Cereal & toast	Scrambled eggs	Porridge	Cereal & toast	Pancakes	Porridge
LUNCH	Wk1=Sarnies Pasto pesto	Soup & bread	TPM	Noodle soup	Special fried rice	Pick 'n' mix pasta	Pizza	Sandwiches & soup
DINNER	Lancashire hotpot & mash	Chilli con carne & rice	Chicken supreme & peas & rice	Pasta bol.	Wrestlers Beef & dumps. mash	S&S chicken & rice	Veg. curry & rice	Cheese & onion pie & mash
	Sponge cake Fruit & custard	Suet pud custard	Dried fruit crumble & custard	Rice pudding	Apple crumble & custard	Cheese cake	Jam tart & custard	Butterscotch delight
SUPPER	Cheese & crackers Muesli bars	BAKE BREAD Cheese & crackers Peanut butter	BAKE BREAD Fruit cake Cheese & crackers	Scones	BAKE BREAD Fruit loaf Cheese & crackers	Scones	BAKE BREAD Cheese & crackers	Cup-a-soup Cheese & crackers